THE Les Paul GUITAR BOOK

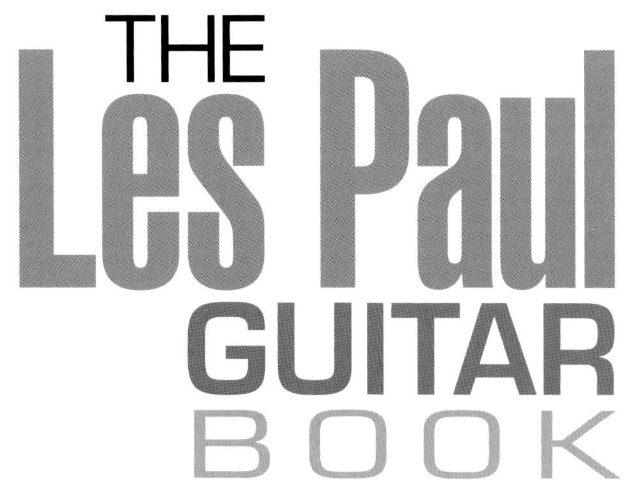

THE Les Paul GUITAR BOOK

A COMPLETE HISTORY OF GIBSON LES PAUL GUITARS *TONY BACON*

THE LES PAUL GUITAR BOOK

A Complete History Of Gibson Les Paul Guitars

by TONY BACON

A BACKBEAT BOOK
This new third edition 2009
First edition (as The Gibson Les Paul Book) 1993;
second edition (as 50 Years Of The Gibson Les Paul) 2002
Published by Backbeat Books
An Imprint of Hal Leonard Corporation
7777 West Bluemound Road,
Milwaukee, WI 53213
www.backbeatbooks.com

Devised and produced for Backbeat Books by
Outline Press Ltd
2A Union Court, 20-22 Union Road,
London SW4 6JP, England
www.jawbonepress.com

ISBN: 978-0-87930-951-0

DESIGN: Paul Cooper Design
EDITOR: Siobhan Pascoe

Origination and print by Regent Publishing Services Limited, China

09 10 11 12 13 5 4 3 2 1

CONTENTS

the fifties

"Carved top, great neck, cool sound, wild look ... this brand new Les Paul electric guitar really does have it all."

Guitar Slim ▶

Few guitars excite the same kind of passion among players as a Gibson Les Paul, whether it's an original 1959 sunburst-finish Standard – the holy grail of solidbody electric guitars – or even a brand new Les Paul Studio just shipped from Gibson's Nashville factory yesterday afternoon. However, there are still fans of this illustrious piece of instrumental perfection who are unaware that Les Paul is not only a name emblazoned in script lettering on the head of each one of these guitars, but also a real person.

The man himself was born Lester William Polfuss in Waukesha, Wisconsin, in 1915, and started professional life in his teens. By age 17, he was broadcasting on local radio stations, playing country guitar as Rhubarb Red, and adding jazz to his expanding repertoire. The kid had an apparently natural technical ability, which he applied to music as well as to making his own bits and pieces of instrumental and electrical gadgetry. Like a number of performers in the 30s, the young Lester soon became interested in amplifying his guitar. He recalled later that in his early teens he'd managed to create a pickup out of a telephone mouthpiece and an amplifier from his parents' radio, allowing him to bring his guitar to the attention of the audience at a local roadhouse gig.

It was around this time that companies such as Rickenbacker, National, and others began to sell the first commercial electric guitars. These were regular archtop acoustic instruments with electric pickups and controls fixed on to them. By the middle of the 30s, the Gibson company of Kalamazoo, Michigan, had joined in with what they called an "Electric Spanish" guitar and amplifier, and so too had Gibson's biggest competitor, Epiphone of New York City.

Meanwhile, Lester Polfuss had permanently adopted a suitably shortened version of his name – Les Paul. For three years from 1938 he led a jazz-based trio broadcasting out of New York on the Fred Waring show. He shifted from an acoustic archtop model to various Gibson electrics, including an ES-150, an experimental L-7 and L-5, and an ES-300. But he wanted something more – something that none of the guitar companies seemed to want to produce.

"I had in mind a guitar that sustained and reproduced the sound of the string with nothing added: no distortion, no change in the response," said Les. Those early hollowbody electrics of the 30s suffered from feedback and poor tone. "I wanted the string to do its thing. No top vibrating, no added enhancement – either advantageous or disadvantageous. I wanted to be sure that you just plucked the string and that's what you heard. That was my whole idea. So I just went on my way."[1]

Later, Les would visit the empty Epiphone factory at weekends to experiment with instrument ideas. The result was what he called the 'log' and a few 'clunkers'. The log nickname came from a four-by-four solid block of pine that he fitted between two sawn halves of a dismembered Epiphone body, adding a Gibson neck, a Larson Bros fingerboard, a Kauffman vibrato, and some pickups. Les would play his semi-solid Epiphone clunker and his singing guitarist partner Mary Ford her Epi clunker or modified Gibson L-12 regularly, on stage and in recording studios, into the early 50s. Les Paul knew that Gibson was the biggest operator in the guitar business of the 40s. After all, he'd appeared in the company's catalogues and ads as a famous player, both as Rhubarb Red and as Les Paul, and had played various Gibsons.

Now Les decided to try to interest Gibson in his log. The company was big and undoubtedly successful. It had begun in Kalamazoo in 1902 and soon gained an enviable reputation among musicians for fine, attractive, potent instruments, with the mandolins in particular widely popular. Guitars had grown in importance during the 20s and 30s, and any maker that wanted to succeed among guitarists had to be seen as inventive and forward-thinking. Gibson certainly obliged, offering many six-string innovations, including the notable L-5 archtop of the early 20s.

The Chicago Musical Instrument Company (CMI) acquired a controlling interest in Gibson in 1944. CMI had been founded some 25 years earlier in Chicago, Illinois, by Maurice H Berlin. Under the new deal, Berlin became the boss of Gibson's parent company. The manufacturing base remained at the original factory, purpose-built in 1917 at Kalamazoo, an industrial and commercial centre in a farming area, more or less halfway between Detroit and Chicago. Gibson's new sales and administration headquarters at CMI was in Chicago.

It was probably around 1946 that Les took his experimental log to Maurice Berlin in Chicago, hoping to convince him to market such a guitar as a Gibson model. No doubt with all the courtesy that a pressurised city businessman could muster, Berlin showed Les Paul the door. "They laughed at the guitar," Les remembered.[2]

Making the home-studio hits

Les Paul was becoming famous. He was a member of the original Jazz At The Philharmonic touring-and-recording supergroup organised by Verve Records boss Norman Granz. During World War II, he was in the Armed Forces Radio Service, operating out of their headquarters in Hollywood and entertaining the troops. Among the singers he backed was Bing Crosby.

After the war, Les played prominent guitar on Crosby's 1945 Number One hit 'It's Been A Long Long Time', which was credited to Bing Crosby With The Les Paul Trio. It brought Les to a much wider audience. Crosby showed a keen interest in new recording developments and from 1947 was an early user of tape-recording machines for his radio show. He encouraged Les to build a studio into the garage of the guitarist's home in Hollywood, California.

It was in his small home studio that Les Paul hit upon some effective recording techniques – at first using discs, then tape. Les's method was to build up multiple layers of instruments by using two recording machines. He would add new material to an existing recording at each pass of the tape and could vary the tape-speed to produce impossibly high and fast guitar passages. With this homegrown technology – and later with the

● **Les Paul & Mary Ford** on-stage (left) around 1950 with Les's 'clunkers', two guitars he modified with bolted-on pickups and semi-solid bodies. Les's **clunker** is pictured (right), with Bigsby pickup and Kauffman Vibrola. Les first endorsed Gibson guitars back in 1940 (**ad**, above left). The company marked his growing success with this early-1952 **ad** (above right) that mentions the "wonderful new Gibsons now under construction for you and Mary". It was the first official sign that Gibson Les Paul guitars would be launched later that year.

● This crude '**log**' (left) was Les Paul's first experiment with a semi-solid body. He put it together in the 40s using a Gibson neck, Larson Bros fingerboard, and Epiphone body, adding his own vibrato, pickups, and 4x4 solid central section.

facilities afforded by a single, modified tape recorder – Les created on record a magical orchestra of massed guitars playing catchy instrumental tunes.

Capitol Records signed Les Paul and his 'New Sound'. His first multi-guitar single, 'Lover', became a Number 21 hit in 1948. Jazzman Sidney Bechet had done a technically similar thing seven years earlier for his multi-instrument 'Sheik Of Araby', and singer Patti Page's hit 'Confess' later in 1948 used the same recording techniques. But it was Les Paul who made overdubbing his own.

After a long break to recover from a bad car accident, he found even greater fame when he added vocalist Mary Ford to the act. He'd known Ford (real name Colleen Summers) since 1945, but they didn't hook up officially until 1949. Their marriage, Les's second, took place in December, and the following year the duo released their first joint single, pairing 'Cryin'' and 'Dry My Tears'. Guitars and now Mary's voice too were given the multiple recording treatment, and big hits followed for Les Paul & Mary Ford. 'The Tennessee Waltz' went to Number Six in the US charts in 1950, but it was 'How High The Moon' that struck gold for the duo, going to Number One in April 1951.

Today, it's perfectly normal and commonplace for musicians to build up recordings at home using multiple parallel tracks, usually on a computer now, but back in the early 50s it must have seemed as if some kind of witchcraft was involved. At least one reviewer was mystified by the sound of 'High How The Moon' and how it was put together. "Beyond revealing that there are 12 guitar parts and nine vocal parts on it," he wrote, "and that Les works out his trick formula with the aid of a tape-recorder at home, Capitol refuses to divulge information it obviously regards as top secret."[3] Appearing on a television show in 1953, Les told the presenter that the maximum number of dubs he could get on to tape with his scheme was 14.

There were more hits using the "trick formula". 'The World Is Waiting For The Sunrise' went to Number Two in 1951, as did 'Tiger Rag' the following year, and 'Bye Bye Blues' got to Five during 1953. 'Vaya Con Dios' was the duo's second Number One, in 1953, while the same year 'I'm Sitting On Top Of The World' went to Number Ten, and 'I'm A Fool To Care' reached Six in 1954.

The duo made a host of personal appearances and performed at plenty of concerts. They were heard on NBC Radio's *Les Paul Show* every week for six months during 1949 and 1950 and starred in a networked TV series, *The Les Paul & Mary Ford Show*, which began in 1953 and ran until 1955, filmed at their new luxury home in Mahwah, New Jersey. Les Paul & Mary Ford, "America's musical sweethearts", were huge 50s stars.

Meanwhile, people were exploring the idea of a fully solidbody electric guitar, notably at Bigsby and Fender, both in California. A solidbody electric was appealing to manufacturers because it would be easier to construct than an acoustic guitar, using a body or body-section made of solid wood to support the strings and pickups. For the player, it would cut down the annoying feedback produced by amplified acoustic guitars. A solidbody guitar reduced the effect that the body had on the instrument's overall tone –

and for players of electric hollowbody guitars, that's a problem. But the solid body had the benefit of more accurately reproducing and sustaining the sound of the strings, and many guitarists would come to value this quality.

In 1950, Fender – a small company making amplifiers and electric lap-steel guitars – launched on to an unsuspecting market the world's first commercially available solidbody electric 'Spanish' guitar. This innovative musical instrument was originally called the Fender Esquire or Broadcaster but soon was renamed the Fender Telecaster. Fender's burst of activity failed to instantly convert guitarists everywhere to the new tones and the potential to play safely at higher volumes afforded by the new solidbody instruments. At first Fender's novel electrics were used by a handful of country players and western swing guitarists, mainly in areas close to the company's workshop in Fullerton, California. But slowly the word spread. Fender's rise to the top of the electric guitar market had begun.

Such a success, even if modest at first, was quickly picked up by other guitar makers. Valco of Chicago offered a cheap new single-pickup solidbody electric early in 1952 for both of its principal guitar brands – National, with the Cosmopolitan model, and Supro, with the Ozark. By the summer 52 music-trade show, the other two big US guitar manufacturers had their own new solidbody electrics: Kay offered the Thin Twin; Harmony the Stratotone. Over in Kalamazoo, Gibson too had their ears to the ground.

In summer 1950, Ted McCarty was made president at Gibson. He had joined the company in March 1948, having worked at the Wurlitzer organ company for the previous 12 years. McCarty later recalled that Maurice Berlin, head of Gibson's parent company CMI, in Chicago, had appointed him expressly to improve Gibson's business performance, which had been suffering since World War II. The company had suspended most of its musical instrument production during the war, instead undertaking government electronics work for radar installations. This selfless activity earned Gibson three Army & Navy 'E' Awards for productivity.

Gibson was finding it hard in the post-war years to get back into full-scale guitar production. McCarty's immediate targets when he joined were to increase the effectiveness of supervision in the factories, to bolster efficiency, and to improve and widen internal communication. "I went there on the 15th of March 1948," he remembered. "We lost money in March, we lost money in April; we made money in May, and we made it for the next 18 years that I was there."

By 1950, Gibson's electric guitar line consisted of seven models, from the ES-125 retailing at $97.50, through the ES-140, ES-150, ES-175, ES-300, and ES-350, up to the ES-5 at $375. These were all archtop hollowbody guitars, complete with f-holes and fitted pickups and controls.

Then along came that Fender solidbody electric from California. McCarty remembered the reaction at Gibson. "We were watching what Leo Fender was doing, realising that he was gaining popularity in the west," said McCarty. "I watched him and watched him, and said we've got to get into that business. I thought we were giving him a free run, and he

● Gibson launched the new Les Paul guitar in summer 1952, setting the list price at $210 – about $20 more than a Fender Telecaster of the time. Les Paul himself received some early samples of the instrument in May and played it in public for the first time a month later at the Paramount Theater in New York City. This **1953 Goldtop** (below) is a fine example of the first version of the new guitar, with its two P-90 pickups and associated selector switch, a volume and tone control per pickup, and of course that distinctive gold-painted top.

● This **1952 ad** (above) shows Les Paul, the most famous guitarist in America at the time, proudly playing the instrument that bore his name. The **1952 Goldtop** (right) is a rare left-hander.

IN THE BEGINNING 1952–53

● The first Gibson Les Paul solidbody electric guitar, called the Les Paul Model but known now as the Goldtop, went on sale in 1952. This **1952 Goldtop** (main guitar) was among the first ones produced. We can tell this because it has an unbound fingerboard and the bridge pickup has fixing screws in each corner. Those features were soon revised, as seen on the two slightly later guitars here. Les Paul's only contribution to the design of the new guitar was the 'trapeze' bridge/tailpiece; the **patent** is pictured above.

was about the only one making that kind of guitar with that real shrill sound which the country and western boys liked. It was becoming popular. We talked it over and decided to start out and make a solidbody for ourselves. We had a lot to learn about the solidbody guitar. It's different to the acoustic," McCarty emphasised. "Built differently; sounds different; responds differently."

McCarty's recollection was that Gibson started work on its own solidbody guitar project soon after the appearance of Fender's Broadcaster in November 1950, and that he and the company's top engineers were involved in the project. "We designed the guitars," McCarty explained. "And we started trying to learn something about a solidbody guitar. I was working with the rest of the engineers and we would sit down, like in a think tank, and we would talk about this guitar: let's do this, let's try that."

It's unclear exactly how many people at the company were involved in the design of the new instrument, which was to become the Gibson Les Paul Model. McCarty thought there were at least four: himself, John Huis, who was McCarty's number two and in charge of production, "plus one of the fellows in charge of the wood department and one of the guitar players in final assembly". McCarty also mentioned Gibson employees Julius Bellson and Wilbur Marker as being "in on the thing", and it's likely that Gibson's sales people were consulted at various stages through Clarence Havenga, the company's vice president in charge of sales.

"We eventually came up with a guitar that was attractive," said McCarty, "and as far as we were concerned it had the tone, it had the resonance, and it also had the sustain – but not too much. As far as I can remember, to get to that point took us about a year."[4]

An article early in 1952 in Gibson's local paper, the *Kalamazoo Gazette,* noted that the company had files bulging with instrument ideas that musicians had sent in. There were enough suggestions, the piece continued, "to create the combined pandemonium of a four-alarm fire, dog fight, curfew chorus, and mouse-frightened female". According to McCarty, the paper reported, "only a few of the ideas" were impractical.[5] Presumably, somewhere in those files there still lurked Les Paul's idea for a semi-solid electric guitar, his 'log' that he'd taken to the company years earlier. He'd been turned away then. But things were changing fast.

"We thought we had our guitar," said McCarty, "and now we needed an excuse to make it. So I got to thinking. At that time Les Paul and Mary Ford were riding very high – they were probably the number one vocal team in the United States. They were earning a million dollars a year. And knowing Les and Mary, I decided maybe I ought to show this guitar to them."[6]

Les Paul's recollections of the events that led to Gibson producing the Les Paul guitar are different. He told me that Gibson first contacted him early in 1951, when Fender started making early examples of its solidbody electric. He remembered that Maurice Berlin, boss of Gibson's parent company CMI, told his second-in-command Marc Carlucci to get in touch with "the fellow with the strange log guitar" whom they'd seen briefly back in the 40s. "They said to find that guy with the broomstick with the pickups on it," Les laughed. "They came round right away, soon as they heard what Fender was doing. And I said well, you guys are a little bit behind the times, but OK, let's go."

Les said that after Gibson contacted him in 1951 about their interest in developing a solidbody electric, a meeting was set up at CMI headquarters in Chicago. Present were Berlin, Carlucci, and CMI's attorney, Marv Henrickson, who also represented Les. "They finalised their deal," Les said, "and hammered out the specifics of the new guitar's design. Then, the research and development began in earnest."[7]

Gibson and the Stroudsburg deal

McCarty's story of how he came to show the first prototype of the Gibson Les Paul guitar to Les Paul takes him away from the Gibson factory. Accompanied by Les's business manager, Phil Braunstein, McCarty took the prototype to Les and Mary at a hunting lodge in Stroudsburg, Pennsylvania, near the Delaware Water Gap park, probably in late 1951 or early 1952. The lodge was owned by Les's friend, publisher Ben Selvin, and Les had turned the living room into a studio, taking advantage of the quiet isolation of the building for an ideal recording retreat. On this occasion, Les and Mary were there to record together with Mary's sister Carol and her husband Wally Kamin. Carol would sing harmony parts off-stage on the duo's live appearances to help recreate their multiple-recording sound, and Wally played double-bass.

McCarty said he went to the Stroudsburg lodge to interest Les in publicly playing the new guitar in return for a royalty on sales. Les too recalled that the lodge was where he saw the first prototype of what became the Gibson Les Paul. McCarty remembered that Les loved the prototype, saying to Mary: "I think we ought to join them; what do you think?" She said she liked it too. Neither McCarty nor Les could remember for sure, but that prototype was probably very similar to the eventual production model, except that it may have had a normal Gibson tailpiece of the period (as for example on a Gibson ES-350) with a separate bridge.

Ted McCarty, Les Paul, and Phil Braunstein sat down and worked out a contract. First they decided on the royalty Gibson would pay for every Les Paul guitar sold. Les said it was five per cent. The term of the contract was set at five years. McCarty remembered: "Braunstein, Les's business manager, said he wanted one extra paragraph in there, saying that Les Paul had to agree that he would not play any guitar other than a Gibson in public during the life of the contract. If in the fourth year he appeared playing a Gretsch, say, it would cancel the whole thing – he wouldn't get a dime."

Braunstein explained that this was to save on tax commitments, and to assure money for Les and Mary when their income from records and concerts might reduce in later years. McCarty said that there was also a clause in the contract stating that Les should act as a consultant to Gibson. "We agreed that night," McCarty recalled. "We each had a copy, written out long-hand. Les could take it to his attorney and I could take it to ours, and if

● The Custom was Gibson's $325 marketing-led reply to the popularity of the original Goldtop. The Custom was fancier, with a black finish, gold-plated hardware, and an all-mahogany body (the Goldtop had a maple cap on a mahogany base). This first-year **1954 Custom** (above) shows the pickup layout of P-90 at the bridge and Seth Lover's "louder" Alnico at the neck. Note also the Custom's distinctive block markers on the fingerboard .

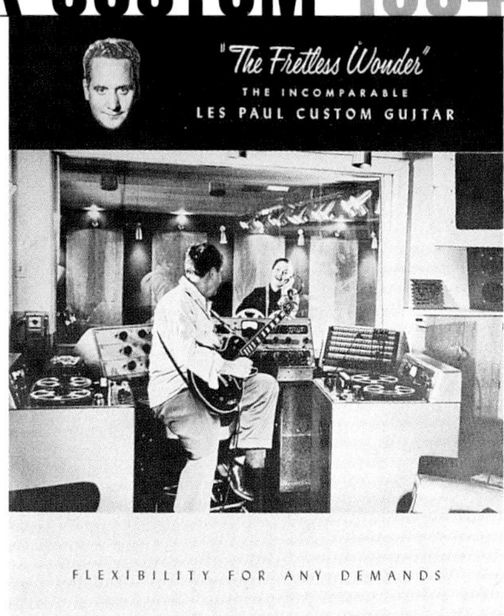

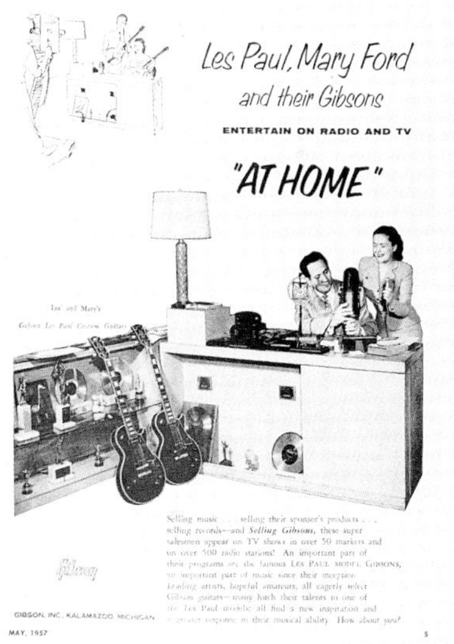

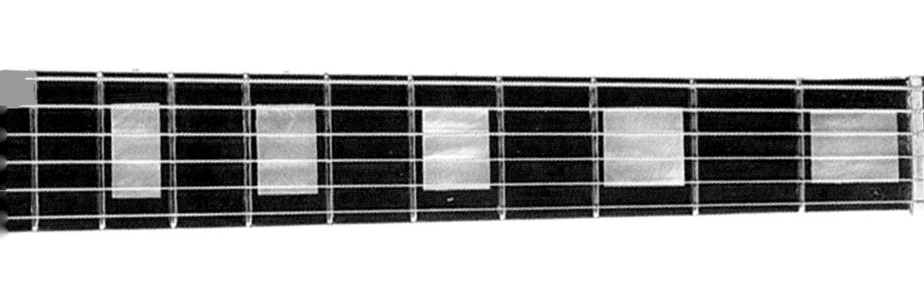

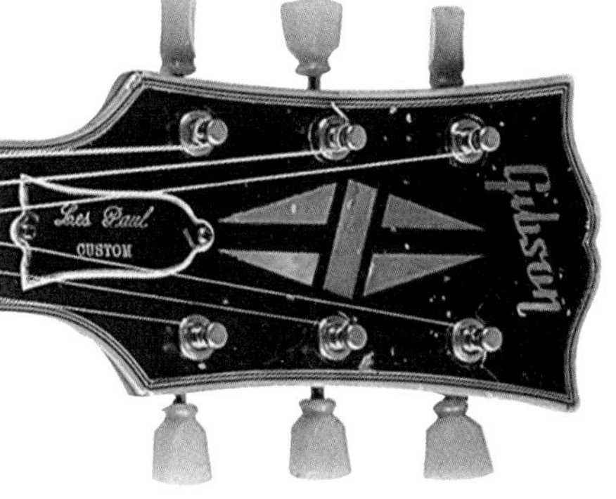

● The Custom was upped to three humbuckers in 1957. Keith Richards used this **1957 Custom** (main guitar) with The Rolling Stones in the late 60s, complete with personalised paint job and bottle-top-converted control knobs. **Les Paul** was another keen guitar modifier and a pioneer of home recording. The guitarist is pictured (above) laying down tracks in the 50s with a typically modified Custom and 'at home' in some cosy scenes with musical and marital partner Mary Ford (right) at their luxury abode in New Jersey.

there were any questions then we would get together and work them out. But not a single word in that contract was changed. So anyway, I came back to the factory. Now we had a Les Paul model."[8]

Les said that he had a much bigger involvement in the design of the Les Paul guitar than McCarty's story allows. Les told me categorically: "I designed everything on there except the arched top. That was contributed by Maurice Berlin. Mr Berlin told me he liked violins and took me by his vault to show me his collection. And he said that Gibson had something that nobody else had, a shaper that could make a 'belly' on that guitar, and it would be very expensive for Fender or whoever to make one like it. He asked if I'd have any objection to a violin top, and I said no, that was a wonderful idea. So then they introduced me to Ted McCarty, and we signed the agreement with Gibson."[9] But McCarty was adamant. "I have told you exactly how it got to be a Les Paul. We spent a year designing that guitar, and Les never saw it until I took it to Pennsylvania."[10]

Looking at photographs of Les playing Gibson Les Paul guitars in the 50s (and later) suggests that he continued to have his own ideas about what a solidbody electric guitar should be, usually contrary to Gibson's. Often his instruments were specially made with unique flat tops, where the production Les Pauls had carved tops. Les nearly always modified his Gibsons in some way. As the diehard tinkerer said: "By early 53, Gibson was shooting guitars to me all the time, and I was still cutting them up and modifying the pickups, bridges, controls, and just about everything else."

After the deal was made between Les and Gibson, the company requested that he change the logo on the modified Epiphone 'clunker' models that he and Mary Ford were still using on-stage. "Gibson asked me if, until they made the Les Paul model for me, I would agree to play my Epiphone but put the name Gibson on it," explained Les. "You could just pull off the Epiphone plates with a screwdriver, which I did. Then I suggested to Ted McCarty that he send me some Gibson decals, which we put on the guitars so they would say Gibson prior to the solidbody coming on the market."[11]

The Les Paul was not Gibson's first guitar named for a musician. Today it would be called a signature model. Gibson's first signature instrument was the Nick Lucas acoustic flat-top, launched back in 1928. There are some parallels with the Gibson–Les Paul association. Lucas, touted as the "singing troubadour", was the first American to become a big star through popular guitar-and-vocal records, notably his big hits 'I'm Looking Over A Four-Leafed Clover' and 'Tiptoe Through The Tulips', though he also made some nifty guitar-loaded solo tracks like 'Pickin The Guitar' and 'Teasin The Frets'. Despite the signature model, Lucas continued to play his favoured Gibson L-1 flat-top.

Perhaps it will never be clear exactly who designed what on the original Gibson Les Paul model, but my own view is that Gibson was responsible for virtually all of it. What we can be certain about is that Les's respected playing and commercial success plus Gibson's weighty experience in manufacturing and marketing guitars added up to a strong and impressive combination.

The new Les Paul guitar was launched by Gibson in the summer of 1952, listing at $210, about $20 more than Fender's Telecaster. (In today's money, you'd need to spend around $1,700/£1,150 now to match the buying power of $210 in 1952.) Early samples of the new guitar were shipped to Gibson's case manufacturer, Geib, at the end of April, and to Les Paul himself late in May. Some dealers began to receive stock in June.

Come see the new electronic guitar

The official unveiling of new musical instruments would usually be reserved for the annual convention of NAMM, the National Association of Music Merchants, which all the important instrument-business people would attend. In 1952, it was held at the Hotel New Yorker in New York City from July 27th to the 31st. Gibson instruments were shown at the CMI exhibits in rooms 611 through 615. But Gibson also hosted a special pre-NAMM musicians' clinic at the nearby Waldorf Astoria on the Thursday and Friday before the convention, July 24th and 25th.

The idea, reported *The Music Trades,* was that professional musicians, who couldn't officially attend the NAMM show, as well as local dealers, would have the opportunity to preview and play the latest Gibson instruments. "Especially Gibson's new Les Paul model electronic guitar," noted the trade magazine. The new GA-40 Les Paul amplifier was also shown. "Tiger Haynes, reported to be the premier colored guitarist, spent at least an hour on the Les Paul Model," the reporter continued, "and we doubt that suite 4-V will ever be the same again."

Other guitarists who visited and tried the new Les Paul included a cross-section of sessionmen and jazzers such as George Barnes, Mundell Lowe, Tony Mottola, and Billy Mure. "W.B. 'Doc' Caldwell demonstrated the tone and volume controls on the guitars," the report concluded, "and adjusted the new amplifiers to the tastes of the musicians."[12]

Les Paul himself began using the new Gibson solidbody immediately, in line with his endorsement contract. He said he used one for the first time in June 1952, on-stage at the Paramount Theater in New York. Les and Mary toured Europe that September, and a British musicians' newspaper noted the unusual new instruments that the "guitar boffin" and his singing partner were playing. "He'd brought his own special amplifiers," wrote the reporter, "and four specially-made and surprisingly small guitars with cut-away shoulders to help with the high-speed treble, plus plenty of spare tubes."[13]

Today, a gold-finish Les Paul model is nearly always called a Goldtop thanks to its gold body face, and that's what we'll call them, too, throughout this book. The new Goldtop's solid body cleverly combined a carved maple top bonded to a mahogany base, a sandwich that united the darker tonality of mahogany with the brighter sonic 'edge' of maple. Les said that the gold colour of the original Les Paul model was his idea. "Gold means rich," he said, "expensive, the best, superb."[14]

Gibson had made a one-off all-gold-colour hollowbody guitar in 1951 for Les to present to a terminally ill patient whom he had met when making a special appearance at a

● Gibson's new cheaper Les Paul models were the Junior, launched in 1954, and the TV and Special, which emerged the following year. They were simple guitars with uncarved tops and plain appointments. At the time they were at the bottom of the pricelist but have since become revered for their direct rock'n'roll spirit. This **1956 Junior** (above) is in the original sunburst finish, while the **1956 TV** (right) has that model's unusual yellow-cum-beige paintwork. The TV name was an allusion to Les Paul & Mary Ford's popular 50s television show.

● The Les Paul Special first appeared in 1955, effectively a two-pickup version of the Junior and TV. It shared most of those models' humble specs, including the 'slab' body, but with the crucial extra P-90 and controls, plus a little reworking of the five-ply plastic pickguard to accomodate the revised arrangement. This first-year **1955 Special** (top) would have sold to a lucky 1955 buyer for just $182.50, which placed it somewhere between the $110 TV or Junior and the $325 Custom. Different pick-strokes for different folks.

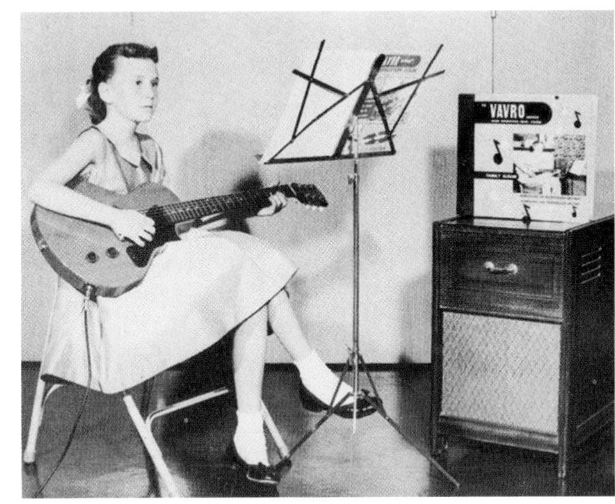

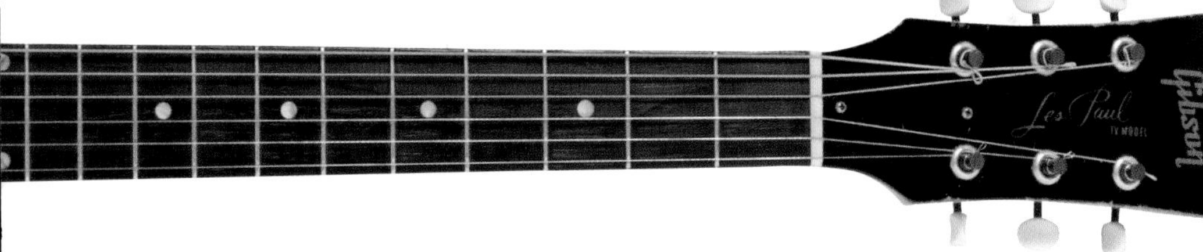

● The Les Paul Junior, TV, and Special guitars were designed by Gibson to be 'student' models. Guitar-teaching schools in stores across the country were hungry for cheap, functional instruments. Gibson knew it was a lucrative market. A **promo photo** (above) shows exactly what Gibson had in mind. Later, however, switched-on rock players would discover other uses.

hospital in Milwaukee. That presentation guitar probably prompted Gibson's all-gold archtop electric ES-295 model of 1952, and most likely was the inspiration for the colour of the first Les Paul model too.

Underlining the origin of the guitar from within Gibson, almost all other design elements of the first Les Paul have precedents in earlier Gibson models, although of course the solid body was a first for the company. The layout of two P-90 single-coil pickups and four controls (a volume and tone knob for each pickup) had been a feature of the previous year's L-5CES and Super 400CES models. The general outline of the single-cutaway body and the construction of the glued-in mahogany neck followed established Gibson traditions, while the crown-shaped inlays on the rosewood fingerboard had first appeared on a revised version of the ES-150 model first seen in 1950. Several Gibson acoustic guitars had already appeared with the Les Paul's particular string-length (the distance from nut to bridge saddle).

Correcting the pitch, fixing the bridge

The production Les Paul Model came with a new height-adjustable combined bridge-and-tailpiece. The part where the strings made contact was bar-shaped, and joined to this were two long metal rods that went down to anchor the unit at the bottom edge of the guitar. This 'trapeze' was without doubt designed by Les Paul, and was originally intended for use on archtop guitars. Gibson also sold it separately as a replacement accessory.

The earliest Goldtops had a very shallow neck pitch – that is, the neck joined the body at a gentle angle. This was a mistake in the design. It meant that the strings were almost flat on to the body as they came off the neck. This precluded use of existing Gibson hardware, and so the new bridge/tailpiece was chosen as the only suitable item. But even with this at its lowest setting, the string action was still too high, so Gibson had no choice but to adapt the bridge and wrap the strings around underneath it. This was contrary to the way the unit was designed to be used, with the strings feeding over the top – as on some of Gibson's archtop, hollowbody electric models of the period including the ES-295 (introduced 1952) and ES-225 (1955).

This bridge arrangement on early Les Paul Goldtops meant that sustain suffered, intonation was inaccurate, and popular hand-damping techniques were virtually impossible. It was clearly unworkable, as Les Paul pointed out to Gibson. "They made the first guitar wrong," he remembered. "I don't know how many went out wrong that weren't playable. When they sent me mine, I stopped them, said this won't even play. They had run the strings under the bridge instead of over, and hadn't pitched the neck. They had it all screwed up."[15]

During 1953, Gibson dropped the original bridge–tailpiece unit – usually known as a trapeze, because of the shape of the long rods – and replaced it with a new specially-designed single bar-shaped bridge–tailpiece, the 'stopbar', that mounted on the top of the body, using twin height-adjustable studs. *Down Beat* magazine's preview of Gibson's exhibit at the July 1953 NAMM show in Chicago highlighted the Les Paul's "new adjustable metal bridge and tailpieces". It was a more stable unit, and the strings now wrapped over the top of the bridge, providing improved sustain and intonation. Also, the guitar's neck pitch was made steeper. The result was a much happier and more playable instrument.

The original Goldtop sold well in relation to Gibson's other models during these early years. In 1954, Gibson's historian Julius Bellson charted the progress of the company's electric instruments, both solidbody and hollowbody. Consulting records, Bellson estimated that back in 1938 electric guitars had made up no more than 10 per cent of Gibson guitar sales, but that the proportion of electrics to the rest had risen to 15 per cent by 1940, to 50 per cent by 1951, and that by 1953 electric guitars constituted no less than 65 per cent of the company's total guitar sales. The buoyant Les Paul model must have helped considerably.

Custom and Junior too

With that success in mind, Gibson issued two new Les Paul models in 1954, the Custom and the Junior. As Ted McCarty described it: "You have all kinds of players out there who like this and like that. Chevrolet had a whole bunch of models, Ford had a whole bunch of models. So did we."[16] The two-pickup Custom looked classy with its all-black finish, multiple binding, block-shaped position markers in an ebony fingerboard, and gold-plated hardware, and was indeed more expensive than the Goldtop. Les said that he chose the black colour for the Custom. "When you're on stage with a black tuxedo and a black guitar, the people can see your hands flying with a spotlight on them."[17]

The Custom had an all-mahogany body, as favoured by Les Paul himself, rather than the maple–mahogany mix of the Goldtop, giving the new guitar a rather mellower tone. Les insisted that Gibson got the timber arrangements the wrong way around, and that as far as he was concerned the cheaper Goldtop should have been all-mahogany, while the costlier Custom should have benefited from the more elaborate maple-and-mahogany combination. The Les Paul Custom was promoted in Gibson catalogues as "the fretless wonder" because of its very low, flat fretwire that was different to the wire used on other Les Pauls at the time. Some players favoured this style for the way it helped them play more speedily.

The budget Junior was designed for and aimed at beginners. It did not pretend to be anything other than a cheaper guitar. The outline shape was the same as the Goldtop and Custom, but the most obvious difference to its Les Paul partners was a flat-top solid mahogany body. It had a single P-90 pickup, governed by a volume and tone control, and there were simple dot-shaped position markers along the unbound rosewood fingerboard. It was finished in Gibson's traditional two-colour brown-to-yellow sunburst and had the wrap-over bar-shape bridge–tailpiece ('stopbar') like the one used on the latest Goldtop. The September 1954 pricelist showed the Les Paul Custom at $325 and the Les Paul Junior at $99.50. The Goldtop meanwhile had sneaked up to $225.

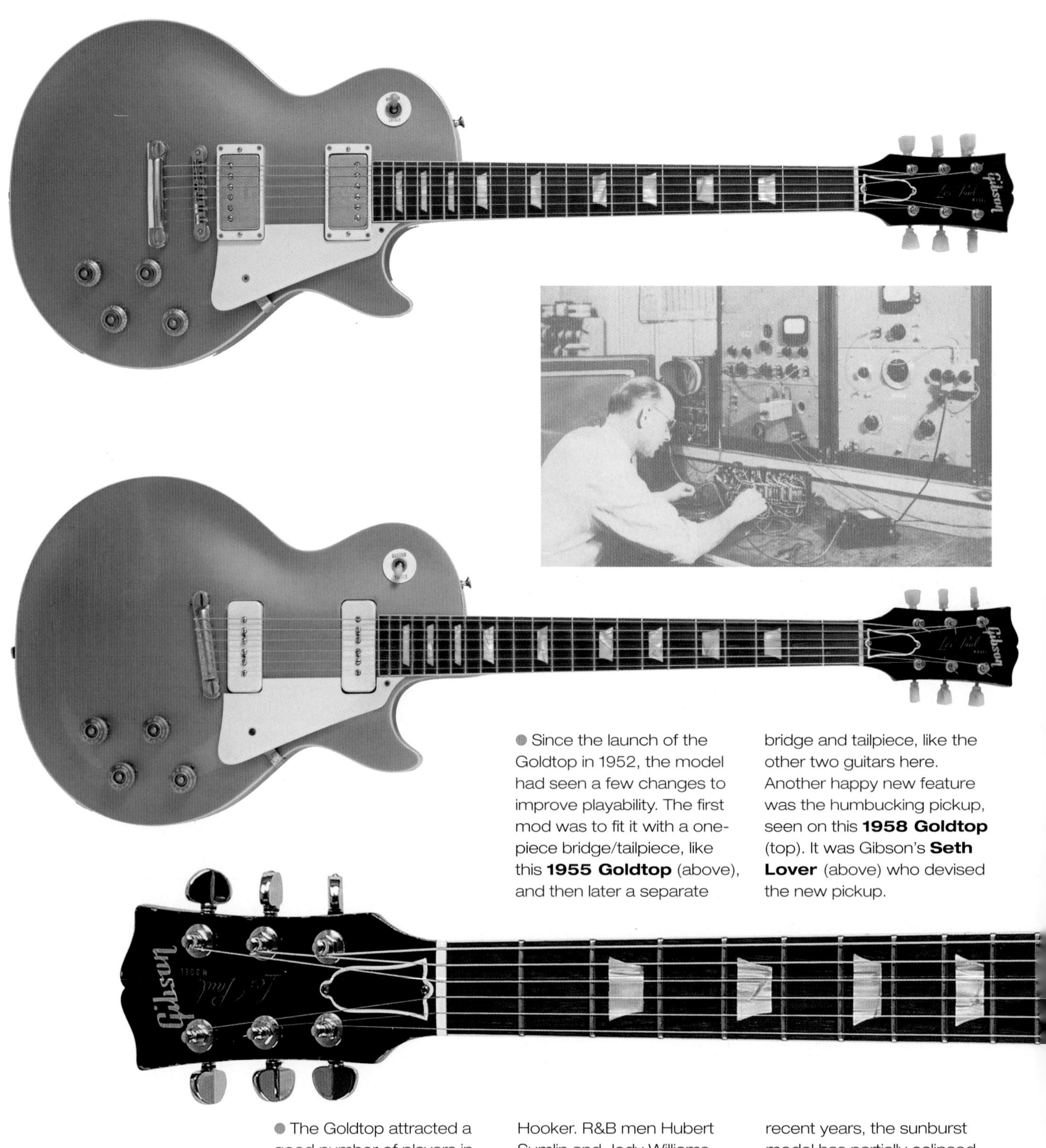

● Since the launch of the Goldtop in 1952, the model had seen a few changes to improve playability. The first mod was to fit it with a one-piece bridge/tailpiece, like this **1955 Goldtop** (above), and then later a separate bridge and tailpiece, like the other two guitars here. Another happy new feature was the humbucking pickup, seen on this **1958 Goldtop** (top). It was Gibson's **Seth Lover** (above) who devised the new pickup.

● The Goldtop attracted a good number of players in the 50s, including a host of great bluesmen such as Muddy Waters, Guitar Slim, Freddie King, Buddy Guy, B.B. King, and John Lee Hooker. R&B men Hubert Sumlin and Jody Williams each played a Goldtop with Howlin' Wolf, and rockabilly rebel **Carl Perkins** (opposite) took a shine to the same model. In more recent years, the sunburst model has partially eclipsed the Goldtop for some players, but Paul McCartney owns and plays this lovely left-handed **1957 Goldtop** (main guitar).

In addition to its conventional P-90 at the bridge, the Les Paul Custom featured a new style of pickup at the neck. It was soon nicknamed the Alnico, a reference to the *al*uminium-*ni*ckel-*co*balt alloy used for its distinctive rectangular magnetic polepieces (although alnico is used in many other pickups). The new pickup was designed by Seth Lover, a radio and electronics expert who had worked on and off for Gibson in the 40s and early 50s while he also did teaching and installation jobs for the US Navy. Lover rejoined Gibson's electronics department permanently in 1952.

Lover had been asked to come up with a pickup louder than Gibson's P-90 and louder than the single-coil Dynasonic pickup used by Gretsch, a New York-based guitar maker and a competitor to Gibson. Gretsch's unit was supplied by DeArmond, a pickup manufacturer in Toledo, Ohio. The reason for the rectangular polepieces of the new Gibson pickup was simple, remembered Lover. "I wanted to be different. I didn't want them to be round like DeArmond's," he said. "I don't like to copy things. If you're going to improve something, then I thought you should make it different. Also, by making them that shape, I could put screws between for height adjustment. But that pickup was never too popular, because the players would always adjust them up too tight to the strings. They'd get that slurring type tone and they didn't like that."[18]

The Custom had another new piece of Gibson hardware fitted. It was the first Les Paul model with the company's Tune-o-matic bridge, used in conjunction with a separate bar-shaped tailpiece. Patented by McCarty, the Tune-o-matic offered for the first time on Gibsons the opportunity to individually adjust the length of each string, which improved tuning accuracy. From 1955, it also became a feature of the Goldtop model.

Toothpaste and the TV

Also in 1955, Gibson launched the Les Paul TV, essentially a Junior but with a finish that the company referred to variously as "natural", "limed oak", and (more often) "limed mahogany". Surviving original TV models from the 50s reveal a number of different colours, with earlier examples tending to a rather turgid beige, while later ones are often distinctly yellow.

No one knows for sure where the model's TV name came from. As usual around Les Paul guitars, people speculate and come up with any number of theories – and all without evidence. One such theory says that the TV name was used because the pale colour of the finish was designed to stand out on the era's black-and-white TV screens. This seems unlikely, because pro players appearing on television would naturally opt for a high-end model. An ad that Gibson ran at the time, headed Tennessee Ernie Stars With Gibsons, featured guitarist Bobby Gibbons from *The Tennessee Ernie Ford Show* on NBC television. Gibbons is pictured playing the most expensive Les Paul of the time – the Custom. It's hard to imagine him settling for a lowly TV model.

Others say the guitar followed the look of fashionable contemporary furniture, where the expression 'limed' was used for a particular look. Certainly Gibson promoted the Les

Paul TV as being "the latest in modern appearance". There's also been a suggestion that 'TV' might be a less than oblique reference to the competing blond-coloured Telecaster made by Fender.

The name was probably coined to cash in on Les Paul's regular appearances on television at the time, on *The Les Paul & Mary Ford Show*. This was effectively a sponsored daily ad for a toothpaste company, for which the couple signed a $2 million three-year contract in 1953.

Gibson reasoned that if you'd seen the man on TV, well, now you could buy his TV guitar. Following a reader's enquiry to a 70s guitar magazine, Gibson's spokesman confirmed that "the Les Paul TV model was so named after Les Paul's personal Listerine show was televised in the 50s". That appears to be the most likely story behind the Les Paul TV.

During research for this book, I talked to Tom Murphy who, as we shall discover later, is renowned for his work with modern reissue guitars, especially those with 'aged' finishes. Murphy's speciality is in refinishing and restoring old guitars. I asked him to name one thing he would ask workers about at the 50s Gibson factory, presuming he had the facilities of a time machine at his disposal. Murphy answered immediately. "I'd watch them do a TV finish," he laughed. "I'd like to see the first day they ever tried it. I wonder what discussions took place to make them attempt that original beige colour? And when they went to the real yellow shade in 58, was it because someone said OK, enough is enough … paint it yellow!"[19]

Also in 1955, the original line of Les Paul models was completed with the addition of the Special, effectively a two-pickup version of the Junior, finished in the TV's beige colour (but not called a TV model – a cause of some confusion since). The Special appeared on the company's September 1955 pricelist at $182.50. The following year, Gibson added a Junior Three-Quarter model. It had a shorter neck, giving the model a scale-length some two inches shorter than the normal Junior. Gibson explained in its brochure at the time that the Junior Three-Quarter was designed to appeal to "youngsters, or adults with small hands and fingers".

Meanwhile in the Gibson electronics department, run by Walt Fuller, the industrious Seth Lover started work on another new pickup. This one would turn out to have a far greater and lasting impact than his previous design. He was charged with finding a way to cut down the hum and electrical interference that plagued standard single-coil pickups, including Gibson's ubiquitous P-90, designed by Fuller. Lover contemplated the humbucking 'choke coil' found in some Gibson amplifiers, installed to eliminate the hum dispensed by their power transformers. "I thought," recalled Lover, "that if we can make humbucking chokes, why can't we make humbucking pickups?" No reason at all, he concluded, and started to build prototypes.

The humbucking name comes straightforwardly from the ability of such devices to buck or cut hum. The design principle too is reasonably simple. A humbucking pickup

Gibson was on a roll in 1958, with the weird-shape Explorer and Flying V and the radical 335. In the Les Paul line, Gibson adapted the 335's double-cutaway body shape and applied it to the student models, such as this **1960 Junior** (here) and **1959 Special** (centre).

The TV also went double-cutaway along with its fellow students: the Junior and TV gained the extra high-fret access in 1958, the Special in 1959. This **1958 TV** (below) shows the more yellow hue adopted by the paint shop at Gibson HQ in Kalamazoo, Michigan. The double-cut student Les Pauls would be gone from the Gibson line by 1961, replaced by the company's new SG design.

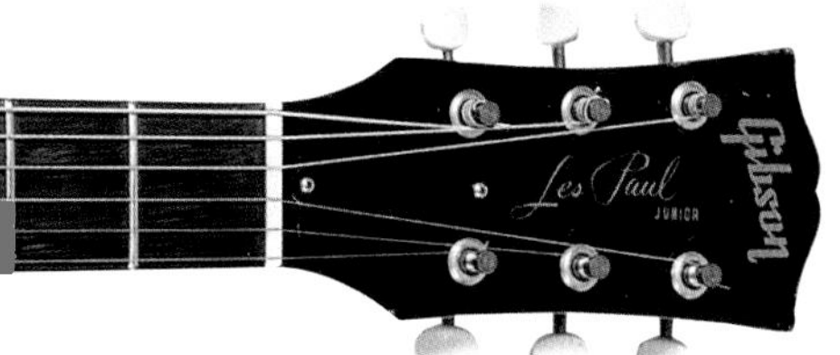

● The **1959 Special** pictured on the far right is one of the short-scale "three-quarter" models, with a scale-length two inches shorter than normal, designed for those of us with smaller hands. Meanwhile, a page from Gibson's **1958 catalogue** (right) details two models from the Les Paul line: the $247.50 Goldtop and the $179.50 Special. A case, too, sir? Just add $42.

The Les Paul Guitar

This beautiful solid body Les Paul guitar incorporates many unusual Gibson features. Gold-finished carved maple top, mahogany body and neck with Les Paul name on peghead. Combination bridge and tailpiece is another Gibson first • tailpiece can be moved up or down to adjust tension • Tune-O-Matic bridge permits adjusting string action and individual string lengths.

Graceful cutaway design with ivoroid binding around top • bound, rosewood fingerboard with pearled inlays. Two, powerful humbucking pickups with individually adjustable polepieces • separate tone and volume controls for each pickup which can be preset • three-way toggle switch to activate either or both pickups. Nickel-plated metal parts • individual machine heads with deluxe buttons • padded leather strap included.

SPECIFICATIONS
12¾" wide, 17¼" long, 1¾" thick, 24¾" scale, 22 frets

Les Paul – Mahogany with Gold Top............$247.50
No. 535 Case – Faultless, plush lined........... 42.00
No. ZC-LP – **Zipper Case Cover**............... 21.50

The Les Paul Special

The Les Paul Special combines tone, versatility, slender neck and low, fast action with a moderate price • solid Honduras mahogany body and neck finished in highly polished, limed finish • black Royalite pickguard and unit covers • nickel-plated metal parts.

Graceful cutaway design • Gibson Adjustable Truss Rod neck • bound, rosewood fingerboard with sparkling pearl dot inlays. Two, powerful pickups with individually adjustable polepieces to balance each string • separate tone and volume controls for each pickup which can be preset • three-way toggle switch to activate either or both pickups; unique combination metal bridge and tailpiece, adjustable horizontally and vertically; enclosed individual machine heads; and padded, adjustable leather strap.

SPECIFICATIONS
12¾" wide, 17¼" long, 1¾" thick, 24¾" scale, 22 frets

Les Paul Special – Limed Mahogany Finish.......$179.50
No. 535 Case – Faultless, plush lined........... 42.00
No. 115 Case – Durabilt...................... 13.50

G-16

● This **1959 Special** has a TV-style finish – the cause of much confusion ever since. A single-pickup student model is a Junior, unless in the beige or yellow finish, when it becomes a TV. A two-pickup model is always a Special.

employs two coils with opposite magnetic polarity, wired together so that they are electrically out-of-phase. The result is a pickup that is less prone to picking up extraneous noise, and one that in the process gives a wonderful clear tone. Original humbucking pickups and the single-coil units of the day offered different tonal characteristics – although today those differences have become blurred as technology has developed.

Lover provided additional screening for Gibson's original humbucking pickup with a metal cover, as he explained. "The cover helps shield away electrostatic noises from fluorescent lamps and so forth," he said. "I needed a material with high resistance so it wouldn't affect the high-frequency response, and I considered non-magnetic stainless steel. But you can't solder to it. German silver [an alloy of copper, nickel, and zinc] has high resistance, and you could solder to it, so I used that. The prototype didn't have adjusting screws, but our sales people wanted them – so that they would have something to talk to the dealers about. The screws were added before we went into production. For a two-pickup guitar, I set the pickups in the guitars with the screws toward the bridge on the pickup nearest the bridge, and toward the fingerboard on the other. Want to know why I did that?" He laughed, and answered his own question. "For decorative purposes."

Patently devious

Gibson began to use the new humbuckers in the early months of 1957 and started to replace the P-90 single-coil pickups on the Les Paul Goldtop and Custom during that year. The Custom was promoted to a three-pickup guitar in its new humbucker-equipped style. Players gradually came to appreciate that humbuckers and a Les Paul guitar made for a congenial mixture, and today many guitarists and collectors covet the earliest type of Gibson humbucking pickup. This is known as a PAF because of a small label with the words Patent Applied For attached to its underside.

Lover was not the first to come up with the idea of humbucking pickups, as he discovered when he came to patent the design (as assignor to Gibson). The filing office made reference to no fewer than six previous documents, the earliest dating from the 1930s – probably Armand F. Knoblaugh's 1935 patent for Baldwin, apparently made with an electric piano in mind but specifically offered as appropriate to other steel-string instruments.

"I had a hell of a time getting a patent," Lover remembered, "and I finally got one with more or less one claim: that I'd built a humbucking pickup." Ray Butts came up with a similar principle around the same time while working with Gretsch, for whom he designed the Filter'Tron humbucking pickup. Lover's patent application had been filed in June 1955, and was eventually issued in July 1959. Which explains that PAF label. Or does it? The PAF labels appear on pickups on guitars dated up to 1962 – well after the patent was issued.

Lover explained this. "Gibson didn't want to give any information as to what patent to look up for those who wanted to make copies. I think that was the reason they carried on with the PAF label for quite a while." When they did eventually get around to putting a patent number on the pickup, Gibson again deterred budding copyists by 'mistakenly' using the number for Les Paul's trapeze bridge-and-tailpiece patent.

Some players say they prefer the sound of original PAF-label humbuckers (and the subsequent 'patent-number' pickups). They consider later humbuckers to have a poorer tone, apparently caused by small changes to coil-winding, magnet grades, and wire-sheathing. Seth Lover could not recall any alterations made to his invention during the transition from those that had the PAF label to the later units that were stamped with patent numbers. "The only change that I'm aware of," he said, "is that from time to time Gibson would use gold plating on the covers, and I think if the gold plating got a little heavy then the pickups would tend to lose the high frequencies, because gold is a very good conductor."[20]

The July 1957 Gibson pricelist details the Les Paul line as follows: Junior (sunburst) $120; Three-Quarter (sunburst) $120; TV (beige) $132.50; Special (beige) $179.50; Les Paul Model (Goldtop) $247.50; and Custom (black) $375.

Sales of the original Les Paul guitars in general reached a peak in 1956 and 1957, with the Junior hitting a record-so-far 3,129 units in 56. But famous musicians were still generally cautious of the relatively new-fangled solidbody electric guitar, although there were clearly a number of more adventurous players who recognised the musical benefits – and that a guitar as flashy as a Goldtop could make them look good, too. Bluesmen such as Muddy Waters, Guitar Slim, Freddie King, and John Lee Hooker were seen with Goldtops during the 50s, as were R&B supremo Hubert Sumlin (guitarist with Howlin' Wolf) and rockabilly rebel Carl Perkins.

Among the most prominent of the new rockers using a Les Paul was Frannie Beecher of Bill Haley & His Comets. The group had introduced many record-buyers to the new rock'n'roll with 'Rock Around The Clock', a Number One on both sides of the Atlantic in 1955. Beecher effectively became the first big-name official endorser of Les Paul guitars – after Les Paul himself, of course, although the popularity of Les & Mary's rather polite records was waning now that raucous rock was evidently here to stay. Beecher had played with western-swing groups and in Benny Goodman's big-band before joining Haley, following the death of original Comets guitarist Danny Cedrone in 1954. Beecher began the job with an acoustic archtop Epiphone guitar with added pickup, but it didn't take long for him to realise that his Epi wasn't up to the job.

"At the volume we had to play, I just couldn't do it," Beecher explained later. "Loud wasn't the word for it. Jeez!" Gibson then provided the band with guitars and amplifiers – Haley himself had an L-7, while Beecher played the top-of-the-line Les Paul Custom. "If there was anything wrong with it or I didn't like it," said Beecher, "I'd send it back and Gibson would send us another one."[21] In return, Gibson used the band in ads in the 50s.

Gibson decided to remake the Goldtop with a sunburst finish in 1958. The result was not an important guitar for Gibson at the time, but rather an attempt to improve sales of a flagging model. It didn't appear in promo material until the company's **1960 catalogue** (top of page), but it was dropped later that year. Since then, examples like this **1958 Standard** (main guitar) are rated as among the greatest electrics ever made.

Gibson executives pictured (right) at the 1958 NAMM trade show in Chicago. They are (left to right) Julius Bellson, Clarence Havenga, and Ted McCarty. It was at this show that Gibson introduced its customers to the new sunburst-finish Les Paul – although there is unfortunately no sign of the instrument in this photo. No doubt 30 seconds after the picture was snapped, each man grabbed one of the Bursts just out of shot and blew through a dirty low-down blues medley.

Gibson made around 1,500 sunburst-finish Les Paul Standard models between 1958 and 1960. All the features are clear on this **1958 Standard** (below), including the red-to-yellow sunburst, which allows a view of the maple underneath, and the two 'PAF' humbucking pickups. The rear (right) shows the cherry-stained mahogany body, the access plates for the control systems, and the ink-stamped serial number near the top of the headstock. Most collectors now call such a guitar a Burst, short for sunburst.

This was one of the first rock endorsement campaigns. "Bill Haley recommends that you see the magnificent Gibson line at your local dealer," ran the copy, with Beecher and his Les Paul Custom clearly visible at Haley's side. It was the model for the way that electric guitars would be promoted for decades to come.

In 1958, Gibson made a radical design change to three of the Les Paul models and a cosmetic alteration to another. "Guitarists the world over are familiar with Gibson's famous series of Les Paul Guitars," the company proclaimed in its promo magazine, *The Gibson Gazette*, at the end of 1958. "They include some of the finest solidbody instruments manufactured today – and lead the field in popularity. It is with great pride that Gibson announces exciting improvements."

The Junior, Junior three-quarter, and TV were revamped with a completely new double-cutaway body shape. The Junior's fresh look was enhanced with a new cherry-red finish. The TV adopted the new double-cutaway design as well, with a more yellow finish (Gibson called it "cream"). The new double-cutaway Special was offered in cherry or the new TV-style yellow.

"This instrument is a true beauty ... "

The Goldtop was the model that fell victim to the small cosmetic alteration. The *Gazette*, under the headline 'Les Paul Guitar In Cherry Red', continued: "A beautiful red cherry sunburst finish is the news here! This guitar now has a rich, rubbed appearance that cannot be equaled at any price, and [has] the 'new look' that is tops with today's guitarists. If the illustration above were in color, you would see exactly what we mean – this instrument is a true beauty. In the future, all Les Paul guitars will be shipped in cherry sunburst finish – there will be no increase in price.

"All other features of this wonderful guitar will remain exactly the same. Two powerful humbucking pickups give the instrument increased sustain and a clear sparkling tone. Any guitarist will appreciate the wide range of tonal colorings produced by the Les Paul. Tune-o-matic bridge permits adjusting string action and individual string lengths for perfect intonation. Graceful cutaway design with attractive inlaid rosewood fingerboard. Separate tone and volume controls for each pickup that can be preset – three-way toggle switch to activate either or both pickups."[22]

Sales of the Les Paul Goldtop model in particular had begun to decline, so naturally the feeling at Gibson was that something needed to be done to stimulate renewed interest in this relatively high-price model. They decided that the unusual gold finish was at fault, figuring that some players found it too unconventional. So Gibson changed the look, applying this new "cherry sunburst" finish in a bid to attract new customers. The first two sunburst Les Pauls – known today as Standard models – were shipped from the factory on May 28th 1958, logged in Gibson's records simply as "LP Spec finish". Gibson had the new look ready to show off in Room 727 at the Palmer House in Chicago during the summer NAMM show in 1958, which took place from July 21 to 24. The new look would last only until 1960. It was the first time Gibson had used this type of sunburst. Their regular sunburst resulted in a brown-to-yellow effect, as on the single-cutaway Les Paul Junior. But Gibson introduced a new red-to-yellow sunburst for the Standard. The maple body cap was now clearly visible through the finish. On Goldtops, the maple had always been hidden under the opaque gold paint.

Now that the Standard showed off its maple through the virtually transparent sunburst finish, Gibson's woodworkers were usually a little more careful with its appearance, often bookmatching the timber.

Bookmatching is a technique where a piece of wood is sliced into two, then opened out down a central join (like a book) to give symmetrically similar patterns on the wood's surface. Gibson had already used such a look – bookmatched maple, sunburst finish – on a handful of its guitars, including a couple of solidbody electric steel models: the relatively broad-bodied Doubleneck Electric Hawaiian back in the late 30s, and the more recent Royaltone, produced for a couple of years from 1950. The backs of archtop hollowbody Gibson guitars were regularly made from carved bookmatched maple, often using spectacularly beautiful timber.

Some of the Les Paul Standards made between 1958 and 1960 also display some astonishing patterned maple. The woodworker's term for these patterns on the surface of timber is figure. ('Grain' is something different, usually the lines in the wood that travel 'across' any figuring.) Any tree can potentially provide figured timber, but it's actually an unpredictable fluke. Some trees will have it, some will not. It's caused by a sort of genetic anomaly in the growing tree that makes ripples or rays in the cells of the living wood.

The visual effect of figure is also determined by variations in the colour and density of the tree's growth, the effect of disease or damage, and, significantly, the way in which the timber is cut from the felled tree. Quarter-sawing – cutting so that the grain is generally square to the face of the resulting planks – often provides the most attractive figured wood, sometimes giving the illusion of roughly parallel rows of three-dimensional 'fingers' or 'hills and valleys' across the face of the timber. In extreme cases it can look dramatic.

Figured maple is also called many (non-technical) names, like curly, or fiddleback, or tigerstripe, but the most common word among guitar people is flame or flamed. So a Standard might be said to have a flame top. Such figured timber is still highly prized at Gibson. "Flame can look like one thing on the raw billet and then turn out to be a totally different animal once it's carved," explained Rick Gembar of the Custom division.

"I had one very established collector who had been talking about this 'holy grail' piece of wood he'd been hoarding for years," Gembar continued. "So I asked him to bring the wood in and offered to build him a Les Paul out of it. Sure enough, this piece of maple was highly flamed from top to bottom with beautifully spaced lines. It looked like what we would call a 'killer' top. We took it and started carving the dish for the top … and you could see the flame start to melt away. The depth of the flame is the key to whether or not it's going to remain figured during the entire process from board to guitar top."[23]

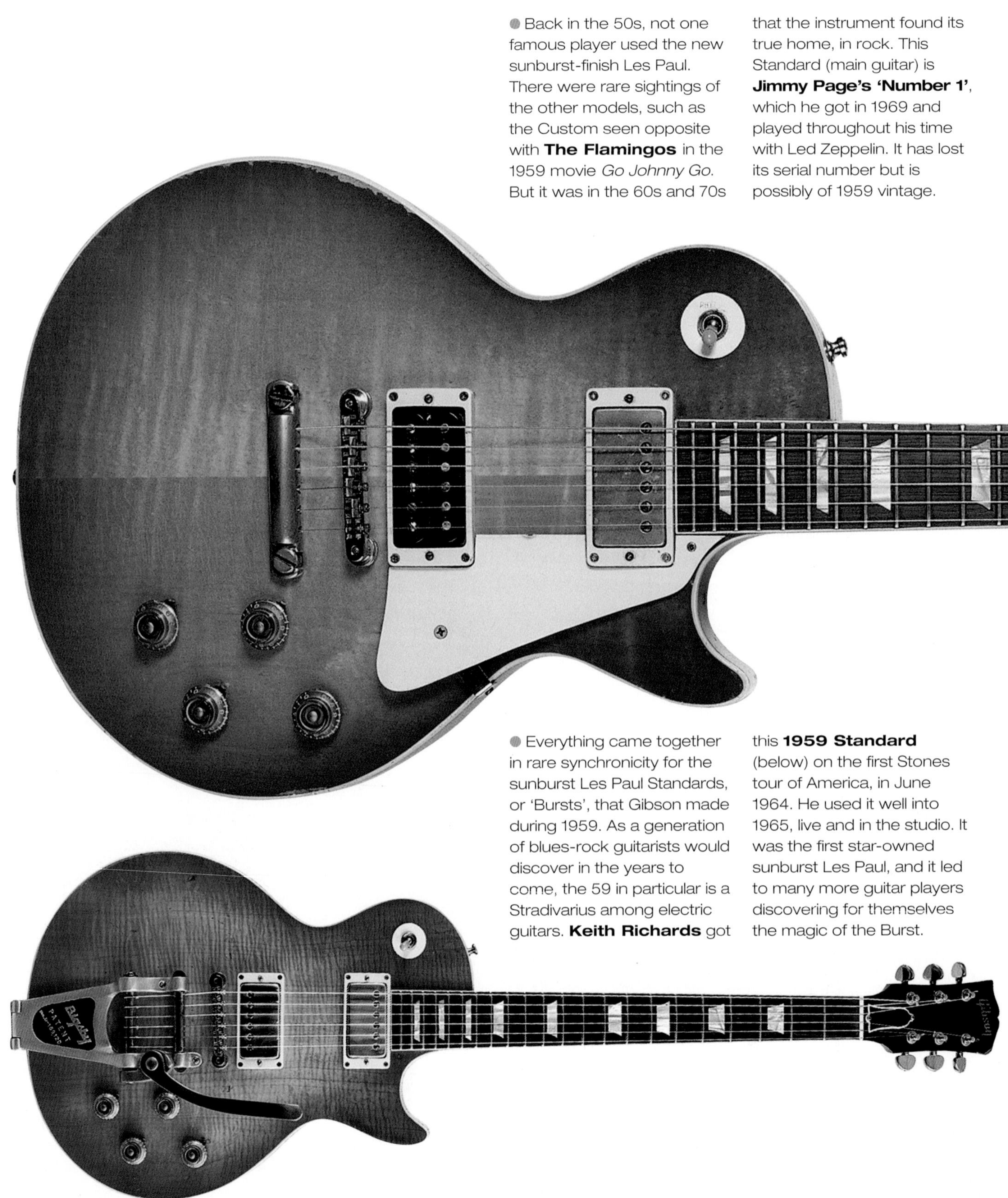

● Back in the 50s, not one famous player used the new sunburst-finish Les Paul. There were rare sightings of the other models, such as the Custom seen opposite with **The Flamingos** in the 1959 movie *Go Johnny Go*. But it was in the 60s and 70s that the instrument found its true home, in rock. This Standard (main guitar) is **Jimmy Page's 'Number 1'**, which he got in 1969 and played throughout his time with Led Zeppelin. It has lost its serial number but is possibly of 1959 vintage.

● Everything came together in rare synchronicity for the sunburst Les Paul Standards, or 'Bursts', that Gibson made during 1959. As a generation of blues-rock guitarists would discover in the years to come, the 59 in particular is a Stradivarius among electric guitars. **Keith Richards** got this **1959 Standard** (below) on the first Stones tour of America, in June 1964. He used it well into 1965, live and in the studio. It was the first star-owned sunburst Les Paul, and it led to many more guitar players discovering for themselves the magic of the Burst.

● **Peter Green** bought this **1959 Standard** (above) in 1965 and played it with John Mayall and then on nearly all the great Fleetwood Mac records and gigs. Green passed it on to Gary Moore, who also made good use of the guitar. Moore owned it from about 1970 to 2006.

Back at Gibson in the late 50s, Les Paul Standards continued to come off the line. The quality of the maple used for their tops was never advertised or promoted by Gibson, because it was simply down to the wood that happened to be available, whether figured or plain. No priority was given to the Standards. After all, Les Pauls had not been selling. The new-look Standards were almost an afterthought. If a good-looking one happened to come along now and again, well, that was a bonus. At the time, timber was cut and shaped in the 15,000-square-foot wing that had been added to Gibson's original 1917 Kalamazoo factory in 1945, just behind the famous chimney. From the guitars of the period that turn up today, it's clear that Gibson's most impressively figured maple was reserved for the backs of archtop models. Nevertheless, some Les Paul Standards were astonishingly attractive. And some were extremely plain.

At first, Gibson's hunch about a different look for the guitar was proved right. They knew that sales of the Goldtop had declined from a high of 920 during 1956 to just 434 in 1958, the year of the new Standard. After the revised model appeared, sales climbed to 643 in 1959 – but they would dip again in 1960. Gibson then decided it needed something more than the change of finish, and that the only way to attract new customers was to completely redesign the entire Les Paul line. We'll look at that in more detail in the next chapter, which covers the 60s. The result of that decision was that the original sunburst Les Paul Standard was only produced from 1958 to 1960.

In December 1958, Gibson set the list price of the 'new' sunburst model at $247.50 (which, translated to today's buying power, is the equivalent of about $1,800, or £1,200). Among players and collectors, the sunburst Standard has since become the most highly prized solidbody electric guitar ever. 'Bursts', as these sunburst models are now known, regularly fetch huge sums, presently well into six figures, far in excess of almost all other collectable guitars. The factor that often determines the magnitude of their value is usually related to more than the sound or playability of a particular example: the individual quality and visual impact of the maple top. Those with especially outrageous figure visible through the top's finish are rated most highly. Like collectable violins, some of the most celebrated Bursts are even given names.

Unbursts, zebras, and killer tops

There is another factor that can make Standards look different from one another today. The coloured paint used to create the sunburst effect can fade in varying ways, depending primarily on how a particular guitar has been exposed to daylight during its lifetime. Some apparently sharp-eyed collectors even claim to be able to tell how long a particular guitar spent in a shop window or a smoke-filled club. In some cases the original shaded sunburst will have almost totally disappeared, leaving a uniform and rather pleasant honey colour on such guitars (now affectionately known as 'unburst' examples).

A further cause for excitement among collectors – even some players – is the different pickup bobbins that became evident years later with an Eric Clapton-led fashion for removing pickup covers. In the very late 50s, manufacturer Hughes Plastics and its distributor Eastman Chemical ran out of the black Tenite plastic they used to make Gibson's pickup bobbins. They substituted white plastic for a while.

Today, some people insist that dual-coil Gibson pickups from the period with all-white or white-and-black ('zebra') bobbins are somehow better. The pickup's inventor, Seth Lover, was amused by the idea. "Yes, our supplier ran out of black material, but they did have cream. We were not going to stop production just for that," he laughed. "So we got some cream bobbins. I couldn't tell any difference one from the other – although I think cream was a better colour for winding the wire on to the pickups, because you could see the wire in there a lot easier than you could with the black."[24]

Those who do get the chance to play Les Paul Standards, rather than consign them to bank-vaults as part of an investment portfolio, have noted a number of minor changes over the three production years: smaller frets in 1958, bigger during 1959–60; and a chunky, round-backed neck over the 1958–59 period compared to a slimmer, flatter-profiled version in 1960. But as one US guitar dealer put it: "It seems like the top more than anything else will sell those guitars. If it has a killer top but it's beat to hell and refinished, it'll still sell for more than one that's plain. The high prices seem due in part to non-players paying the most money for them, and often it seems that these people go solely for the look. I've seen them buy those guitars without even plugging them in. And they've missed some great guitars, because they've looked … and then said no, not interested. No top!"

Gibson's November 1959 pricelist shows seven Les Pauls: Junior (cherry, double-cutaway) $132.50; Junior Three-Quarter (cherry, double-cut) $132.50; TV ("cream", double-cut) $132.50; Special (cherry or "cream") $195; Special Three-Quarter (cherry) $195; Les Paul Model (sunburst, known as Standard from following year) $265; and Custom (black) $395.

These sunburst Standards have turned into some of Gibson's most sacred sleeping giants. Almost ignored at the time, the instruments have now become ultra-collectable icons. Players and collectors came to realise that their inherent musicality, as well as a short production run – around 1,450 were made between 1958 and 1960 – added up to a modern classic. As we'll discover in the next chapter, this re-evaluation was prompted originally in the middle and late 60s when a number of guitarists discovered that Gibson Les Pauls had enormous potential for high-volume blues-based rock. It turned out that these guitars' inherent tonality, coupled with the humbucking pickups and played through a loud tube or valve amp, made a wonderful noise.

the sixties

"Wind it up through a stack and there's this great over-the-top sound that Les Paul never even dreamt of."

Eric Clapton, Cream ▶

Considering all Gibson's various Les Paul models as a whole, sales declined in 1960 after a peak the previous year. By 1961, Gibson had decided on a complete redesign of the line in an effort to rekindle interest in the Les Pauls. The company had started a $400,000 expansion of its factory in Kalamazoo during 1960 that more than doubled the size of the plant by the time it was completed in August. It was the third addition to the original 1917 factory, with other buildings added in 1945 and 1950. The new single-storey brick-and-steel building meant that Gibson's entire plant now covered more than 120,000 square feet and extended for two city blocks at Parsons Street in Kalamazoo. Clearly, the firm would be needing instruments that sold in big numbers to keep the new factory at peak performance.

One of the first series of new models to benefit from Gibson's expanded production facilities were the revised Les Pauls. The SGs had a completely new highly-sculpted double-cutaway design. At first, Gibson continued to call them Les Paul models, so guitars of this new style made between 1961 and 1963 with suitable markings are now known as SG/Les Pauls. But by 1963, the Les Paul name was gone and the models officially continued as SGs. The SG name stands for Solid Guitar.

Ted McCarty, still president at Gibson, said Les Paul's name was taken off the guitars because the association was now less of a commercial bonus than it once had been. Les's popularity as a recording artist had declined: he and Mary Ford had no more Top 40 hits on Capitol after 1955 and left the label three years later. They recorded for Columbia from 1958 to 1963 with little commercial impact.

But the main reason that Les Paul's name was dropped from Gibson guitars in 1963 relates to his divorce. The news was noted in the record-trade magazine *Billboard* in May 1963, under the headline 'Les And Mary Say Bye-Bye', where it was reported that Miss Ford was now living in California while Mr Paul was living in New Jersey.

The couple were officially divorced by the end of 1964, and Les retired from most playing and recording for about ten years from 1965. "The contract came due I think in 1962," Les told me, "right at the time that Mary and I decided to split."

He agreed with Gibson to wait until the divorce was over before starting further discussions because he did not want to sign any fresh contract bringing in new money while the divorce proceedings were underway. "[Mary's] lawyers would ask for part of it in the divorce settlement," he said. "So my contract ended in 62, and Gibson could not make any more Les Paul guitars."[1]

Les said also that he didn't like the design of the new SG/Les Paul models and that this was another reason why his name was removed from them. "The first [SG/Les Paul] I saw was in a music store," Les said later, "and I didn't like the shape – a guy could kill himself on those sharp horns. It was too thin, and they had moved the front pickup away from the fingerboard so they could fit my name in there. The neck was too skinny, and I didn't like the way it joined the body: there wasn't enough wood, at least in my opinion. So I called Gibson and asked them to take my name off the thing. It wasn't my design."[2]

Les was seen regularly in the 60s in official Gibson promo photos with the SG/Les Paul models, and held one on the cover of his 1967 album *Les Paul Now*. Yet when he played the occasional live appearance he would still use his old-style Gibson Les Pauls. It was clear that, like many other musicians in the 60s, he considered a proper Les Paul to be the one with the traditional single-cutaway design.

Gibson did manage a slight increase in production when the new SG designs were introduced, with output of all Les Paul models from the Kalamazoo factory settling at just under 6,000 units each year in 1961, 1962, and 1963. The September 1963 pricelist is among the last in the early 60s to feature Les Pauls, and it itemises three models: the SG/Les Paul Junior (cherry) $155; SG/Les Paul Standard (cherry) $310; and SG/Les Paul Custom (white) $450. With the contract now expired, from 1964 until 1967 inclusive there were no guitars in the Gibson line bearing the Les Paul name, either on the guitars themselves or in the company's literature.

All change at Gibson

In the United States, sales of guitars in general – including acoustic as well as electric instruments – climbed throughout the early 60s and hit a peak of about a million and a half units in 1965, after which the figure declined, falling to just over a million during 1967. CMI's sales of Gibson guitars and amplifiers hit a peak of $19 million-worth in 1966 but then began to fall in line with the general trend, down to $15 million by 1968.

As well as this general decline in demand for guitars, Gibson's production was hit by a number of strikes in the 60s, including a 16-day stoppage in 1966 which, reported *The Music Trades*, resulted in a "turnover of skilled personnel" (they fired people) and "production efficiency at Gibson remaining at relatively low levels throughout the year" (output was down). Gibson was hindered by a spate of bad weather, and matters were hardly improved when a trucking-industry strike in the Chicago area "interrupted the flow of merchandise in and out of the company's distribution center".[3]

Gibson had built a new home for its electronics department in 1962 and added a separate factory for making amps, strings, and pickups in 1964. Guitar manufacturing remained at Parsons Street, Kalamazoo. Gibson president Ted McCarty and his number two, John Huis, left in 1966 after buying the Bigsby musical accessories company of California, which they re-established in Kalamazoo.

In February 1968, after a number of short-stay occupants in the job, Stan Rendell was appointed president of Gibson. Rendell had worked for CMI since 1963 and at the time of his new appointment was vice president of manufacturing. He told his boss, Maurice Berlin, that he was tired of travelling so much between CMI's factories, including plants for Lowrey organs and Olds brass as well as Gibson. Berlin offered Rendell the chance to run Gibson – a challenge, as it turned out.

"Mr Berlin said we're not doing too well with Gibson," Rendell explained. "They had lost a million dollars at the factory for the two prior years."[4] So Rendell was made president

● Among the guitarists who found the various Les Paul models sympathetic to their requirements was the great **Freddie King** (right). He made nearly all his bustling bluesy instrumentals with the Goldtop he's pictured with here, not least the classic 'Hide Away', which he recorded in summer 1960. It was a big American hit the following year, grazing the pop Top 30, and it reached the ears of just about any blues player you care to name – including an Englishman called Eric Clapton, who noted the master's choice of guitar with great interest.

● Many Standards from the last year of the model's production period have slimmer necks and appeal to players who like that feel. The **1960 Standard** shown here (below) belongs to Paul McCartney, and it is certainly the most famous of the three 60s pictured across these pages. It's also a particularly rare example of the Standard in that it's left-handed – only a very few were made, and Gibson clearly did not think it worth going to the trouble of moving the 'Les Paul Model' logo the right way up on the guitar's headstock.

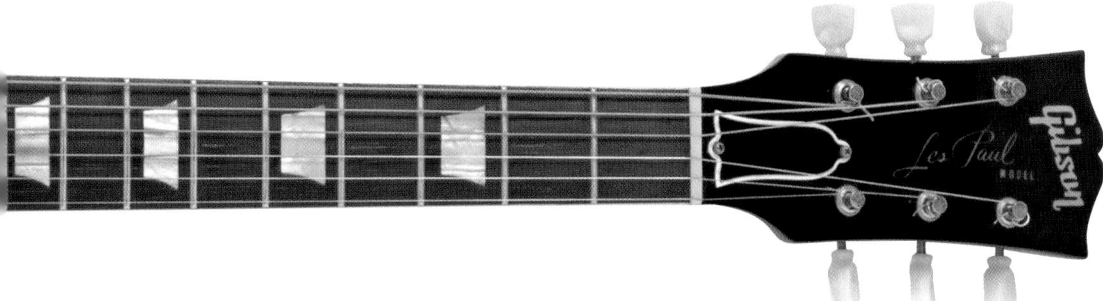

● Gibson at this time was not the kind of company to let a model ride for years to see if its fortunes might change. As soon as the sunburst Standard began to dip in sales, it was deleted from the catalogue. These two **1960 Standards** (main guitar, and above) show the different levels of 'flame' that can occur in the maple tops. Gibson stopped making all its original-design Les Paul models, in fact, and it seemed as if these single-cutaway carved-top models were history. And so they would be – but without the emphatic full-stop that Gibson intended in the early 60s.

of Gibson and faced the usual brief handed to incoming presidents: make sure you improve the company's fortunes.

Guitarist Bruce Bolen, born in England and raised in Chicago, joined Gibson in 1967 to run promotional shows and concerts and, as he described it, "to be a representative player for Gibson". Gradually, over the years, he took on more responsibility, eventually becoming involved in guitar design and marketing. Back in the late 60s when he joined Gibson, Bolen saw a company in poor condition.

"One of the reasons I was hired was because Gibson's electric sales were floundering," he said. "All we had in solidbody electrics were SGs, plus the archtop and thinline instruments, and they weren't selling all that well. The mainstay of the company at the time was the flat-top acoustics. So I was hired basically to go out and sell electric guitars."

He found that management at Gibson and its parent company CMI were generally unaware at the time of the growing interest among rock guitarists in the original pre-1961 Les Paul models. "I was just a punk kid, and most of the people there were in their fifties or older," Bolen recalled. "I don't think they had a great grasp on how important that guitar was becoming once again. Mike Bloomfield, Eric Clapton, guys like that – they'd found it to be something really precious that offered a sound that was very conducive to their form of music."[5]

And God created sunburst

Starting around 1965, there was a boom in blues-based rock music, originating in Britain. Many white guitarists were at the core of this new musical movement, and some were naturally inspired to find the guitars used by their black American influences. They discovered that a Gibson Les Paul overdriven through a stack – a powerful tube (valve) amplifier with multiple loudspeaker cabinets – produced a wonderfully rich, emotive sound that was well suited to this fresh musical setting.

The most notable member of the Les Paul guitar appreciation society was Eric Clapton. He said later that his best Les Paul was the sunburst Standard he acquired around the end of May 1965 while he was playing with John Mayall's Bluesbreakers. "I bought [it] in one of the shops in London right after I'd seen Freddie King's album cover of *Let's Hide Away And Dance Away*," said Clapton, "where he's playing a Goldtop. It had humbuckers and was almost brand new – original case with that lovely purple … lining, just magnificent. I never really found one as good as that. I do miss that one."[6] The guitar was stolen as he began rehearsals with his new band, Cream, in summer 1966.

Many, many Standards have since been hopefully offered as the famous ex-Clapton guitar, but no proof has ever accompanied such instruments. Clapton in fact played a number of Standards in the 60s, probably two more following that original, as well as a three-humbucker Custom. But as a member of Mayall's Bluesbreakers, Clapton had played that first Standard through a small Marshall amp to great effect on the group's *Blues Breakers* LP. This famous 'Beano' album (Clapton reads a *Beano* comic on the front) came out in July 1966, and the rear of the jacket pictured Clapton with his original Standard. Even though the photograph only showed part of the back of the guitar, keen-eyed fans could work out what it was. Some people argue today that this one image began the entire vintage-guitar fashion, a trend based on the notion that old guitars are inherently better than new ones.

Whatever the arguments, it was certainly Clapton more than any other musician who turned the ears of fellow players toward the new sound of the old Les Paul guitars, particularly when his innovative, sweet, flowing sound was introduced to the world on Cream's 1966 hit 'I Feel Free'. This he recorded on his second Standard, which he bought from future Police guitarist Andy Summers around September 1966. "I am playing more smoothly now," Clapton explained. "I'm developing what I call my 'woman tone'. It's a sweet sound, something like the solo on 'I Feel Free'. It's more like the human voice than a guitar. You wouldn't think that it was a guitar for the first few passages. It calls for the correct use of distortion."[7]

The search for old Les Pauls grew ever more urgent as a queue of respected players formed to take up the aging model. In fact, Clapton hadn't been the first to realise that the old, discontinued Les Paul models played so well. Keith Richards of The Rolling Stones was the first star guitarist to be seen with an old-style Les Paul. He acquired a 59 sunburst Standard during the group's first US tour, in June 1964, and used it into the following year (the guitar is pictured elsewhere in the book). Jimmy Page was playing a three-humbucker Custom by late 1964 when he was a busy session player on the London recording scene.

Clapton's replacement in Mayall's band, Peter Green, got a Standard in late 1965 and used it to great effect in that group and also in Fleetwood Mac, which he fronted for three years from 1967. Jeff Beck, too, was inspired to get a Les Paul after seeing Clapton play his with the Bluesbreakers in London, and Beck bought his first Burst at the end of February 1966 when he was playing with The Yardbirds.

Beck explained later that he wanted a Les Paul for its sonic qualities. "They had this deep sound, and I really needed that power in a three-piece, to help fill out the sound. There was a guy at Selmer's shop in London, said he'd got a good one at home. That was the shop to go to. So it was: Meet me at so-and-so and I'll bring along the guitar."[8] Beck said this first Les Paul was a 1959 model that cost him about £175. It's all over the *Yardbirds* album, known as *Roger The Engineer*, which was made in mid 1966.

Beck left The Yardbirds by the end of 66, put together The Jeff Beck Group, and continued to play his Standard, stripping its sunburst finish himself in 1968. He used it on the fine *Truth* album of that year. By October, the guitar had suffered damage and Beck bought a second one, from future Cheap Trick guitarist Rick Nielsen, but he never recorded much with it. He got a third Les Paul in late 1972, when he was in Beck Bogert & Appice. This was a converted mid-50s Goldtop, modified with two humbuckers and a heavy dark-brown refinish to the body, which Beck called an 'oxblood' colour. He used it for some of the classic *Blow By Blow* album of 1974.

As Gibson changed style, players found joy in original-style Les Pauls. **Michael Bloomfield** (left) plays his Goldtop on a UK tour with The Paul Butterfield Blues Band in late 1966, while sessionman **Jimmy Page** (above) clutches his Custom in 1965.

● Gibson redesigned the Les Paul line with a new sculpted body shape. At first, the Les Paul name was retained on these new guitars, but Gibson later called them SG models. As a result, these early instruments, made between 1961 and 1963, are known as SG/Les Paul models. This **1961 SG/Les Paul Custom** (above) and the others pictured on these two pages are examples of the original SG/Les Pauls. In 1963, Gibson removed the Les Paul name, and from then they became, simply, Gibson SGs. Meanwhile, the first 'name' player to discover the old-style Les Pauls was **Keith Richards**, pictured in March 1965 (below) with sunburst Standard.

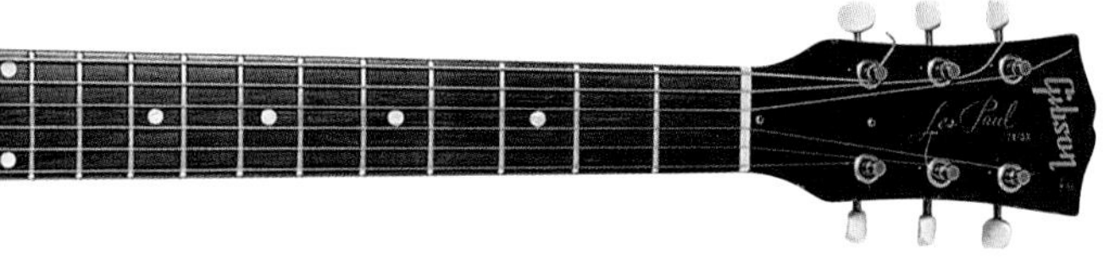

● Two more fine examples of the new-style models: a simple, potent **1961 SG/Les Paul Junior** (above) and a **1961 SG/Les Paul Standard** (below), complete with 'sideways' Vibrola.

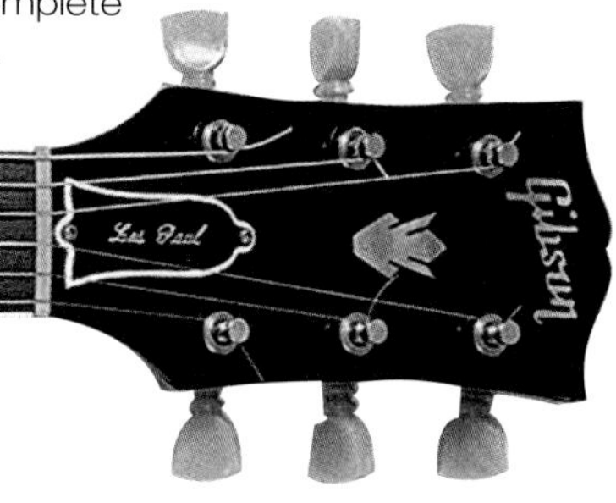

In the USA, Michael Bloomfield, with the Butterfield Blues Band and then Electric Flag, had a similar effect. Bloomfield started in the Butterfield band with a Telecaster, which he used for their debut album of summer 1966, but then shifted to a P-90 Goldtop, inspired by his beloved Chicago blues guitarists who also played Goldtops. His Goldtop can be heard on the band's remarkable *East-West* album of summer 1966.

When the Butterfield band played in the UK late in 1966, Bloomfield took along his Goldtop, but witnessed Green and Clapton playing their sunburst Les Pauls. "I wondered to myself how they knew that this guitar had all the inherent qualities of sustain, volume, and tone that was just better than any other possible rock'n'roll guitar at that time," said Bloomfield. He acquired a Burst of his own around May 1967, debuting it with his new Electric Flag band at the Monterey Pop festival the following month. "All of us ... were playing the same model guitar."[9]

Billy Gibbons, who would go on with ZZ Top to do much for the popularity of Les Paul Standards in future decades, recalled how his passion began. "I stand among the many who seemed to think that the appearance of Clapton on the reverse side of the Mayall *Blues Breakers* album, that first disc, was indicative, because the sound was so fierce and so attractive. The photograph was a clue and has been reproduced many times. Ah, look at that: they don't make those any more – but it's *one of those old Les Pauls.*"

Gibbons followed his nose and sought a sunburst Standard of his own, encouraged when his band supported The Jeff Beck Group and Beck told him a Les Paul–Marshall combination was impossible to beat. A false alarm led Gibbons to a Flying V, but around late summer 1968 he acquired what became known as Pearly Gates, his luscious 59 sunburst Standard.

It was the guitar that Gibbons would go on to play with ZZ Top, the instrument that would make his name. "I'll tell you, man, that is some kind of guitar," he said. "I've wondered along the way why this particular example of the Burst is so robust. Really, the only explanation is that it just happened to be put together on the right day. The particular day that all of the disparate elements came together was just that magical moment, I suppose. It was all guess work back in those days."[10]

Prices for used Les Pauls had gradually been moving upward and reports were appearing in the music press. One of the first to identify the trend was the British magazine *Beat Instrumental*, in summer 1966. "Les Paul Customs are in great demand!" shrieked a headline. "If you have a Les Paul Custom you want to sell, come to London and get a very good price for it from almost anyone. Rarest of the lot seems to be the three-pickup job which Jimmy Page uses. If you have one of these you are rich."[11]

Letters pleading for help began to appear, too. "I am having great difficulty in obtaining a Gibson Les Paul Custom guitar," wrote a *Beat* reader. "Have you any idea where I can obtain one? If you think this is impossible, perhaps you could tell me which guitar is similar in tone?" While a Custom was specified, most guitarists would have been pleased to find any original Les Paul model. The magazine replied: "The Les Paul Custom is a much sought after instrument. It is impossible to obtain a new one, and even secondhand models are very scarce. If you want one, then you will have to be very patient."[12] The editors recommended as an alternative one of the slowly growing band of Japanese-made copy guitars on sale in Europe and the USA. These oriental 'replicas' were of pretty poor quality at the time – but at least they looked similar and were available.

The search for Les Pauls continued. In a news item later in 67, a reporter contemplated the sorry state of supply and demand. "So many people are interested in obtaining one of the almost legendary Les Paul guitars that we've done a bit of checking. Some guitarists insist that new Les Pauls can still be bought, but they're wrong ... so if you're offered a guitar, and told it's a Les Paul, be very wary."[13]

Gibson at last woke up to all this interest and decided to do something about its deteriorating position in the electric guitar market – and specifically about the increasing demand for its old Les Paul guitars. Bruce Bolen, Gibson's 'guitar-playing representative', remembered that one day soon after he started working for the company in 1967, vice president Marc Carlucci asked if he'd mind staying late that evening at the CMI headquarters in Chicago.

"Marc told me they had someone coming in and wanted my opinion on what he had to show us," said Bolen. "I asked who it was, and he told me it was Les Paul. Now, when I was a kid, six years old, Les Paul was my first guitar hero, so I was thrilled to have the chance to meet him. Gibson still wasn't too sure they wanted to reintroduce the Les Paul guitar. I was going: Please!"[14]

Les Paul's musical activities had been very low-key since the mid 60s, but in 1967 he released *Les Paul Now*, his first album for some time. This meeting that same year marked the start of his new association with Gibson and the beginning of the reissue programme for Les Paul models. Les's recollection of the circumstances was typically forthright. "I called Gibson and said hey, Fender's here bugging me and they want to make a deal, and my divorce is over. I asked if Gibson wanted to make a deal. And Mr Berlin said it was odd that I should call, because they were striking all electrical instruments from the Gibson line. He told me the electric guitar was extinct. So I asked if he could meet me that Friday in Chicago. I said I wanted to buy him a cup of coffee. We stayed up for 24 hours, and I convinced him to go back and make the electric guitar."[15]

Maybe Berlin was thinking about "striking all electrical instruments from the Gibson line" but there's little evidence the company really was contemplating such a move. Certainly Gibson negotiated a new contract with Les. The royalty agreed was five per cent of the 'standard cost' of each Les Paul model – that is, the internal price at which Gibson sold the guitar to CMI, around a third of retail. Such a calculation meant that he would receive about \$6.50 for each Les Paul model typically selling then for \$395 retail.

By the time Stan Rendell had become president of Gibson in early 1968, the decision to re-commence the manufacture of Les Paul guitars had already been made by CMI management in Chicago, principally by Berlin and Carlucci. At the Gibson plant in

Kalamazoo, Rendell and his team had their own difficulties. Rendell recalled the position when he joined Gibson. "We had all kinds of quality problems. We had production problems. We had personnel problems. We had union problems. We had problems that wouldn't end."

Rendell, the new broom, set to work. He developed a structure for supervision in the Kalamazoo factory, he instigated manufacturing schedules, improved inspection routines, installed a separate stock room, held regular meetings, and bought, as he puts it, "a ton of new equipment, all sorts of stuff. Mr Berlin said that in the first five years I was there, there were more new ideas, new machinery, and new products than in the entire history of the Gibson company prior to that. We just had a ball. And if we didn't know how to do something, we found out".[16]

Bruce Bolen, meanwhile, had a showstopper for his Gibson promotional concerts. He'd taken out on the road a prototype of the forthcoming reissue Les Paul Custom, as far as he can remember by very late 1967. "People were just falling apart about it. They couldn't wait to get one."

"Okay, you win ... Les Pauls available now"

Gibson decided to reintroduce the relatively rare two-pickup Les Paul Custom and the Les Paul Goldtop with P-90 pickups and Tune-o-matic bridge. At first, there was some discussion about making the Custom in white, like the SG/Les Paul Custom, but the white lacquer proved sensitive to contamination, so the company went with the 'correct' black.

Gibson formally launched the two new models at the June 1968 NAMM trade show in Chicago. The company's pricelist from that month showed the two revived Les Pauls for the first time: the Custom was pitched at $545 and the Goldtop (they called it the Standard) at $395. Les Paul was at the NAMM show to promote the new guitars for Gibson by doing what he's always done best – playing the things. Bolen remembered: "I provided the rhythm section for Les, and it was the first time in years that he'd got on a stage. We had a lot of fun."[17]

Gibson's press advertisement publicising the revived guitars, headlined Daddy Of 'Em All, admitted that Gibson had been forced to reintroduce the guitars. "The demand for them just won't quit," ran the blurb. "And the pressure to make more has never let up. OK, you win. We are pleased to announce that more of the original Les Paul Gibsons are available. Line forms at your Gibson dealer."

Around the time of that summer 68 NAMM show, production of the new Customs and Goldtops was started at Kalamazoo. Jim Tite of Gibson said at the time that production was expected to start in June. "The revival of these instruments answers a pressing need," he admitted. "It will soon be no longer necessary to search for used models that sell in auction for $700 to $1,000 in the United States."[18]

Rendell told me that the first run, which took 90 days to get from wood shop to stock room, was for 500 guitars: 400 Goldtops and 100 Customs. "By the time we had that started, CMI wanted 100 a month of the Goldtop and 25 a month of the Custom, and before we were finished with that we were making 100 Les Pauls a day. That's out of a total of 250, 300 instruments a day."[19] Gibson clearly had a success in the making. The only mystery as far as many guitarists were concerned was why they'd waited so long – and why they reissued the wrong Les Paul models. Where was the sunburst with humbuckers?

An important change to Gibson's ownership occurred in 1969. The company's new owner, Norlin Industries, was born in 1969 following the merger of CMI and ECL, an Ecuadorian brewery. ECL simply bought enough of CMI's publicly traded stock to gain control of the company. The Norlin name was made by combining the first syllable of ECL chairman Norton Stevens's name and the last syllable of that of CMI founder Maurice Berlin. Norlin was in three businesses: musical instruments, brewing, and 'technology'. The takeover was formalised in 1974 and Maurice Berlin, a man widely respected in the musical instrument industry, was moved sideways in the new structure, away from the general running of the company.

Many people who worked for Gibson at the time have said how, when the change of ownership occurred, there was suddenly a new breed of employee to be seen. The most common description – and indeed the most polite – is of a Harvard MBA with suit, slide-rule, and calculator at the ready. To translate, that's a Master of Business Administration graduate from the Harvard Business School, armed with the tools of his trade. Or, as one long-serving Gibson manager of the time put it: "I'd think about people, about machines, about parts ... and these new guys would 'solve' all the problems with a calculator. They had nothing to offer other than that they were looking for a place to invest their money and gain a profit. That was their motivation."

Stuck in Kalamazoo with the Norlin blues again

Gibson president Stan Rendell said that the new owners made a fundamental change to the way his business operated. "When they came in, they said we're going to change Gibson from a profit centre to a cost centre. Before, we sold guitars to CMI, which meant that we could make a profit at the factory. And with that profit we were able to buy machinery, improve the benefits to the employees, increase the rates of pay – everything that a company that makes a profit can do. But when they changed us to a cost centre we had no sales – they just paid our bills. And when they did that they destroyed the initiative. If someone runs up a bill, it's paid. So the person running up the bill doesn't have any incentive to not run it so high or not run it at all."[20]

Some of those at Gibson during this period feel that there was a move away from managers who understood guitars to managers who understood manufacturing. Some of the instruments made during the period soon after Gibson was taken over have a bad reputation today. The new owners are generally felt now to have been insensitive to the needs of musicians. One insider remembered: "Up until about 1974, everything was hunky dory, and then it began to change. Too many people were doing too few things, too much money was being spent on too little," our insider continued, "and it started to affect the infamous bottom line."

This air of retrospective uneasiness is mirrored in the case of two other American guitar-making giants who also were taken over during this period: Fender, by CBS in 1965, and Gretsch, by Baldwin in 1967. Clearly this was a sign of the times, as economic analysts advised big corporations to diversify into a range of different businesses, pour in some money ... and sit back to wait for the profits. At any rate, Gibson was not alone in feeling the effects of the new management methods.

The shift during the 70s toward a 'rationalisation' of production meant that changes were made to some Gibson guitars at that time (and, to some extent, into the 80s). Generally, these alterations were made for one of three reasons. First, to save money. Second, to limit the number of guitars returned for work under warranty. And third, to speed up production. One of the most common things guitarists say about Gibson Les Pauls from the 70s is a generalisation: many of them are relatively heavy when compared to examples from other periods. This was partly due to an increase in the density of the mahogany that Gibson was buying, but also to a change in body construction that lasted from about 1969 to 1973.

Instead of the traditional maple-and-mahogany or all-mahogany construction, an elaborate multiple sandwich was developed (also used, from 1969, for the new Custom). It consisted of a maple top with twin layers of mahogany above and below another layer of thin maple. If you look at the side of a Les Paul made in this way you should be able to see the extra central strip of maple. Adding an extra piece of timber like this, with a contrary grain pattern, is known as cross-banding.

Gibson's internal ECN, or Engineering Change Notice, said that it was done to strengthen the body, to prevent cracking and checking. "It's a standard practice in the furniture industry," said Stan Rendell. "It ties the wood together." It may also have simplified Norlin's timber buying, because it meant that the thinner pieces of mahogany already assigned for necks could now also be used for bodies. However, by about 1973 the cross-banding was stopped. There were complaints from players and dealers about shrinkage around the obvious joins, but the extra labour costs involved in preparing the sandwich priced it out of existence anyway.

Gibson changed the way they constructed guitar necks, also from around 1969. The move was from the traditional one-piece neck to a stronger three-piece mahogany laminate, and on to three-piece maple around 1974, intended to give even greater strength. From about 1969, Gibson also added a volute to the back of the neck. A volute is a triangular 'lump' just below the point where the neck becomes the headstock, designed to reinforce this notoriously weak spot. Another change made at the time to minimise problems in the same area was a slight decrease in the angle at which the headstock tips back from the neck. Such practical changes did nothing to enhance Gibson's reputation among those who liked the older guitars.

The busy guitar-design department at Gibson next changed the style and name of the recently reissued Les Paul Goldtop-style model, meaning that the first type only lasted a short time in production. In 1969, the Les Paul Deluxe took its place, marking the first new name for a Les Paul model in 14 years. The Deluxe was prompted by calls from Gibson's marketing managers, who were being told by dealers that players wanted the Goldtop model with humbucking pickups rather than the single-coil P-90s of the reissue. And ideally they'd like a sunburst finish, not gold, because that's what Clapton and Bloomfield and the rest used.

Jim Deurloo had joined Gibson back in 1958 as a factory worker. He moved through the ranks and by 1969 headed up the pattern shop at Kalamazoo, where he was given the task of providing the planned Deluxe with humbuckers ... but without incurring costs for new tooling. The only way he could do this was to fit a humbucking pickup into the space already being routed for smaller P-90s. He considered a few options and eventually came up with the solution of using a mini-humbucking pickup of a type that appeared on some Epiphone models of the time.

Gibson had acquired Epiphone and began producing guitars with the brand in Kalamazoo during 1958. According to Ted McCarty, who was president at the time of the purchase, Gibson thought that they were buying Epiphone's double-bass business. What they actually got was virtually the entire company: guitars, parts, machinery, and all.

"We only discovered this when they shipped the whole thing back to Kalamazoo in a big furniture truck," McCarty told me. He had to rent space in another building in Eleanor Street in Kalamazoo so that Epiphone parts could be prepared before final assembly at Parsons Street. "I put Ward Arbanas in charge of it, and we made the Epiphone guitars just the way Epiphone made them, with every detail exact," McCarty claimed.[21]

Production of Gibson-made Epiphones started during 1958 – and by 1961 totally at Parsons Street. Many fine guitars were produced. But by 1969, the Epiphone line was being run down, because by then Epiphone prices more or less matched those of Gibson. Customers would naturally opt for the highly-rated Gibson, meaning a drop in demand for Epiphone. Something had to be done, and by 1970 Gibson took the decision to phase out US production of Epiphones, instead applying the brandname to cheaper guitars imported from oriental factories. No proper Les Paul-style Epiphones would be made until the 80s.

Back with the Gibson Les Paul Deluxe, in 1969, and Jim Deurloo managed to accommodate an Epiphone mini-humbucker by taking a P-90 pickup cover, cutting a hole in it, and dropping in the small Epiphone unit ... of which Gibson now had surplus stocks. The result pleased everyone: the look was relatively traditional, the pickup was a humbucker, and there were no extra tooling costs. At first, the Deluxe was only available with a gold top, but gradually sunbursts and other colours were introduced, and the model lasted in production until the mid 80s (and again from the early 90s). It appeared on Gibson's pricelist for September 1969, its year of introduction, at $425.

● Finally, after Keith and Peter and Michael and Eric and the rest proved the sonic efficacy of those early-style Les Pauls, Gibson reintroduced the original design – but they missed the obvious one. This **1968 Goldtop** (above) and **1968 Custom** (right) were the Gibson choices, and perfectly fine guitars too. But for now there was not a sign of the sunburst Standard that all those great players used.

WELCOME BACK 1968–69

Gibson launched another old-style Les Paul in 1969, and as this **1970 Deluxe** (left) shows, it had the benefit of sunburst finish and humbuckers – but mini humbuckers. Still not quite right. Meanwhile, doing very much the right thing with original old-style Les Pauls were **Jeff Beck** (right), seen here in 1968 fronting The Jeff Beck Group with his Standard, and **Peter Green** (below) recording with Fleetwood Mac in 1969.

On the original 50s models, Gibson had put Les Paul's name on the company's own design. In 1969, however, the roles were reversed, and Gibson put its name on some of Les Paul's low-impedance designs, including this **1978 Professional** (main guitar) and **1969 Personal** (opposite page, above the Professional).

The Goldtop-style model was, as you may remember, one of the two Les Pauls reissued in 1968, with P-90s and a Tune-O-Matic bridge. It was in effect dropped upon the release of the Deluxe in 1969, but Gibson launched a new version around 1971, this time with the wrap-over bar-shaped bridge–tailpiece (the 'stopbar', like the one fitted to the second version of the original 50s model). It had narrow binding in the body cutaway, a characteristic of 50s Les Pauls, prompting suggestions that Gibson was using up old bodies. This style of Goldtop, still with P-90s, lasted for about a year, although it did not appear on the company's pricelists.

Getting down with Les

We know that Les Paul's ideas on guitar design were often quite different from what Gibson felt would be commercially successful. One of Les's more out-of-step preferences was for low-impedance pickups. Today, low-impedance components are more often used in pickups, thanks to technical improvements, but back then Les was pretty much on his own. The vast majority of electric guitars and guitar-related equipment were (and still are) high-impedance.

The chief advantage of low-impedance is wide-ranging tone. That might seem like an advantage, but the tonal range offered isn't necessarily to everyone's taste. A disadvantage is that low-impedance pickups must have their power boosted at some point before the signal reaches the amplifier (unless you plug the guitar straight into a recording-studio mixer, which is what Les Paul would do).

When Les went to Gibson in 1967 to discuss the reissue of Les Paul guitars, he talked with great passion about his beloved low-impedance pickups and how Gibson should use them. He convinced Gibson to go ahead. In 1969, along came the first wave of Les Paul models with low-impedance pickups – the Les Paul Professional and the Les Paul Personal, as well as a Les Paul Bass.

The Personal was, as the name implied, in keeping with one of Les's own modified Les Paul guitars, even copying the unusual feature of a microphone jack on the top edge of the body. The Personal and Professional had a complex array of controls, and Gibson's instruction leaflet reinforced the impression that they were built with recording engineers rather than guitarists in mind. Familiar volume, bass, treble, and pickup selector were augmented by an 11-position Decade control, "to tune high frequencies", a three-position tone selector to create various in and out-of-circuit mixes, and a pickup phase in–out switch. The Personal also provided a volume control for that handy microphone input.

Both guitars required connection using the special cord supplied, which had a built-in transformer that boosted the output from the low-impedance stacked-coil humbucking pickups up to a level suitable for use with normal high-impedance amplifiers. The guitars were unsuccessful – predictably, with hindsight – and they made only a short appearance in the Gibson line. Terry Kath with the group Chicago was one of the few famous players ever seen playing one. Their sombre brown colour, achieved with a natural mahogany finish, was probably a turn-off during an era when competitors were busily turning out simple guitars in bright colours.

Gibson's pricelist from September 1969 listed the two Les Paul low-impedance guitars: the Personal at $645 and the Professional $485. The company also produced a special LP-12 combo amp and LP-1 amplifier, both with switchable high–low impedance that allowed the use of any standard cord. These were listed at $1,110 for the LP-12 and $505 for the LP-1.

Toward the end of the 60s, the fashion for original Les Pauls was showing no sign of letting up. Robert Fripp of King Crimson acquired his 50s Les Paul Custom when he saw it in a London shop window during 1968. It was priced at £400. "The salesman was pretty loathsome," Fripp told me. "But we'd been given a loan, and I had a briefcase with a very large sum of cash inside. I asked about a discount for cash and was refused. So I opened the briefcase and showed the manager the money. I walked out with the Custom for £375. It remains to this day the finest Les Paul I've ever played, and I've played a few."[22]

Jimmy Page had moved from his session-days Custom to a Fender Telecaster when he joined The Yardbirds, and he continued with the Tele in the first days of Led Zeppelin in the late 60s. But soon he acquired an old sunburst Les Paul Standard, and with the enormous rise in Zep's popularity in the 70s, Page became almost synonymous with the glories of overdriven humbuckers, and he was often seen on stage with his favourite Standard.

Page was full of praise not only for the Les Paul guitar but also for Les Paul the musician. He pointed interviewer Steven Rosen in the direction of 'It's Been A Long Long Time', the single that Les made back in 1945 with Bing Crosby and that had gone to Number One. "[Les] does everything on that, everything in one go – he sets the whole tone, and then he goes into this solo, which is fantastic," Page enthused. "I've traced a hell of a lot of rock'n'roll, little riffs and things, back to Les Paul. He's the father of it all. If it hadn't been for him, there wouldn't have been anything, really."[23]

the seventies

"Humbuckers ... single cut ... check that flame ... whack it right up ... OK, let's get down!"

Jimmy Page, Led Zeppelin ▸

In 1970, Gibson launched a peculiar instrument. It was the Les Paul Jumbo, a flat-top acoustic guitar with round soundhole and a single cutaway. It had a low-impedance pickup installed in the top and a row of body-mounted controls – volume, treble, and bass, the 11-way Decade control from the Personal and Professional models, and a bypass switch designed to cut the tone controls from the circuit. Very few Jumbos were made, and it's easy to see why. It made a final appearance on Gibson's November 1971 pricelist, at $610.

Les Paul himself in a 1971 interview hinted at another unusual acoustic, an amplified nylon-strung model that he called the Gibson Les Paul Classical Guitar, but which never reached production. Years later, Gibson did produce a guitar along similar lines, the 1981 Chet Atkins CE. Les also spoke in that 71 interview of developing a special acoustic pickup, one that today we would call a piezo, and suggested combining it with a regular magnetic electric pickup to "give the player both types of sounds".[1] Here again was the avant-garde Les Paul in action, for he was clearly describing the modern acoustic–electric hybrid guitar – which would appear much later, in the 90s.

Gibson made its second attempt at a line of low-impedance solidbody Les Pauls in 1971. The body size of the Professional/Personal style was scaled down virtually to that of a regular Les Paul, and it was given a contoured back. The still-necessary impedance transformer was shifted into the instrument itself, with a switch provided on the guitar for low-impedance or regular high-impedance output. And the guitar's name was changed to Les Paul Recording. Gibson's pricelist for June 1971 showed the Recording at $625; this second wave of low-impedance trickery lasted until the end of the decade. Bruce Bolen thought the failure of these guitars was down to Gibson's inability to grasp what players really wanted. "The high end was so clean on those guitars," he said, "that they just didn't have enough harmonic distortion to relate to the rock players."[2]

The art and science of guitar collecting

As the 70s went on, more guitarists were finding that older instruments could seem somehow more playable and better sounding than new guitars. Some acoustic guitarists had felt this for a while, and a small number of specialist dealers had grown up in the USA since the late 40s to cater for the demand. Harry West in New York and Jon & Deirdre Lundberg in California were among the first.

But now players and dealers were on the lookout for older electrics, too, and 50s Les Pauls were near the top of many a wish-list. Norman's Rare Guitars, established in California during the mid 70s, was one of the newer dealers specialising in the vintage requirements of rock players. Norman Harris was in no doubt why so many guitarists were taking up older instruments. "You simply cannot compare what I have to offer with what the big companies are mass producing today," he said in 1976.[3]

Steve Stills of Crosby Stills & Nash had amassed a collection of some 70 guitars by the middle of the decade. Touring with his solo band at the time, he needed two dressing rooms: one for himself, another for the 17 guitars that accompanied him. Included were two double-cut Les Paul Specials and a sunburst Standard. He was an old-guitar evangelist.

"I don't think they've built anything new that's worth a damn since 1965," Stills said in 1976. "It's all mechanised."[4] If the image of Clapton with his Standard on the 66 *Blues Breakers* album really did start the vintage-guitar trend, then it was this quote from Stills that exemplified the notion that it was somehow only old guitars that were worthy of attention by 'real' players.

Steve Howe was another famous player–collector in the 70s. Like Stills, the British guitarist acquired dozens of guitars because he craved new sounds. Touring the USA regularly with Yes gave him the opportunity to buy instruments from dealers who were busily supplying the growing demand. Howe would visit Silver Strings in St Louis, Pete's Guitar in St Paul, Mandolin Bros or Manny's in New York City, Gruhn Guitars in Nashville, adding guitars to his collection – like the 1956 Les Paul Custom he bought from Gruhn for $800 in 1974.

George Gruhn wrote the first serious magazine piece about this new trend, published in *Guitar Player* at the start of 1975 and grandly titled The Art And Science Of Guitar Collecting. Writing as both a shrewd businessman promoting demand for his wares and an obsessive collector hungry for detailed information, Gruhn emphasised the desirability of old Les Pauls in the article. "There are currently more people looking for Les Pauls than for any other electric guitar," he reported. And the 1958–60 Standard, he said, "is today probably the most sought after of the Les Pauls and has become the standard by which other guitars are judged, at least on the current market".[5]

Gibson itself had reflected the interest in its own history with an amateurish but eagerly devoured booklet, *The Gibson Story*, in 1973. The company was of course in the business of selling new instruments, but noted briefly that some players had "requested the opportunity to purchase certain previously discontinued models",[6] pointing to its recent limited-edition reissues meant to address such demand, such as the Les Paul Custom 54 Ltd Edition, launched in 1972. This was Gibson's first attempt to reissue an old-style Les Paul. It was intended to recall the first version of the Custom, with P-90 at bridge and Alnico at neck, and unusually for the period came with a one-piece neck and no volute. Gibson underlined the special nature of the model by providing a serial number with an LE prefix, for limited edition. The model only lasted another year or so on the catalogue, but clearly the idea was beginning to take hold that there was an important heritage available for further exploitation by the modern Gibson company.

The first published attempt to sort out the various Les Paul models and their dates of manufacture came in Tom Wheeler's *The Guitar Book* in 1974. Further detailed studies would follow later with André Duchossoir's *Gibson Electrics* (1981) and Wheeler's *American Guitars* (1982).

One of the old guard itself was also able to criticise the growth of the vintage-guitar fashion. The ever-cynical Frank Zappa poked fun at the trend when in 1977 he wrote a

● This is **Jeff Beck's 'Oxblood'** Les Paul, a converted mid-50s Goldtop with added humbuckers and very dark brown finish, that he got in 1972. Beck used it for some of his classic *Blow By Blow* album two years later.

● Gibson used '**cross-banding**' (inset above), with an extra layer of maple in the mahogany body, from about 1969 to 1973. Some new Les Paul models featured low-impedance pickups and multiple switching: examples shown here are a **1970 Jumbo** (above), an unusual flat-top, and this **1972 Recording** first version (left).

This **1978 Recording** (right) shows the revised second version of the Recording model. Guitarists, meanwhile, lined up for old-style Les Pauls, and two prime representatives are pictured here. **Duane Allman** (top right) plays the Burst he used for the classic 1971 Allman Brothers LP *At Fillmore East*, but that October he died in a motorcycle accident. **Paul Kossoff** (below right) was a passionate Burst player, with his band Free and solo, but he too succumbed to an early death, in 1976.

typically playful "brief version" of the evolution of the guitar's use in pop music. Zappa wrote: "[The] musical world has reached a point of sophistication that accepts concepts like The Super-Group, The Fastest Guitar Player In The World, and The Guitar Player In The World Who Has Collected The Most Oldest Guitars In The World (some of which have been played by dead guitar players who were actually musicians)."[7]

Gibson's final fling with low-impedance pickups was reserved for the company's thinline electric guitar style, a shallow, semi-hollowbody design that had begun with the classic ES-335 in 1958. That instrument had a central block of timber inside the otherwise hollow body, on which to mount the pickups and bridge. It reduced any tendency to feedback and gave the guitar a musically useful blend of solidbody and hollowbody tones. It was in 1974 that the new two-pickup Les Paul Signature guitar was launched, in thinline style. Bruce Bolen said it was essentially an asymmetric 335, although it didn't have the full centre block like that model, instead featuring a smaller block, below the bridge, which made it more like Gibson's ES-330 model.

Some of the Signature's controls were similar to those found on earlier low-impedance models, but the 11-position Decade control had shrunk to a three-position switch and lost its name. The Signature had a pair of jacks (sockets), one on the side of the body for normal high-impedance output, the other on the top for connection to low-impedance equipment such as a recording mixer. A similar facility was offered on the final version of the Recording model. The gold-finish Signatures never fired players' imaginations, despite their luxurious image, and by the end of the 70s had ceased production. Gibson's February 1974 pricelist showed the Signature at $610.

It occurred to Gibson in 1974 that it was 20 years since the first Les Paul Custom had appeared, so they celebrated by issuing a Custom with a Twentieth Anniversary inlay at the 15th fret, in place of the regular position marker. This was the first Gibson anniversary model. The only precursors in the electric guitar market were Gretsch's four Anniversary models of 1958, issued to celebrate that company's foundation 75 years earlier. The 20th Anniversary Les Paul Custom established a marketing trend, and since that time a number of special anniversary-edition Les Paul models have appeared. This and the Custom 54 marked a new awareness at Gibson that its history could be valuable to its present.

Nashville plans

By now, Gibson employed around 600 people at its Kalamazoo factory, producing some 300 guitars a day. Demand for new guitars had increased during the early 70s and, as a result, the management at Gibson's parent company, Norlin, decided to build a second factory, located in Nashville, Tennessee, which is located many hundreds of miles to the south of Kalamazoo.

No doubt several factors affected Norlin's choice of site, but one that was probably high on its list was that Tennessee was a 'right to work' state. In other words, unions existed but employees could choose whether or not to join. Michigan – and indeed a good deal of the north-eastern United States – had much stronger unions with closed-shop deals in place, meaning obligatory union membership and generally higher wages and insurance rates. Recent strikes at Gibson had cost Norlin dear. Gibson built the big new plant at Nashville not only with increased production in mind but also with a view to reduced costs through advantageous labour deals.

Work began in 1974 on the new facility, five miles to the east of Nashville, and the factory eventually opened in June 1975. Training a new workforce was difficult. Stan Rendell, still Gibson president, recalled that a limited number of people were transferred from Kalamazoo to Nashville in supervisory positions but that no workers made the move. "So everybody there had to be hired and trained," he said, "and that takes time. I think a Les Paul guitar took on average eight or ten man-hours of labour. So if you're going to make, say, 100 guitars a day, you would need maybe 125 or more direct-labour people – and that's without all the support personnel. It takes time to train the management, the workers, everybody. So we shipped some key people down there."

The original intention was to keep both the Kalamazoo and Nashville factories running, with the new Nashville plant producing only acoustic guitars. Rendell said that trying to build acoustics and electrics in the same factory was a bit like trying to build trucks and cars in the same place. They need different kinds of attention at different stages of their construction.

"The real challenge," he said, "was to schedule a flow of work through the factory so that everybody was kept busy. For example, the amount of work needed to finish an electric guitar is tremendous, whereas with an acoustic guitar, about all you've got to do is to put on strings and machine heads. So the types of guitars flowing through final assembly at any one time make a big difference to the workload. I wanted to try to specialise and remove the flat-top acoustic guitars out of the mainstream at Kalamazoo and get a group of people who lived and breathed nothing but acoustic guitars at Nashville."[8] In fact, that would happen years later, when Gibson shifted acoustic-guitar making to a plant in Bozeman, Montana.

Unfortunately, the new acoustic project allocated to Nashville in 1975 was the Mark series, some of the least successful of Gibson's flat-tops. The guitars were fraught with technical and construction problems. One ex-employee describes them bluntly as a fiasco. Following this failure, management decided to transfer to Nashville the production of the bulk of the Les Paul line, by far the most successful Gibson solidbody guitars at the time.

Kalamazoo had always been what is known technically as a 'soft tool' factory. This means that the machines and fixtures used to make the guitars could be modified and adapted at will, as circumstances dictated. In other words, things could be changed easily. Nashville started life as a 'hard tool' facility, which means that it had a lot of heavy machines and fixtures on which the settings were never changed.

This meant that the character of the two factories that Gibson ran during the remaining years of the 70s and into the early 80s was quite different. Nashville was set up

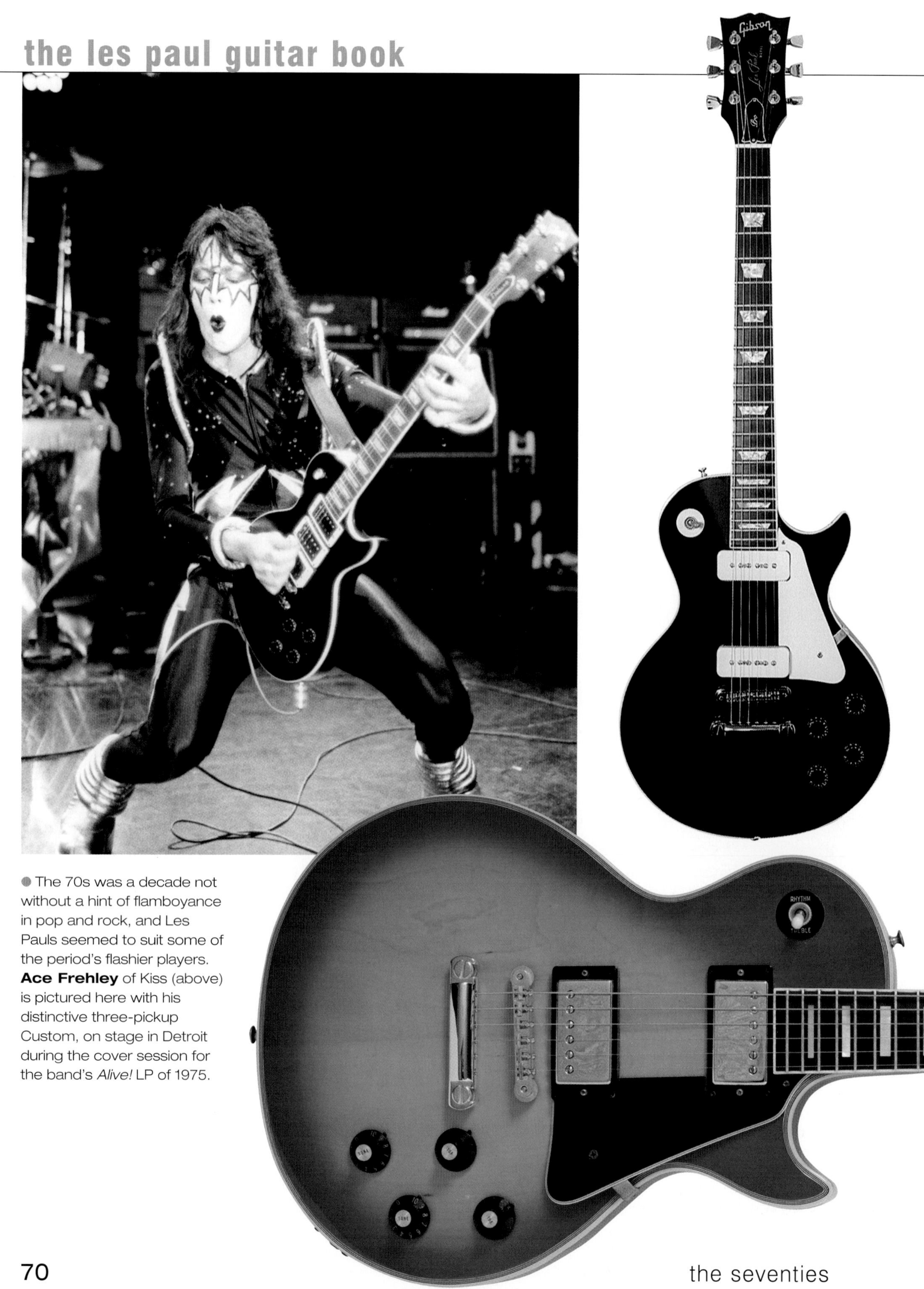

● The 70s was a decade not without a hint of flamboyance in pop and rock, and Les Pauls seemed to suit some of the period's flashier players. **Ace Frehley** of Kiss (above) is pictured here with his distinctive three-pickup Custom, on stage in Detroit during the cover session for the band's *Alive!* LP of 1975.

GLAMOROUS GIBSONS 1974–75

● T.Rex had a run of UK hits in the 70s, with **Marc Bolan** (above) deploying simple and effective pop guitar. He often used this Les Paul, which probably began life as a sunburst or Goldtop. Bolan had it refinished to orange, and an accident resulted in its new Custom neck.

● These three axes were launched in the mid 70s. The **1974 Custom 20th Anniversary** (main guitar) was Gibson's first anniversary guitar, a sign of the company's growing awareness of the value of its history. The **1980 Pro Deluxe** (top left) was in effect a Deluxe with P-90s, and the **1976 Signature** (top right) brought the low-impedance idea to its semi-solid 335-style instruments.

to produce very large quantities of a handful of individual models, where Kalamazoo was more flexible and had the potential to specialise in small runs. Nashville was therefore the obvious choice to produce the highest-volume models in Gibson's solidbody line at the time – the Les Paul Custom and Les Paul Deluxe – along with various other solid models.

As if to highlight the contrast between the capabilities of the plants, Gibson introduced two new Les Paul models in 1976. First was the Pro Deluxe, effectively a Deluxe with P-90 pickups and an ebony fingerboard. It was produced in large quantities at Nashville.

The other was The Les Paul – note that opening *The* – which Gibson first revealed at the 1975 NAMM show. It was a spectacular limited edition notable for the use of fine woods on virtually the entire instrument. Many parts that on a regular electric would be made from plastic were hand-carved from rosewood, including the pickguard, pickup surrounds, backplates, controls, and truss-rod cover. Raw bodies and necks of attractive maple, including the back, and an ornate ebony and rosewood fingerboard were produced at Gibson's Kalamazoo factory. Further work on the multiple coloured binding, abalone inlays, and handmade wooden parts continued at the workshop of freelance luthier Dick Schneider, about a mile from the factory in Kalamazoo. Schneider worked on The Les Pauls together with his brother, Donnie, and Abe Wechter from Gibson.

Very few The Les Pauls were made, and while an unfortunate four-figure misprint in Gibson's own records precludes an exact total, it's likely that well under 100 were produced between 1976 and 1979, with most made during the first year. During the model's life, Schneider moved away from Kalamazoo, and some later examples of The Les Paul were therefore produced entirely at the Gibson factory. As the limited stocks of Schneider's handmade wooden parts ran out, so normal plastic items were substituted, as well as less ornate binding.

Each example of The Les Paul had a numbered oval plate on the back of the headstock. Bruce Bolen remembered flying to Hollywood to present number 25 to Les Paul, just prior to the 1977 Grammy Awards ceremony where Les and Chet Atkins received a Grammy for their *Chester & Lester* album. Why number 25? It was 25 years since the first Gibson Les Paul guitar of 1952.

"That instrument, The Les Paul, was a fun project," remembered Rendell. "They were gorgeous guitars: the wood was so beautiful. I remember saying nothing to CMI about it until we had it done. We showed it at NAMM, and I remember Les Propp, president of CMI at the time, asking how much we were going to charge for the guitar. Well, I said, it's 3,000 bucks. And he choked," laughed Rendell.[9] That tag put The Les Paul at four times the cost of its nearest Les Paul rival on the 1976 pricelist – but not far from what some players were paying for Gibson's precious old Les Paul Standards.

Despite ventures like The Les Paul, it seems there was too little of the fun projects to maintain Stan Rendell's interest as president of Gibson, and in November 1976 he resigned. After a number of short-stay presidents, Marty Locke would move over from CMI's Lowrey organ business to head up Gibson in 1980.

During the mid to late 70s, Gibson indulged in more theme and variation within the Les Paul line – but there was little innovation. The company could hardly have failed to notice the continuing interest in older Les Pauls in general and the Standard in particular. Duane Allman had used a Goldtop and a Standard with The Allman Brothers before his untimely death in 1971, while Duane's bandmate Dickey Betts had several 50s Pauls and came to prefer a Standard for slide and a Goldtop for regular lead work.

Lusting for old Les Pauls

Toy Caldwell of The Marshall Tucker Band decided to leave his old Les Pauls at home as he went out on tour, after losing two to thieves on the road. For live work, he opted instead for a two-year-old stock model fitted with 50s humbuckers, reserving his more precious instruments for the studio. As the values of vintage guitars increased, this would become a practical necessity for other players, too.

Then there was Joe Walsh, with The James Gang and Barnstorm, who was an especially enthusiastic original-Standard fan. "I can't live with anything but a Les Paul," he said in 1972.[10] He persuaded others, too, by distributing Standards to player friends and acquaintances, notably Jimmy Page, who was using Walsh's gift to great effect in the world-dominating Led Zeppelin.

Page acquired his Standard from Walsh at one of Led Zep's early dates in the USA, probably in late April 1969. The guitar, later nicknamed Number 1 and taking on almost mythical status among Les Paul fans, arrived in time to be heard on the band's classic second album and on every major tour and album following that. Page got a backup Burst during the 70s, 'Number 2', and a cherry red Standard, but Number 1 remained his favourite.

Mick Ronson with David Bowie, at the time aka Ziggy Stardust, played a recent black Custom but had it stripped to reveal the natural-wood top, and Marc Bolan in T.Rex also had his Les Paul refinished. Southern-boogie star Charlie Daniels had an original 58 Standard, and while he told a 70s interviewer that he didn't particularly care about the date of manufacture, he added: "It just happens that most guitars that sound good and play good are old ones."[11]

But the sunburst and humbucker'd Les Paul Standard was still notably absent from the current Gibson line. Nonetheless, the model was available as a special order. Roger Matthews of Gibson said in 1974: "We are producing a Les Paul Standard model which could be related to the instrument produced in the latter part of the 50s. The limited edition that is now in production has the large humbucking pickups and is available in [sunburst] finish."[12]

One of the first to prompt this sideline at Kalamazoo was a dealer, Strings & Things, set up by Chris Lovell in Memphis, Tennessee, in 1971. Lovell ordered a small number of Standards – the best estimate puts the total at 24 – with custom specs that set them a little closer to the 50s originals. This short run, made from about 1975 to 1978, is now recognised as one of the first attempts to recreate the hallowed 59 Burst.

● This **1979 KM** (top) was an early half-hearted stab at a Burst reissue. The Les Paul – note the definite article – was a luxurious limited-run model made from the best timbers Gibson could find at the time. Shown here are a **1976 The Les Paul** (opposite) in natural and a **1978 The Les Paul** (left). The fine work added up to a $3,000 price-tag. Complex electronics were a feature of this **1979 Artist** (below), borrowed from Gibson's RD series. The knobs control volume, bass, and treble; the switches control brightness, expansion, and compression.

THE DEFINITE ARTICLE 1976–79

There was a heady mix of music about in the late 70s, and guitarists from many different areas were drawn to the special qualities of this or that Les Paul model. **Bob Marley** (opposite, left) opted for a much-modified single-cut Special for his reggae rhythm role. In mainstream rock, **Gary Rossington** of Lynyrd Skynyrd (opposite, right) went for the great sunburst Standard. **Steve Jones** of The Sex Pistols (below) favoured a white Custom, seen here with Jones on-stage at the 100 Club in London during the punk summer of '76.

At last, in 1976, Gibson officially added the Standard to its pricelist, at $649, as a straightforward sunburst model with two humbuckers, but still it ignored the precise requirements of vintage fans. Some players were prepared to pay as much as $2,750 for one of the original 1958–60 sunburst Standards.

Meanwhile, down at the low end of Gibson's market in the 70s, oriental makers were providing well-priced copies of many classic American guitar designs, Gibson Les Pauls included. Some of them were cheap in both price and quality, but brands such as Ibanez were beginning to produce good instruments. By the end of the 70s, a 'Made In Japan' label was no longer the sign of an also-ran. Ibanez, Yamaha, Aria, and others had turned the oriental guitar into a well-made, competitive instrument on the world market.

Ever more aware of the value of its own history, Gibson intended its new 25/50 model to celebrate Les Paul's 25th year with Gibson (presumably it was planned for 1977) and his 50th year in the music business. There was plenty of the silver and gold associated with those anniversaries in the guitar's nickel and gold-plated hardware, while Chuck Burge in Gibson's R&D department (research and development) designed the special intricate inlay in pearl and abalone on the guitar's headstock. The instrument had a three-digit edition number on the back of the headstock as well as a standard serial number, and Les Paul was presented with number 001 at a party given in his honour by Gibson upon its launch in 1978.

Despite its relatively high price of around $1,200, the Kalamazoo-made 25/50 sold well, bringing into focus for Norlin the ready market for more costly Les Paul models. Management was also swayed by the opinions of Gibson's salespeople about what the market wanted. An example from this period was the figured-top Les Paul KM model, also made at Kalamazoo and one of a series of six otherwise uninspiring instruments made for a southern sales region.

Junior in bad company seeks special pistols

Gibson reissued single and double-cutaway versions of the Les Paul Special in the mid 70s. Many players were wallowing in the rock'n'roll glory of old Juniors and Specials, the straightforward uncarved-top models that Gibson had at first intended for beginners. Original 50s examples were plentiful and nowhere near as expensive as the now hallowed Standards, with price tags as little as $75 if you were lucky. But it was the raw sound of the P-90 pickups and the responsive playability of the guitars that appealed as much as any financial advantage they offered.

Leslie West with his classic early-70s rock trio Mountain had directed the attention of many a player to the little Junior he drove so hard. One such was Mick Ralphs, who developed a masterful vibrato on his Junior, playing with Mott The Hoople early in the decade and then the generally more raucous Bad Company from 1973. Reggae master Bob Marley favoured the two-pickup Special for his electric work among The Wailers, one of the tightest bands of the 70s, but it was the punk explosion later in the decade that saw more players discovering the bare power of the flat-bodied Les Pauls.

In the USA, Johnny Thunders paved the way with his Junior in The New York Dolls. In Britain, Mick Jones of The Clash also came to love the power of his Junior, and Steve Jones of The Sex Pistols could often be seen with a Special. In fact, Jones was hardly the typical punk thrasher, having a refined taste for his Gibsons. As well as the Special, Jones was fond of a white Les Paul Custom and another in sunburst with a Bigsby, and he also found room for an occasional Firebird and SG Standard.

Flicking the synth switch

Tim Shaw joined Gibson in 1978, having worked in California and in Kalamazoo as a guitar repairer and maker. His first few months with the company were spent in Gibson's pickup plant in Elgin, Illinois, but by early 1979 he was working with Bruce Bolen in R&D at Kalamazoo. Together with Chuck Burge and Abe Wechter, Shaw built prototypes and artist instruments and worked on new designs. One of the first prototypes he worked on became the Les Paul Artist, a model with a system of active electronics originally developed for Gibson's RD models.

Synthesizers were becoming big business in the late 70s, and Norlin figured that if Gibson was to hook up with Moog, one of the synth field's most famous names, it might re-capture some of the ground that guitars were apparently losing to the new keyboards. Gibson's resulting RD line was issued in 1977 but failed to sell well. Many guitarists disliked the active circuitry, which could be harsher than regular tone controls and proved a factor in the downfall of the series. Gibson believed the radical styling of the RD models was more to blame and that the solution was to transplant the technology over to its more traditional guitar designs.

Shaw explained: "In 1979, Gibson decided to expand the RD concept into two of their more mainstream series, the ES and the Les Paul. We had to redesign the circuit board, because the original RD board is too big for almost anything. So we transferred the circuitry into two boards, which still meant we had to take a lot of wood out of the Artist guitars. But something I didn't fully appreciate until later was that guitar players are really conservative folks, and nobody really wanted a Les Paul that did all that. Somebody once said that with one of those Artists, you were a flick of a switch away from total disaster."[13]

The Artist hobbled on to 1981, when it was quietly dropped. A happier project was the Les Paul Heritage Series, one of the first conscious attempts to try to make Les Pauls in a way that many people thought was no longer possible at Gibson. Chuck Burge began to build prototypes in 1979, but we'll meet the production models in the next chapter.

the eighties

"That '59 vibe can't be beat. Bottle it in a brand new guitar, and you'll have lines around the block."

Slash, Guns N' Roses ▶

During 1979, Chuck Burge in Gibson's R&D department started building some prototypes for a new line of Les Paul models, the Heritage Series. His colleague Tim Shaw remembered: "They were our first stab at asking questions like: What's the best this guitar ever was? Are we building it like that now? And if not, why not? Management didn't want to hear that at first, so we fought tooth and nail to do it."[1]

The R&D team used a 1954 pattern sample to provide the carving of the Heritage's body top, and they changed the neck construction to three-piece mahogany. They disposed of then-current production oddities such as the volute below the back of the headstock, and they moved a little closer to older pickup specifications. They chose pretty figured timber for the tops of these new Heritage Series Les Pauls.

Bruce Bolen, head of R&D by then, managed to persuade Norlin to put the vintage-flavoured Heritages into production – not as standard Les Pauls, however, but rather as separate, premium items, touted as limited editions and not included on the company's general pricelist.

Launched in 1980, there were two Heritage Series models, the Standard 80 and the Standard 80 Elite, the latter with an ebony fingerboard, one-piece neck, and even fancier quilted-figure top. A year later the Standard 80 Award was added, 'awarded' to dealers who stocked or sold a number of the regular Heritage models. The Award had gold-plated hardware. The Heritage models lasted in production for just a couple of years, but they were important markers of the way Gibson was gradually changing it's attitude to consider the way it might recreate its own traditions and legacy.

Whether as a direct result of the influence of the Heritage models or a general awareness of market demands, Gibson began to move away from some of the production quirks it had introduced during the 70s. For example, the volute was removed, and gradually there was a change back to one-piece mahogany necks. In 1982, Kalamazoo made the limited-run Les Paul Standard 82, distinguished from the Heritage Standard 80 primarily by its one-piece neck and its manufacture in Kalamazoo.

The regular July 1980 pricelist had six Les Paul models: Deluxe, listing at $799; Standard $849; Pro Deluxe $889; Custom $899; Artisan (a sort of decorated Custom) $1,099; and Artist $1,299.

We've already seen how, during the 70s, some US dealers who specialised in older instruments had begun to order selected Les Pauls with 'vintage correct' appointments from Gibson's Kalamazoo plant. Since the opening of Gibson's new Nashville factory in 1975, the original Kalamazoo plant had leaned more heavily toward shorter, specialised runs of guitars.

Jim Deurloo, who by the early 80s was plant manager at Kalamazoo, remembered dealers such as Leo's of California, Jimmy Wallace of Texas, and Guitar Trader of New Jersey ordering special vintage-style Les Paul Standards. These stores and their customers were looking for features like exact old-style carving and a particular neck feel, as well as a slew of small visual details. Kalamazoo provided an approximation.

Dave DeForrest started the Guitar Trader store in Red Bank, New Jersey, around 1970, and Timm Kummer joined as manager later in the decade. Kummer recalled that someone from Gibson came to Guitar Trader to measure some 1958–60 Bursts, resulting in the KM model of 1979.

Kummer was clearly a critic of the KMs. "They had a maple three-piece neck, a huge volute, and a headstock the size of a heliport. No 'dish' to the top. I believe the fella that did the research probably lost his job there. We couldn't sell 'em. Very few had any flame in the top. Customers were a little too fussy."

Maybe Guitar Trader's customers were fussy – or perhaps they, like many other guitarists, thought that Gibson ought to be making guitars like they used to. Specifically Les Paul sunbursts. Surely it couldn't be that hard? It seemed obvious to everyone else what was wrong with Gibson's current Standard model, even the well-intentioned Heritage 80s and the one-off projects such as the KM and the Standard 82. If the critics had been asked to sum up the problem, they probably would have said that Gibson was failing to exercise enough attention to detail.

Kummer said: "Everything was falling on the deaf ears of those people who were running Gibson, which was Norlin at the time – and CBS, too, who were running Fender. They were pencil-pushers and they just didn't get it."

So Guitar Trader struck a deal to do the research, to give Gibson the specs they needed to make what they hoped would be a proper sunburst Standard reissue. "We thought we had an exclusive with them," remembered Kummer, "although they started selling these specials to other dealers, like Jimmy Wallace in Texas and Leo's out in California." As with the earlier Strings & Things custom instruments, the specials that Gibson made for Guitar Trader and others were turned out in relatively small numbers. Kummer's best guess was that Guitar Trader ended up with 53 of these reissues.

A typical ad for Guitar Trader's dealer specials came in its May 1982 newsletter. "Guitar Trader and Gibson Guitars announce the ultimate Les Paul reissue," claimed the blurb, alongside a repro of the original Standard entry from Gibson's 1960 catalogue. A list of features followed: "Dimensions as per 1959 model shown; 'painted-on' serial number; original style bridge; two-piece highly figured tops personally selected by our luthiers. These instruments will be produced in strictly limited quantities at the original Gibson factory in Kalamazoo, MI, and represent a special investment value."

Guitar Trader added that if you ordered your "59 Flametop" immediately for summer 82 delivery, they would install original 50s PAF patent-applied-for pickups, subject to availability. Kummer estimated that this happened for the first 15 lucky customers. The price (with case) was $1,500, although it later crept up to $2,000. In the same newsletter, Guitar Trader was happy to offer an original and entirely real 1959 Standard with "tiger-striped curly maple top", for $7,500. By the end of the year, Aerosmith's Brad Whitford was pictured taking delivery of his Guitar Trader Flametop. "Hasn't felt this good since 59," he reckoned.[2]

● The importance of the old Les Paul models was steadily growing among musicians, and the Heritage Series marked a new awareness by Gibson. Pictured here are a **1980 Heritage Standard 80** (above) and the fancier-wood **1980 Heritage Standard 80 Elite** (below). The Heritage guitars disposed of some of the constructional oddities of the 70s, and the vibe if not the fine detail pointed to the revered 58–60 Standards.

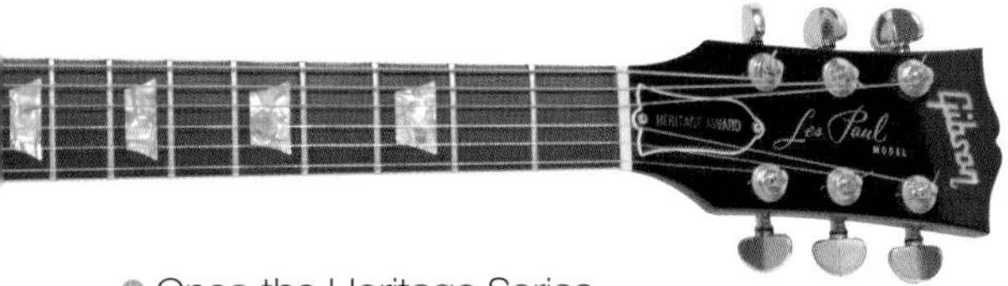

Once the Heritage Series had been selling for a year or so, Gibson came up with a special model that it gave as an 'award' to dealers who sold a significant number of Heritage guitars. This **1982 Heritage Standard 80 Award** (centre) is one of about 50 of the limited-run model that Gibson made.

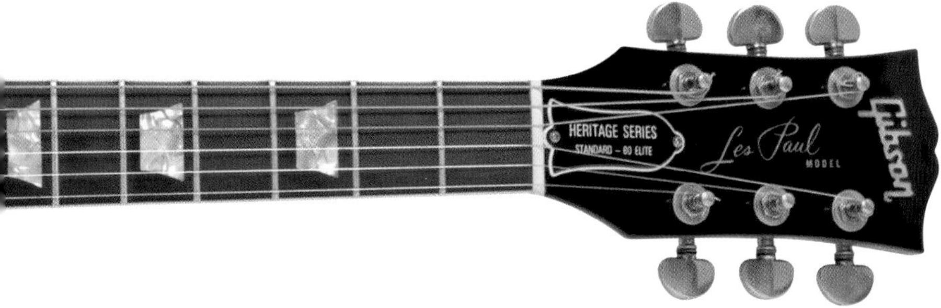

Joe Walsh is pictured (above) on-stage with The Eagles in 1980. He'd joined the California supergroup in 1976 and stayed on until the early 80s. Walsh, seen here playing one of his beautiful original Bursts, was a great evangelist for the Les Paul Standard, famously providing Jimmy Page with the Zep man's beloved 'Number 1'.

Jim Deurloo recalled that the dealer specials were selected from the production line at Gibson but were custom-built to some degree. "It was at a time when we weren't making a vintage-looking instrument," he said. "We were making what was in the catalogue at the time – and not the guitar with the washed-out top. I remember that Guitar Trader selected each top, and they were very picky about the colour."[3]

Kummer said they would go to the factory and select particular planks of wood, before they were cut to size, and photograph them. Customers could then check these photos back at Guitar Trader to select which planks they wanted their instrument's top to come from. "I guess the biggest risk was what it was going to look like once the finish was applied. Because a bare piece of maple, even though we intensified the effect by wetting it with some fluid, well ... you can never know exactly what you're going to get."

Guitar Trader's deal with Gibson lasted only a couple of years. Who bought these guitars? "A lot went to guys who couldn't afford the 5,000 or 6,000 that a real Burst was," said Kummer. "Brad Whitford, who was on a sort of hiatus from Aerosmith at the time, was a good customer. But he was probably the only name player. I don't know if his endorsement did a whole lot. That's a tough thing to gauge. Guys who bought them were running restaurants, they were dentists, players, every walk of life. These were certainly not cheap guitars."[4]

Around 1980, Norlin had decided to sell Gibson. A report in *The Music Trades* said that by 1981, Norlin Industries had incurred "excessive debt through substantial losses in its music divisions" and that this forced the sale of its profitable technology and beer divisions in 1982. As well as Gibson and Gibson Accessories, Norlin's music divisions included Lowrey organs, Moog synthesizers, and a Band & Orchestral division.

As a symptom of Norlin's troubles, Gibson sales fell 30 per cent in 1982 alone, to a total of $19.5 million, against a high in 1979 of $35.5 million. Of course, Gibson was suffering along with everyone else in this decline. The US guitar market in general had virtually imploded, and most other American makers were suffering in broadly similar ways. Their costs were high, economic circumstances and currency fluctuations were against them, and Japanese competitors increasingly had the edge.

Norlin's overall losses in its music divisions were high, according to a 1982 message to shareholders from chairman Norton Stevens. "The operating loss was $11 million before a goodwill write-off of $22.6 million," he said. Norlin had "lean music businesses whose break-even has been reduced significantly in the last few years," continued Stevens, putting a brave face on the company's position. He claimed that Norlin's objective was "to put our capital base to work for growing future earnings". By 1984, Stevens was off the Norlin board after a hostile takeover that year by Rooney Pace, a New York-based financial firm.

Norlin relocated some of its sales, marketing, administration, and finance personnel from Chicago to Nashville around 1980. All the main Gibson production was now handled at the Nashville plant, while Kalamazoo, as we've seen, had become a specialist factory making custom-order guitars, banjos, and mandolins. Plant manager Jim Deurloo said at the time: "The plant is now mainly manufacturing specific models that we call custom shop editions, built in small runs of 25 to 100, sometimes more. Kalamazoo is more of a giant custom-job shop, and we are proud of our heritage and workmanship."

The closing of Kalamazoo

In July 1983, Gibson president Marty Locke informed Jim Deurloo that the Kalamazoo plant would close, and the last production was in June 1984. The plant closed three months later, after more than 65 years of worthy service since the original building had been erected by Gibson. It was an emotional time for the managers and workers, many of whom had worked in the plant for a considerable time.

One employee said that people there knew the closure was inevitable. "You added it all up, and the Kalamazoo factory was falling apart, a very old building, steeped so heavily in tradition and history. The Nashville plant was brand new, in 17 acres, a very beautiful facility. What it boils down to is that the business could not support the two facilities, and there was really only one choice." The same observer also noted that the business would now be easier to sell, with only the Nashville plant and its more amenable labour relations and lower costs.

Tim Shaw, too, recalled those last years. "Jim Deurloo, to his great credit, had fought a hard battle to keep Kalamazoo open, and he lost. But when the announcement came down, he got the entire factory together and said look, they've made the decision to close this place. You people have been with the company for a long time, he said, and I'm very sorry that it's worked out this way. But you're all professionals, you've worked here a long time, you have a heritage to be proud of, and as we downsize and as we close I want you to remain professionals. Basically, Deurloo told them to go out there and smile. And I think, to a large part, they did.

"But it hurt every time you looked around on a Friday and 30 to 60 people would disappear," said Shaw. "I think Deurloo did all that was humanly possible in terms of keeping morale up and trying to set a tone in a very professional framework."[5]

Some of the key people were offered positions at Nashville. But Deurloo, together with Marv Lamb, who'd been with Gibson since 1956, and J.P. Moats, a Gibson employee of equally long standing, decided to leave. They rented part of the Kalamazoo plant and started the Heritage guitar company in April 1985. The business continues today, with a line of over 20 models. As Marv Lamb put it: "We all grew up building guitars and we didn't know too different. We could have searched for another job, but we wanted to do what we know how to do best."[6]

Although the emphasis at the Nashville plant was on large runs of a small number of individual Gibson models, this had to change gradually as it adjusted to its new role as the company's sole factory. A striking example came along in 1983, when Nashville produced the $1,299 Spotlight Special, a limited run designed to use up various components. It was exactly the kind of job that Kalamazoo would normally have done. Tim Shaw said: "It was

● In the absence of suitable guitars in Gibson's own line, some US dealers began to order custom Burst-like models in limited runs. One such was Guitar Trader, of New Jersey, and this **1982 Guitar Trader** shows the effort that went into the detail. A high-profile customer for the Guitar Trader was **Brad Whitford** of Aerosmith, pictured (left) at the store with his model from the run.

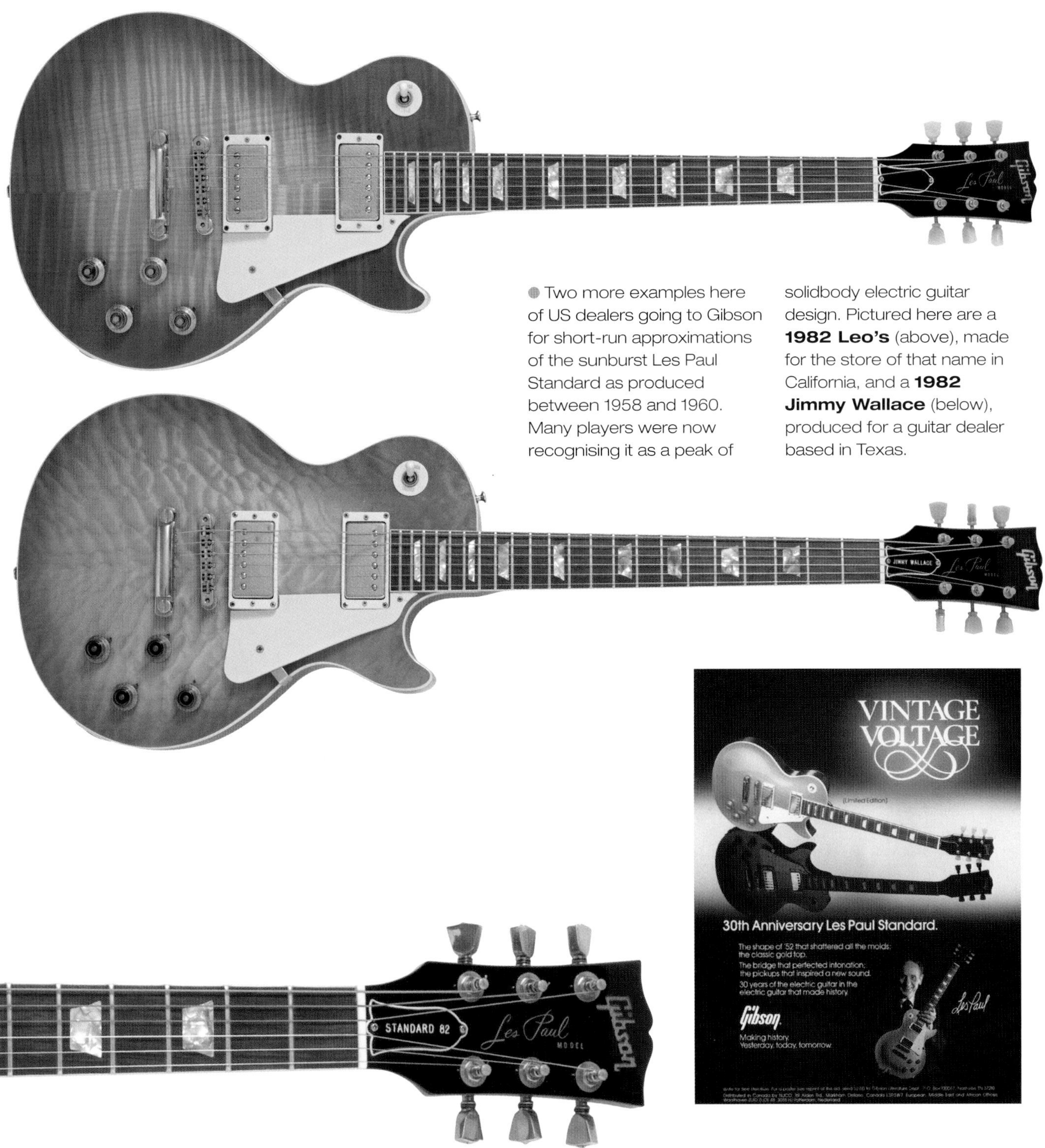

● Two more examples here of US dealers going to Gibson for short-run approximations of the sunburst Les Paul Standard as produced between 1958 and 1960. Many players were now recognising it as a peak of solidbody electric guitar design. Pictured here are a **1982 Leo's** (above), made for the store of that name in California, and a **1982 Jimmy Wallace** (below), produced for a guitar dealer based in Texas.

● Gibson had been making its own efforts at re-creating the delights of the old Les Pauls produced during the late 50s and into the early 60s. Early attempts such as the KM led to the serious Heritage line in 1980, and also to the main guitar pictured here, a **1982 Standard 82**, which unlike the Heritage models had a one-piece neck and was manufactured in Gibson's old (and soon to be closed) Kalamazoo factory. Gibson had begun to mark its history too with birthdays of key models, such as this '82 **ad** (above) for the 30-year-old Goldtop – although in '57 style.

an entirely Nashville-developed design, which was unusual for the time because all the design would typically come from Kalamazoo."[7]

Gibson had some walnut left over from production of two discontinued models – The Paul and The SG – and a number of narrow pieces of curly maple were picked out from some unused timber stock. Nashville managers combined these elements and adapted some headstock veneers and dark binding from a Chet Atkins model.

The resulting concoction was the Les Paul Spotlight Special, announced in the summer 83 number of *The Gibson Gazette*, which commented: "You really have to see this one." The mahogany-base body displayed a distinctive centre stripe of walnut between two maple 'wings', visible through an antique natural or antique sunburst finish, along with gold-plated hardware, usually a one-piece mahogany neck, and 'vintage style' headstock.

The 1983 Spotlight Special seems to mark the start of an official Custom Shop at Nashville, although one observer said the model was made on the regular production line, so it may just have been the beginning of an idea rather than the start of a physical shop. The model carries a Custom Shop logo on the rear of the headstock plus an edition number showing "83" for the date plus a three-digit serial. Records indicate that a little over 200 were made. (Gibson produced a re-creation of the sunburst Spotlight in 2008, calling it the Spotlight Flame.)

At last, the new old reissue

Also in 1983, Gibson finally began to make an official early-style Standard and Goldtop. The company was now well aware of the continuing demand at the monied end of the market for vintage Les Pauls.

The Heritage Series had turned out to be only a half-hearted attempt at a proper reincarnation of the most celebrated old Les Pauls. Now, here was a pair of 'Les Paul Reissue Outfits' – so-called on Gibson's pricelist because the price included a case, which was unusual at the time.

They came in curly maple top or gold top finish, and when they appeared on pricelists in 1985 were pitched at $1,599 and $1,299 respectively. Regular production versions at the time listed at $999. There was some way to go before detail-conscious customers would be happy with the reissues, but Gibson had at least made a start.

Another new model for 1983 that would have a long and important life in the Les Paul line was the Studio. Gibson decided it needed a cheaper Les Paul and, as one person involved in the design puts it, "we stripped off the gingerbread". Primarily, this meant no binding on the body or fingerboard, giving the instrument a basic, straightforward look.

Bruce Bolen remembered trying to devise a name for the model at a meeting he was going to have to leave for an urgent visit to a recording studio. "A little lightbulb came on in my head, and I thought let's call it the Studio. What could be more closely associated with Les than a studio?"[8] By the mid 80s, Bolen had become vice president of marketing and R&D at Gibson. He left the company in 1986, after 19 years of sterling service.

The Les Paul Studio was announced in *The Gibson Gazette* for summer 1983 and first appeared on a pricelist that year at $699, which made it $300 cheaper than any other carved-top Les Paul at the time. Still in the line today, the Studio went through several changes after its launch. It started with a body of normal size but, unusually for Gibson, the timber was alder. However, aesthetic problems with the type of lacquer used prompted a quick change to Gibson's established maple–mahogany combination. This new body was around an eighth of an inch thinner than other Les Pauls, which led to a reduction in production costs and weight.

Around 1987, some Studios began to appear with ebony rather than rosewood fingerboards – which, on the face of it, seemed a luxurious feature for such a relatively cheap guitar, although lower-grade ebony was used (as well as rosewood, depending on availability). The earlier Studios also have dot fingerboard markers, generally reserved for Gibson's cheaper models, but around 1990 the fancier 'crown' type was adopted, a marketing decision to give the guitar a little more visual appeal. A version with bound neck and body, the Studio Standard, came along for a couple of years from 1984, and there have been other variants over the years.

Gibson for sale: only two previous owners

Alert readers may recall that Norlin had put Gibson up for sale around 1980. By summer 1985, a buyer was finally found. In January 1986, Henry Juszkiewicz, David Berryman, and Gary Zebrowski completed their purchase of the entire Gibson operation. They paid a sum undisclosed at the time but now generally acknowledged to be $5 million. Norlin's main business was in printing, and Gibson was the last part of its once-large musical empire to be sold off.

Juszkiewicz, Berryman, and Zebrowski had met while studying at the Harvard Business School in the late 70s, since when Juszkiewicz had been in engineering and investment banking, Berryman in accountancy, and Zebrowski in marketing. Crucially, Juszkiewicz was also an enthusiastic guitarist who loved Gibson instruments. "He's a fan," as one Gibson employee put it. The three had gone into business together, teaming up in 1981 to turn a failing Oklahoma electronics company into a successful operation.

When they bought Gibson in 1986, Juszkiewicz became president and Berryman vice-president of finance and accounting, while Zebrowski continued to run the trio's electronics business. The most immediate effect of the new ownership was that a lot of people were fired, including the plant manager, the quality control manager, and many others. One could hardly expect this to have been a popular first move. "It was pretty scary," admitted one insider. "But Henry got what he was after. If you judge it on results, he brought the company back from the dead."

Juszkiewicz told a reporter early in 1986 that he was, as he described it, in the process of restructuring Gibson's production operation. He said that the new Gibson set-up would be extremely aggressive in developing and introducing new products, and insisted that

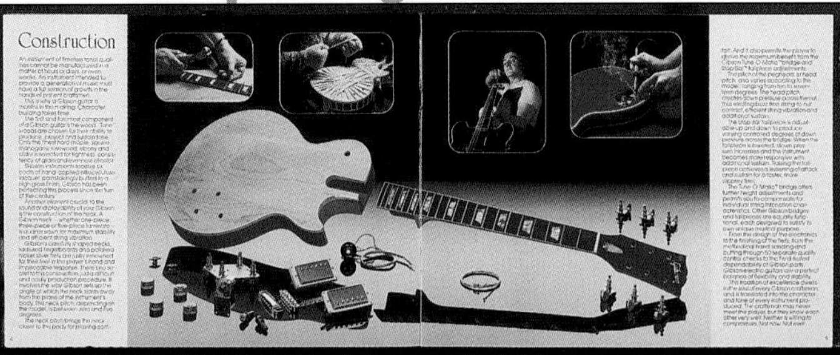
Construction

● At last, in 1983, Gibson began to sell a proper reissue of the great landmark in Les Paul history, the sunburst 1958–60 Standard, or 'Burst' as this great guitar is known today. Here are two examples: a first-year **1983 Standard Reissue** (below) and a custom-order quilt-top **1984 Standard Reissue** (right). **Billy Gibbons** (left) played a gorgeous original '59 Burst with ZZ Top, while a contemporary Gibson **catalogue** (top) emphasised the company's heritage.

● As Gibson began its new programme of proper reissues of the most respected old Les Paul models during the early 80s, some experts scoffed at the poor detail of the new guitars, but gradually matters improved. The activity at Gibson was not limited to the sunburst Standard: also in 1983, the company added a '57-style Goldtop to its list, and soon launched others, such as a single-cut Junior (1986) and a double-cut (1987), and an SG/Les Paul Custom (1987). This **1990 SG/Les Paul Custom** (above) shows that Gibson was at least getting the look right.

● Evidence of a less-focussed Gibson came with the Spotlight Special, an unusual limited edition designed to use up some bits and pieces lying around the factory – including a central walnut stripe and some spectacular pieces of flame maple for the outer body cap. Shown here are a **1983 Spotlight Special ANT** (left), the natural-finish version, and a 1983 **Spotlight Special ASB** (right) in sunburst.

Gibson would be more creative in merchandising and marketing than it had ever been, with a more competitive pricing policy.

"It turned out well," Juszkiewicz told me. "But I pretty much knew that it would be two years of sheer hell." As far as the ever-popular Les Paul models were concerned, Juszkiewicz said that he inherited a poor relationship between Gibson and Les Paul himself. "Les obviously had a proprietary interest in the success of his guitars, and they'd killed them, so he was pretty annoyed. Les lives in New Jersey, and [the New Jersey-based maker] Kramer were constantly seeing him. He even did an MTV video saying how nice Kramer guitars were. So I established a rapport with Les early on, and that seemed to solve the problem. I listened to what he had to say. He wanted to see a lower-cost Les Paul instrument in our imported Epiphone line, for example, and we ended up doing that a few years into the business."[9]

There were several changes to the roles of some key guitar-design people around the time of the change of ownership. Tim Shaw moved from the Custom Shop and R&D to an international role for the company, travelling often to Korea to help expand Gibson's Epiphone lines. He left Gibson in 1992, after 14 years' service with the company. J.T. Riboloff joined Gibson in 1987, moving to Nashville from his home in California where he had operated as a guitar maker, repairer, and restorer. He was hired for the Custom Shop and soon began to work on new designs.

Old ladies don't measure up

The new reissue models, effectively an attempt to recreate more accurately the old-style Standard and Goldtop, had been in production since 1983, driven by the persistent demands of customers seeking perfect duplication of the hallowed 50s instruments. "When I went to Gibson in 87, the Les Paul reissue was basically a Standard with a flame top," said Riboloff. "Slowly but surely, they let us get away with a little more."[10] One of the many problems associated with Gibson's reissue programme – and there will be more to come on this subject later – has always been to determine exactly which details to duplicate. Simply put, there is no such thing as a definitive 1958–60 Standard.

Tim Shaw calls to mind the infamous Gibson 'old ladies' who did much of the handwork in the factory at the time of those praised models. "They used to hand-sand the old ones a little bit differently every time," he said. "It used to tickle the hell out of me with all these people saying oh, the placement of the Gibson logo has to be *right here*, and the Les Paul Model logo *exactly there*. And I'd say well, those women who put the decals on – you think they measured? No they didn't." Shaw went on to ask himself an obviously unanswerable question. "What's the correct specifications of an early Les Paul?" He laughed, concluding with another question. "Who knows?"[11]

One aspect of Les Pauls that leaves less room for argument than vintage details is their weight. Some are, without doubt, heavier than others, but generally speaking a Les Paul is a heavy guitar, and examples from the late 70s and early 80s include some of the heaviest.

Gibson was determined to do something about this. The weight is due principally to the relative density of available mahogany.

Riboloff outlined the real extremes. "You can have two pieces of mahogany the same size," he said, "and one might weigh five pounds, the other twenty-five pounds. The difference is due to the amount of minerals drawn into the wood as it grows, especially silica. Of course, we didn't use that extremely heavy stuff. That became fixtures. It's very useful for little wooden mallets."[12]

The new owners of Gibson had inherited an earlier attempt to cut down the weight of the mahogany. Since about 1982, Nashville had drilled a series of small pockets into the mahogany section of Les Paul bodies, uncharitably called the Swiss-cheese effect by some observers. Of course, once the maple top was in place those holes were invisible, except perhaps to touring musicians with a keen interest in airport X-ray systems.

"I don't think it made a bit of difference to the sound," said Tim Shaw concerning the Swiss cheese. "The holes were too small to act as resonant cavities."[13] Gibson's new president, Henry Juszkiewicz, also considered the drilled bodies to have no effect upon the guitar's sound. "It didn't make any difference to the tonal characteristics of the model," he said. "The critical part of the body to the sound is the bridge area. If you do something up where the toggle switch is, say, it won't make any difference to the sound. The maple top is solid, of course, and a lot of the tonal characteristics come from that. So we were making a better guitar: it was more comfortable, and still sounded good."[14]

Another attempt to deal with the Les Paul weight problem came in the form of a new model called the Custom Lite, introduced in 1987. It had a contoured back that was pure Fender in style. The timber lost in this sculpting cut the weight and made the guitar more comfortable. At first it was priced higher than the normal Custom, presumably as a result of extra production costs – in 1987 the basic models were pitched at $1,170 for the Custom and $1,249 for the Custom Lite – but was gone from the line by 1989. A year earlier, Gibson introduced a similarly contoured version of its Les Paul Studio model, the Studio Lite, with an 88 list showing the Studio at $909 and the Studio Lite at $974.

Changes in fashion among guitar-players and guitar-makers had been unkind to Gibson during the 80s. Some of the key musicians allied closely to the original Les Paul had moved on to other models. At a charity benefit show in London in 1983, Jeff Beck, Eric Clapton, and Jimmy Page played together on stage. Beck was playing Fender Stratocasters. Clapton too played a Strat, and for one song he strapped on a lovely Gibson Firebird. Page mainly played a Fender Telecaster, although he did use his Les Paul Standard briefly. Beck and Clapton would go on to work with Fender and produce signature models a few years later.

The new guitar-making trends of the 80s were moving away from the Les Paul style of solidbody electric. There were plenty of odd-shaped axes about, some brief fads for 'headless' guitars, and a few misguided attempts at synthesizer hook-ups. Fender's Stratocaster was the flavour of the decade, and a revised modern offshoot, the so-called

● **Zakk Wylde** (left) plays his decorated Custom with Ozzy Osbourne. Over at Gibson, designers tried to reduce the sometimes oppressive weight of Les Paul models. This **1992 Studio Lite** (right) offered some relief. The first version, launched in 1988, had Fender-style back contouring; this later version, from 1990, had lighter balsa wood inserts in the body.

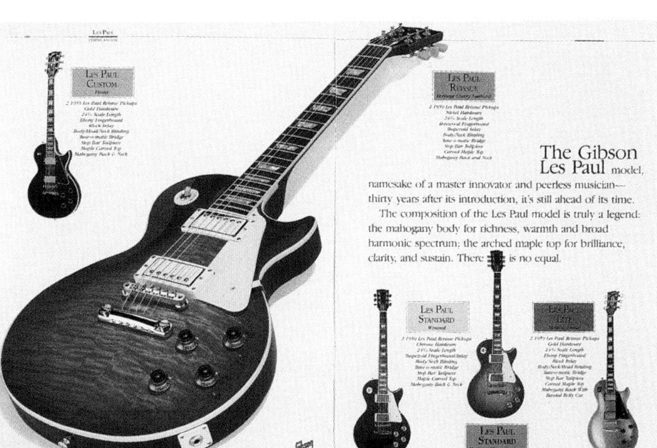

● **Steve Clark** (left) played his last date with Def Leppard in 1988. His Les Paul-fuelled work had helped the band to great success, but in 1991 Clark was dead at the age of just 30. At Gibson, the most expensive model from the original Les Paul line, the Custom, had been largely overlooked in the new reissue programme. But this **1989 35th Anniversary** (right) marked the Custom's birth in 1954 – even if the model itself was based on the three-humbucker '57-style Custom.

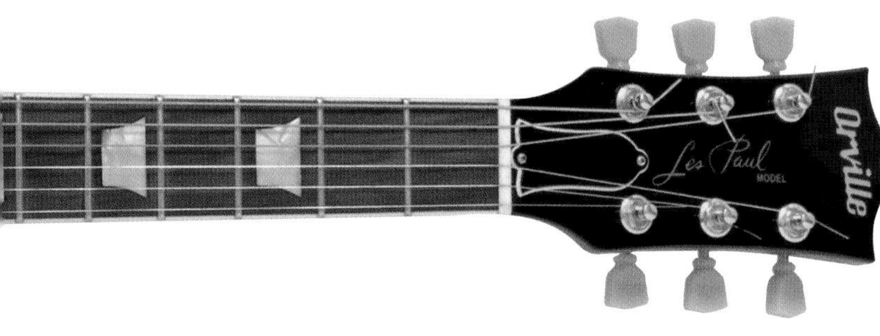

● The Orville brand appeared on a series of instruments made and sold in Japan by Gibson from the late 80s and into the 90s. This **1989 Orville Les Paul** (main guitar) was one of several models built exclusively for the Japanese market, lasting until Gibson began making Epiphone-brand electrics in Japan in 1998.

superstrat, attracted many of the high-octane players who might otherwise have been potential naturals for a Gibson Les Paul.

The superstrat was largely developed by US maker Jackson from the Stratocaster. It offered more frets, deeper cutaways, a drooped pointy-shape headstock, versatile new pickup layouts, a high-performance vibrato system, and bright graphic finishes. In many ways it was the antithesis of a Les Paul Standard – and it came to define the mainstream rock guitar of the 80s.

Jackson and the related Charvel brand attracted important 80s players, especially the talented Eddie Van Halen. But Ibanez too had a highly visible line of superstrats, especially the RG series, and did much to popularise the style. Key 80s guitar heroes Steve Vai and Joe Satriani opted for Ibanez models and helped to design new instruments.

In a 1989 interview, Satriani summed up the way many players and makers were trying to synthesize the best of several instrument styles into a new kind of guitar. "I've tried to get the ultimate Strat sound and the ultimate Les Paul sound from one guitar," said Satriani, "but it's like a jinx."[15]

Of course, some players kept the faith. You would hardly expect such a passionate Les Paul fan as Joe Walsh, for example, to switch allegiance. He'd joined The Eagles in 76 until they disbanded in the early 80s. In 1988, Walsh still defined his all-time favourite guitar set-up as a vintage Les Paul through a pair of Fender Super Reverb amps. "I'm partial to a 59 or a 60," he said. "It depends … 58s are fun too. Les Pauls just really make it for me. I do also love Strats and Teles, though."[16]

When Gibson stumbled on old hand Gary Richrath of REO Speedwagon, who still relied on an enviable collection of old Les Pauls, they got him to endorse their attempt to jump on the superstrat bandwagon, the US-1 model. The resulting 1987 ad displayed Richrath among his vintage collection of seven Standards, a Goldtop, and two Customs – but there he was holding the incongruous-looking US-1.

Slash the saviour

Among all the new shred players lining up for their new superstrats, along came Guns N' Roses to redefine hard rock – and, no doubt to Gibson's delight, guitarist Slash used mostly Les Pauls on which to unleash his aggressive blues-laden licks.

Slash had been influenced to take up Les Pauls by Jimmy Page and Joe Perry. As Guns N' Roses began to sell millions of albums, he assembled a fine collection of guitars, with a good showing of vintage Les Pauls (including one of the earliest-numbered 1958 sunburst Standards). But the guitar he was most often seen with on stage was a regular late-80s Standard – and the one he used to record the band's first hit album, 1987's *Appetite For Destruction*, wasn't a Gibson at all, but a replica. The irony is that the guitar that more or less brought the Les Paul back to public consciousness wasn't actually made by Gibson.

"I'm really attached to my guitars," Slash said recently. "Everything I have in some way, shape, or form is a favourite. I'm partial to Les Pauls, of course. A couple of them are replicas, and one is very dear to me because it's the guitar that really cut the ties between me and any other sort of guitars. It was built by Chris Derrig, and I got it through Guns N' Roses management when we were doing the basic tracks for *Appetite For Destruction*."

Slash said he was experimenting with guitars at the time but didn't have much money, and so he couldn't just go and pick up anything he wanted. Being in the studio for the first time, he realised that he had to get a guitar that sounded really good. "I'd been using Les Pauls, but they'd get stolen or I'd hock them. So Alan Niven, the band's original manager, gave me this hand-made 59 Les Paul Standard replica. I took it in the studio with a rented Marshall, and it sounded great. And I've never really used another. It has zebra-striped Seymour Duncan Alnico II pickups.

"I ended up in the studio with the Les Paul replica," said Slash, "and that was my main guitar through the beginning of the first Guns N' Roses tour. I later got another replica made by someone named Max [Baranet]. I had those two on the road for the first year. Then, when Gibson gave me a deal on two Les Paul Standards, I put away the replicas because I'd banged the crap out of them."[17]

Gibson tried to entice Slash with special models and to have him endorse a signature model. "They offered to make me a Les Paul model to my specs, and that included a thinner low-profile neck with bigger frets," he said. "But I wasn't happy with the sound. In 1989 they approached me to do a Slash model, which included gold hardware and a heavy bookmatched flame top with translucent colours. They were going to be marketed, and ideally I would use them on stage, but again I wasn't happy with the sound."[18] Gibson eventually produced a small run of Slash Les Pauls in 1997, with an Epiphone-brand version following shortly afterward, and then a signature sunburst in 2004 and Goldtop in 2008.

As a difficult decade for Gibson drew to a close, a June 1989 pricelist had eight basic Les Paul models: the Junior, listing at $913; "Junior II" (actually a Special) $913; Studio $1,089; Studio Lite $1,154; Standard $1,263; Custom $1,586; Custom Lite $1,569; Goldtop reissue $1,879; Standard reissue $2,779.

the nineties

"Call it grunge, rock, punk, whatever – good music is good music. But a great guitar is sex."

Stone Gossard, Pearl Jam ▶

Pop's
Love

We know by now that Les Pauls are not necessarily the lightest guitars in the world, and we know how Gibson has tried various remedies to make them lighter. But for a while, in the 90s, an apparently unlikely wood provided a solution for one model. Matthew Klein joined Gibson's small Custom team in 1986, and he brought with him some intriguing experience of balsa wood.

Klein had built for his own amusement a balsa-body Les Paul, discovering that it sustained well and sounded fine unplugged. Balsa has good resonating qualities and, despite a popular misconception, is not cheap. And at about four pounds, Klein's Les Paul was a lot lighter than some Gibsons that were weighing up to eleven pounds thanks to the increasing density of available mahogany.

News of Klein's balsa experiments reached Billy Gibbons of ZZ Top, who promptly ordered from him four white Explorer-shape balsa instruments (two guitars, two basses) for the group's 1985 *Afterburner* world tour. Klein skinned them with thin spruce to help hold screws and prevent paint cracks. "It was like a spruce and balsa sandwich, the filling being the balsa," explained Klein.[1]

The guitars worked well on-stage, playing and sounding good – and were virtually half the weight of regular models. Klein supplied ZZ Top with further balsa guitars – Super 400-style with Firebird headstocks – for their *Recycler* tour. Then Klein joined Gibson, and with his Custom colleagues Mike Voltz and Phil Jones he began to consider the application of balsa to Gibson models.

The first result from the new Gibson team was the maple-skinned-balsa US-1 superstrat-style guitar of 1986, but this turned out to be too difficult to produce and was dropped by 1991. Balsa was then used in the body-wood mix of the Chet Atkins SST model, launched in 1987, and three years later it was applied to the Les Paul's weight problem. The existing Les Paul Studio Lite was modified to incorporate balsa inserts. Gibson renamed balsa as 'chromite', derived from the first word of its Latin names, ochroma pyramidale and ochroma lagopus, perhaps because they feared balsa's 'cheap' image.

The new balsa-enhanced Studio Lite of 1990 was given a regular flat back and a slimmer neck compared to its previous incarnation, losing a couple of pounds in the process. A roughly D-shaped cut-out in the guitar body left the bridge and tailpiece connected to the back, with the space around filled by balsa, which Gibson bought cut to the required dimensions. The model lasted until 1998 – and the balsa experiment was gone from the Les Paul line.

Another attempt at producing a lighter Les Paul came along in 1995 when a model was introduced with hollowed 'tone chambers' inside, the Bantam Elite. The chambers were reminiscent of the sort of thing used in Guild's Nightbird of the late 80s, or even Gretsch's semi-solid Jet models of the 50s. Washburn soon objected to the Bantam name, which it already used for a guitar, and so Gibson quickly released two renamed models, the Florentine Standard or Florentine Plus (the 'Plus' as usual in Gibson terminology indicating a fancier figured top). The Florentines too were gone by 1998, but Gibson did adopt a hollow-body Les Paul for its lower-cost Epiphone brand: first the Custom-style Elite, in 1996, and then the Standard-like ES a few years later.

With the double-cutaway solidbody MIII model of 1991, Gibson launched a radically styled guitar with circuitry more flexible than usual. J.T. Riboloff in the Custom Shop had come up with the original MIII idea, and at first he planned a two-pickup guitar. Management pointed to the popularity of the superstrat's arrangement of humbucker–single-coil–humbucker, and the MIII dutifully appeared in this three-pickup form. "My intention was to get every selection of the Stratocaster and every selection of the Les Paul from a five-way switch," Riboloff said of his ambitious idea.[2] Unfortunately, Gibson's customers felt the design and the electronics of the MIII guitar were too un-Gibson and failed to rush to buy the instrument.

The wiring was adapted into two Les Paul models, the Classic/MIII (1991) and the Studio Lite/MIII (1992), in a move reminiscent of the marriage of RD circuitry and Les Paul Artist ten years earlier. Riboloff felt that the Studio Lite was better suited to the MIII sound, the tone of the lightweight body sitting well with the expanded sonic possibilities of the circuitry. The Classic/MIII was dropped in 1992; the Studio Lite/MIII lasted a further two years. The original M-III guitars (and the later Steinberger trem-equipped M-IVs) had all gone from the Gibson catalogue by 1997.

Reissues: the story so far

Gibson's first official Custom Shop had started in the 60s at Kalamazoo, building one-offs to customers' requirements, although the company had accepted non-standard orders since its earliest days. The idea was revived in the 80s at Nashville, where a small Custom area was set up within the main plant from about 1983.

The present Custom Shop started in a separate building nearby in 1993, continuing the traditional role of making custom orders and developing R&D ideas, as well as fulfilling special dealer orders and contributing its own upscale models to the line. Today, it comes under the auspices of the Custom/Art/Historic division that caters for one-offs, high-end reissues, and many of the signature models.

The idea of reissuing classic models is hardly a new one for the Gibson Les Paul line. We've already met several examples in this book, particularly the way the company eventually reacted to the new popularity of the old Les Paul design in the 60s by reissuing two models in 1968. We also learned how more reissues followed sporadically in the 70s, reproducing the spirit if not the precise detail of the originals.

A number of US dealers then began to custom-order limited runs, because it was clear to them that there was a gap between the 'correct' vintage vibe that some of their customers wanted from a Les Paul and the kind of thing that Gibson was pulling from its production line at the time.

Those customers wanted the 'correct' narrower headstock, the 'correct' thin binding in the cutaway, the 'correct' shape of top carve, plus a host of tiny details. In fact, they

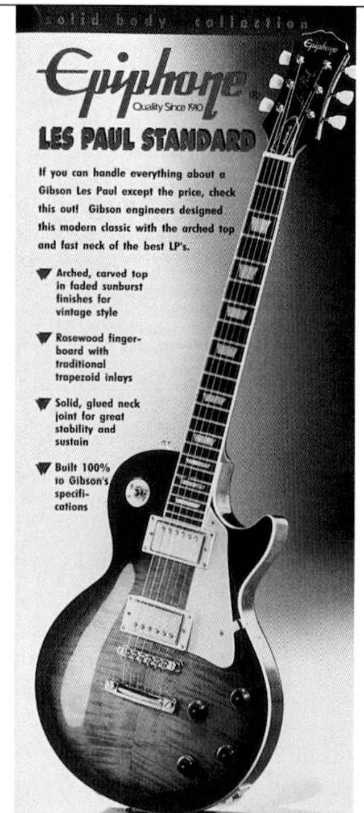

● The reissue programme continued at Gibson into the 90s. A moody shot in the **1991 catalogue** (above left) featured a figured-top Standard. At the other end of the scale, Gibson developed its Epiphone brand into a budget line alongside Gibson, copying some of its most famous models, including Les Pauls. This **1991 flyer** (above) shows the "100 per cent to Gibson specifications" Standard, the first Epi-brand Les Paul.

● Gibson began to offer fancier flame tops from the early 90s, which it rated Plus (better) and Premium Plus (best). Here are two examples: a **1991 Custom Plus** (top) and a **1995 Classic Plus** (main guitar).

A CLASSIC AXE 1990–91

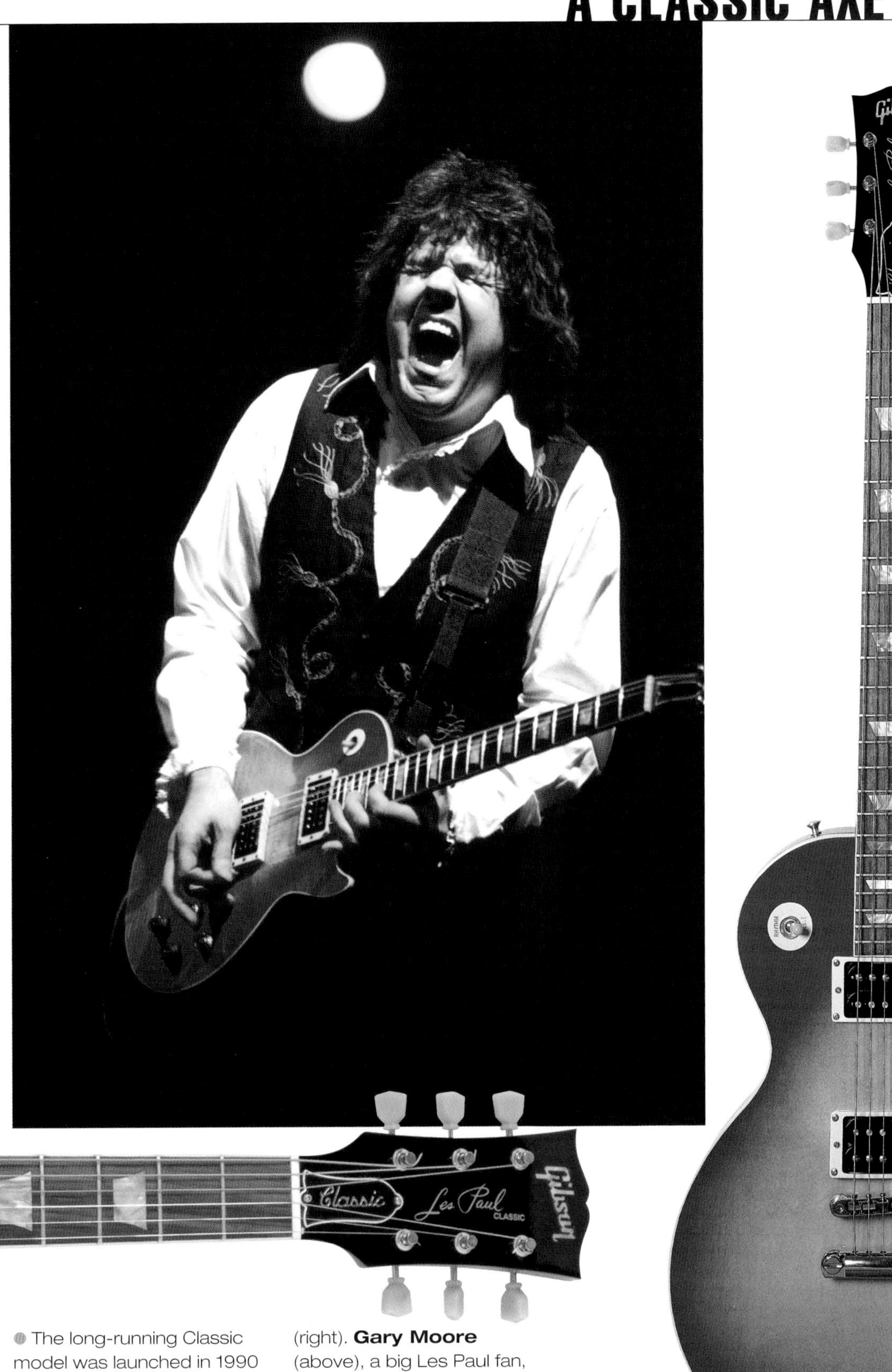

● The long-running Classic model was launched in 1990 as a 1960-flavoured Standard, and at first it had a suitable logo on its pickguard, like this **1990 Classic** (right). **Gary Moore** (above), a big Les Paul fan, turned it up a notch with some blistering humbucker-assisted blues as the 90s got under way.

wanted a Standard exactly like Gibson used to make – and, until 1976, Gibson didn't even have a Standard officially on its list.

As we've seen, the first serious attempt by Gibson at any kind of accuracy in reproducing an old-style Les Paul came with the Heritage Standard models of 1980 – which were good for the time but hardly startling. More dealers became aware of the demand from a particular clientele for the right look – aside from any considerations of playability – and began ordering further small runs of better-spec Standards from Gibson. At last, in 1983, the company reacted and produced the first official Gibson Les Paul reissues, which we discovered in the previous chapter.

Since then, the company's efforts had begun to widen and improve, concentrating on the principal 50s classics: the Standards, the Goldtops, the Customs, and, to a lesser extent, the Juniors and Specials. Of these, it's the sunburst 1958–60 Standard that has generated the most activity. That's no great surprise. After all, this hallowed model pulls increasingly remarkable amounts of money among guitar collectors and is rightly considered by guitarists as one of the prime benchmarks of the great solidbody electric instrument. With today's prices for a fine original well up into six figures, a small but lucrative market has developed for ever-more-accurate Gibson repros at a (relatively) more affordable rate.

Tom Murphy became an important person within the team that developed the reissues. He'd been at Gibson since 1989, and a few years later moved from the finish repair department to the Custom area. As a player, he'd been attracted by several of Gibson's attempts over the years to recapture the holy grail.

"I'd had two of the reissues made for Texas dealer Jimmy Wallace, for example," Murphy recalled, "and I would fantasise that I was getting a really good copy of an old Les Paul. But I'd soon get disenchanted and wonder why I thought they were going to be anything close to the original. They never cut it! Without having any vast knowledge of construction, I found that something just wasn't right with the overall feel.

"I wished someone at Gibson who knew would fix it. Don't they have any old Les Pauls they can look at? Then I thought, well, I guess mother nature never intended for us to have those guitars again. Now, however, I don't know why I thought it was that complicated."[3] Once at Gibson, Murphy began to appreciate the practical (and political) considerations necessary to produce a good, acceptable reissue.

J.T. Riboloff in the Custom Shop had found that a lot of players who asked him to build special one-off Les Pauls were requesting the slimmer-profile neck associated with the 1960 Standard. Gibson boss Henry Juszkiewicz noted the flurry of interest when the company showed an example at a NAMM trade-show and told Riboloff to start work on a production version. This appeared in 1990, called the Les Paul Classic. "One of my main things," said Riboloff, "was to try to get the stock instrument to be just as cool as the custom ones. That's really how the Les Paul Classic came about."[4]

Juszkiewicz had decided that the Classic needed to stand out from the rest of the line, and so insisted on a 1960 logo imprinted on the guitar's pickguard, emphasising the inspiration for its slim neck and 'correct' size headstock. Riboloff's original intention had been to make the Classic with a rather plain top and faded finish, resembling some of the less visually spectacular Standards that notable players would still occasionally take on stage. Later variants with more extreme figured tops were added, such as the Classic Plus and Classic Premium Plus. But among all this retrospection, the sound of the Classic was definitely modern, thanks to some very powerful coverless humbuckers.

A year later, in 1991, the Standard reissue was revised and split into two models, effectively the 59 and the 60. This is where the proper, modern reissue starts. These models adopted the 'correct' details of the Classic, and also came with more traditional-sounding humbuckers, as developed by Riboloff.

Reworking the reissues

Juszkiewicz and his colleagues had owned Gibson now for several years. There was a new awareness of the company's historical importance and an understanding that some old achievements were still highly valued by many players and collectors. Beginning in 1991, Riboloff worked on some commendable reissues of Gibson's revered oddball 50s classics, the Flying V and the Explorer, as part of what Gibson now called its Historic programme.

The accuracy of Riboloff's work set Tom Murphy thinking that perhaps the same thing really could be done with the Les Paul models. "It was like: when are we going to admit it and totally re-do the reissue Les Paul?" Murphy told me. As it turned out, it wouldn't be too long.

There was a significant arrival: a marketing manager who actually owned a 1960 Standard and, for once, understood the arguments. "He spoke the language," explained Murphy, evidently in awe of such an achievement among marketing folk. Murphy was invited to plant-management meetings and presented a list of around 25 important changes that should be made to the Standard reissues.

Gibson people set to work in an attempt to replicate more closely than ever the magic of an original sunburst Standard. Management supported the costly experiments. The 'new' reissue would have more accurate body carving, the smaller-size vintage-style headstock, a fat neck profile, holly veneer for the headstock face with a silkscreened logo, the most attractive figured maple for the top, a slight reduction in neck pitch, proper routing of the control cavity, an early-style Tune-o-matic bridge, and the reinstatement of a longer, wider neck tenon or 'tongue' at the neck–body joint.

"It was a matter of retrieving all those things," said Murphy. "It was almost as if they'd been thrown out and scattered across the plant floor, swept under a table. They were here ... somewhere. I won't take credit for designing the 59 Les Paul," he smiled. "That was done when I was nine years old. But I will take credit in unearthing and finding some of these old key things."[5]

Matthew Klein in the Custom Shop helped to establish the new shape for the revised Standard reissue's body carve – the 'form' as it's known – by measuring every hundred-

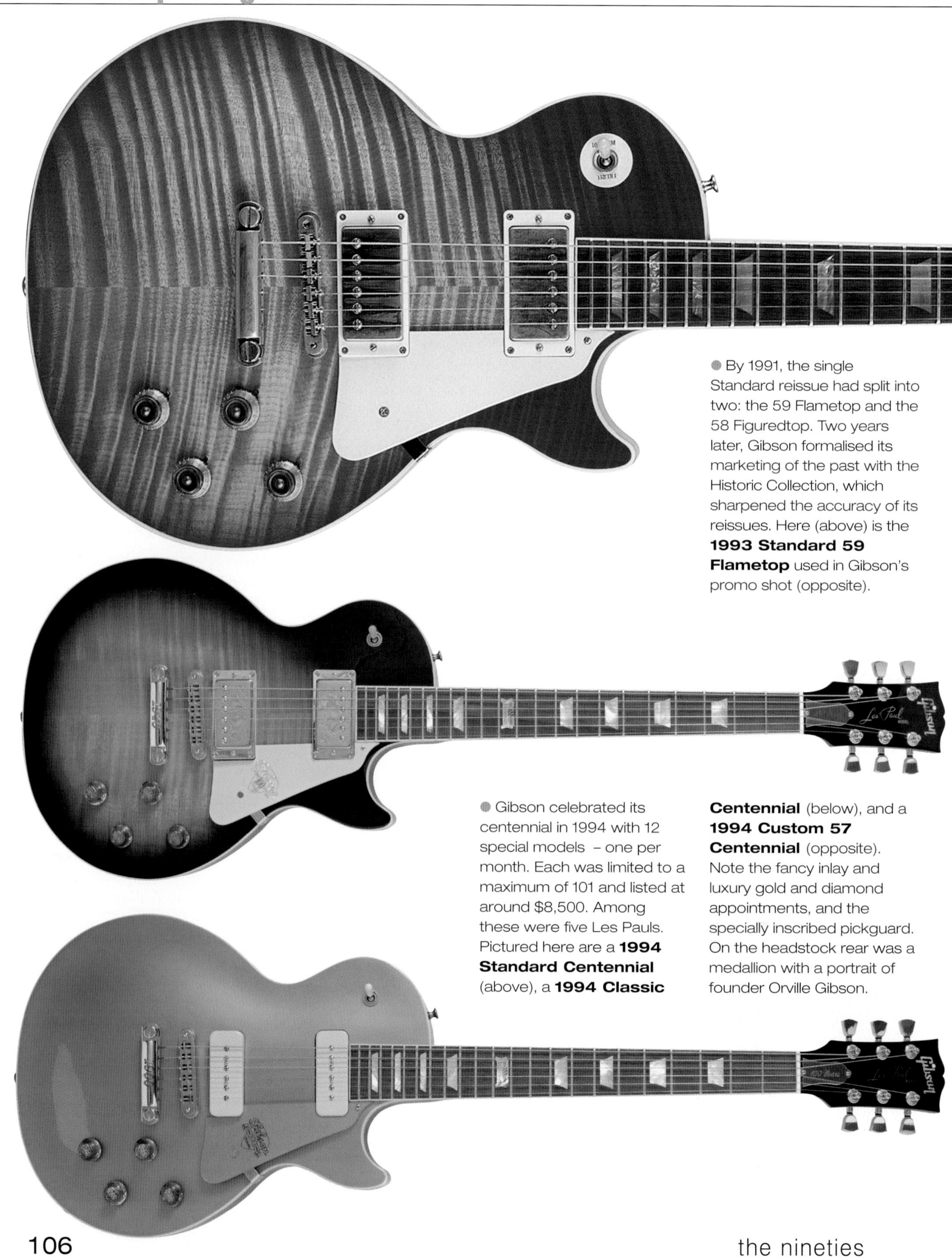

● By 1991, the single Standard reissue had split into two: the 59 Flametop and the 58 Figuredtop. Two years later, Gibson formalised its marketing of the past with the Historic Collection, which sharpened the accuracy of its reissues. Here (above) is the **1993 Standard 59 Flametop** used in Gibson's promo shot (opposite).

● Gibson celebrated its centennial in 1994 with 12 special models – one per month. Each was limited to a maximum of 101 and listed at around $8,500. Among these were five Les Pauls. Pictured here are a **1994 Standard Centennial** (above), a **1994 Classic Centennial** (below), and a **1994 Custom 57 Centennial** (opposite). Note the fancy inlay and luxury gold and diamond appointments, and the specially inscribed pickguard. On the headstock rear was a medallion with a portrait of founder Orville Gibson.

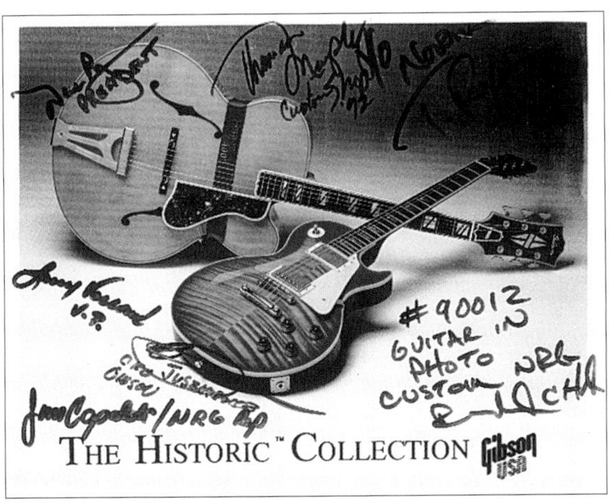

Many musicians had been aware of **Neil Young** (above) since the 60s and his work with Buffalo Springfield and then Crosby Stills Nash & Young, as well as his fine solo tours and albums. By the 90s he'd proved his cred to a new generation, notably with the 1990 album *Ragged Glory*. Some even called him the godfather of grunge. Young nearly always plays this much-modified refinished 50s Goldtop, which he nicknamed Old Black.

thousandth of an inch of the carving on some original Standards to construct a grid from which the production form was developed.

Riboloff reckons he examined maybe 25 different Standards from the 1958–60 era. "They were all different," he laughed, pointing by way of example to his observation that no two headstocks were anything like the same. "The machine heads would be slightly further north or south, the scroll was shorter, and the logo would be different," he said, exasperated. "They were soft-tooled back then, and so every one is different. Really, there is no super-correct one to reissue. So with these 25 to hand, we took the best attributes of each instrument – cosmetics, carving, and all – and combined them."[6]

Edwin Wilson in the Custom Shop offered further insight into reissue lore. "We have never claimed that the reissue was issued as a replica," he said. "What we have continually said is that it is a work in process." He observed how some reissue customers become obsessed with particular details but stressed that, from a production point of view, Gibson have to consider the instrument as a whole. Take neck pitch as an example. There is much debate about the exact number of degrees that this should be. And yet it is another of those variables that differs among original Standards. There is no such thing as the 'correct' measurement.

"Since 1992 we have blueprinted numerous Les Pauls from 1952 to 1960," said Wilson, "and as with all handmade instruments there are variations from instrument to instrument. But the one thing that we have confirmed is that the neck pitch on 1959 and 1960 Standards ranges from four degrees to five-and-a-half degrees, with four being the majority."[7]

Riboloff said the escalating retail price of the Standard reissue was another factor in concentrating their efforts. "It got to the point where we wanted it to be more of a replica rather than a reissue," he suggested.[8] Keith Medley in R&D built the prototypes, and the results were proudly displayed to the public for the first time at the 1993 NAMM show. (The first two prototypes ended up with Slash and Bryan Adams.)

The 'new' revised and improved Les Paul Standard 59 reissue had arrived, along with a similarly ravishing 60, and a new Goldtop 57 reissue. Already in the reissue line were the Goldtop 56 and Customs 54 and 57. Further improvements to details have been made since 1993 and more reissue models added to the line, including in the 90s the Standard 58 Plaintop (1994), Standard 58 (1996), Goldtop 54 (1997), Junior 57 single-cut (1998), Special 60 double-cut (1998), Goldtop 52 (1999), and Standard 59 Plaintop (1999). Another model that might be considered a reissue came along in 1992 with the return of the small-humbucker Deluxe, last seen in the 80s, and it lasted in the line until 2008.

With all this attention to detail and, at 2009 prices, the possibility to own a 'correct' $8,000 Standard 59 reissue as opposed to a $300,000-or-more original, how might a novice tell them apart – or, for that matter, an experienced player ignorant of the constructional details of the late-50s solidbody electric guitar in the Kalamazoo region? The answer is a die-stamped inked number that should be seen in the control pocket of all modern Gibson Les Paul reissues (that's the hole in the back of the body once you take off the panel). There on the lower ledge is stamped R9 for the Standard 59 reissue, R8 for the 58, and R0 for the 60; R2 for the Goldtop 52, R4 for the 54, R6 for the 56, and R7 for the 57; R4 for the Custom 54 and R7 for the 57.

The reissues play very well and sound wonderful. But it's fairly safe to say that no one really knows why the genuine old pickups sound the way they do. "And that's sort of the beauty of it, right?" laughed Murphy. "Maybe mother nature's going OK, go have all the fun you want, but I'm going to keep this one thing – because you're not supposed to have all that stuff. I have said many times to people: this is not a 1959 Les Paul. It's a 2000-and-something Les Paul or whatever. That's not to misunderstand what it's supposed to refer to, and what they want. But it's not a 59!"[9]

At the time of the relaunch of the reissues, Gibson's April 1993 pricelist showed seven basic Les Paul guitars: Studio $899; Special $949; Studio Lite $1,099; Studio Lite/MIII $1,199; Standard $1,599; Classic $2,199; and Custom $2,199. The 'Historic Collection' pricelist showed six basic Les Paul reissues: Standard 59 $5,059; Standard 60 $5,059; Goldtop 56 $2,549; Goldtop 57 $2,549; Custom 54 $2,399; and Custom 57 $2,399.

Let's remember Orville

Gibson has settled upon 1894 as the year that its founder, Orville Gibson, began making instruments commercially, although there's no evidence to pinpoint such a date. He probably began making instruments in his spare time during the 1880s, when he was in his late twenties. The first year that he merits a listing in the local Kalamazoo business directory as a manufacturer of musical instruments was 1896. Whatever the facts, Gibson nonetheless celebrated their centennial in 1994, issuing a series of limited-edition instruments to mark the occasion.

There were 12 special Centennial models produced during 1994 – one per month – and each was limited to a maximum of 101 instruments, serial-numbered 1894 to 1994 and listing at around $8,500 each. Among these were five Les Pauls: the Classic Centennial, the Custom Black Beauty 57 3-Pickup Centennial, two Specials, in single and double-cut style, and the Standard Centennial. They were all decked out with fancy inlay and luxury gold and diamond appointments, as might be expected, including a portrait of Orville on the back of the headstock and an inscribed pickguard. We can only assume that Orville smiled as he looked down from his prime spot in Guitar Heaven.

A further series of decorated upscale Les Pauls came along a couple of years later – the $2,990 Catalina and Elegant and the $7,999 Ultima. Where the Centennials had a circular portrait of Orville on the back of the headstock, these had a pearl Custom Shop banner on the front. All three had the Florentine's 'sound chambers' in the body for weight-saving.

Matthew Klein in the Custom Shop explained: "They had a body hollowed-out to a 'C' shape, from around the switch area, around behind the tailpiece, and then back up toward the horn. It was like a 335, with several things going on to try to make a 'solid' guitar a little lighter."[10] The Catalina came in opaque black, red, yellow, or turquoise finishes,

● For that stadium-rocking sound guaranteed to keep you in the music biz long beyond predictions of a natural sell-by date, this **1995 Joe Perry** signature model (main guitar, above) had a number of unusual features requested by the Aerosmith guitarist. You'll notice that there is plenty of black-plated chrome to enhance the suitably moody appeal of the 'translucent blackburst' finish, and there is an active mid-boost circuit onboard to help shape the guitar's inherent tone.

● This **1996 Ultima** (right) was a luscious Custom Shop special. It was one of the fanciest Les Pauls ever, with swathes of abalone, pearl, and gold, and four optional fingerboard flourishes: this example has the elegant 'tree-of-life' inlay.

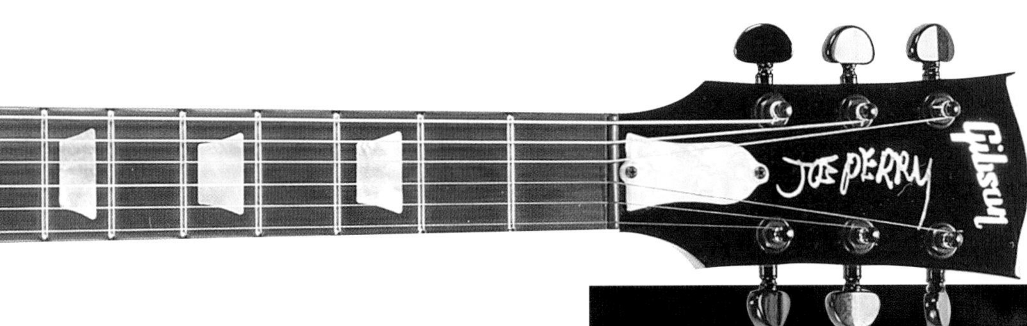

● **Jimmy Page** (right) proved in the 90s there was life post-Led Zeppelin with a number of projects and partnerships, notably with David Coverdale and Robert Plant. Page is pictured here on tour with Plant in 1995, still playing his favoured 'Number 1' Burst that had served him so well in Zeppelin. Gibson produced its first signature-model Les Paul that same year, and the **1995 Jimmy Page** pictured (opposite, centre) shows the guitar's gold-plated hardware and the Page signature on the pickguard. It lasted a few years on the Gibson list, but fans had to wait until 2004 for a proper repro of the famous 'Number 1'.

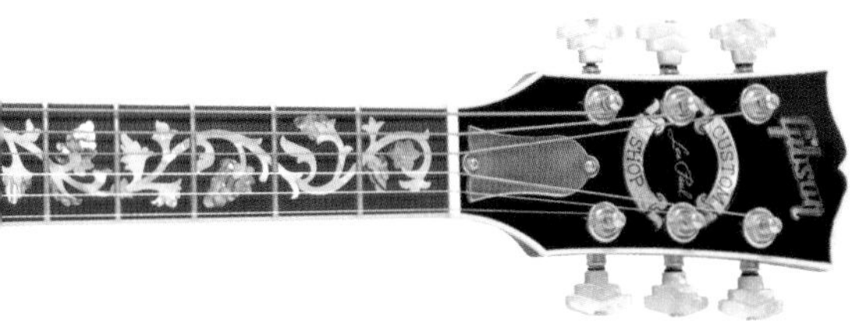

while the Elegant had top-quality flame maple and abalone fingerboard markers. The Ultima was one of the fanciest Les Pauls for some time, with swathes of abalone, pearl, and gold, and it had four optional fingerboard flourishes: flames, tree-of-life, butterflies, or harps. The Catalina was gone from the line by 1998, the Ultima two years later, while the Elegant Quilt, a figured-top version, remained on the catalogue until 2005.

Further down at a relatively affordable level was the Studio – the basic model first seen back in the early 80s that still provides many players with their first experience of a Gibson Les Paul. It remains a straightforward, less expensive alternative to the regular Standard, and the model consistently comes near the top of Gibson's sales charts. Independent polls in the late 90s confirmed the Studio as a Gibson bestseller, although then it was still trailing Fender's all-conquering Stratocaster.

Gibson scored too with its sister brand, Epiphone, and a line of affordable Les Pauls. Since 1970, with a few exceptions, Epiphones were made for Gibson by various oriental factories. In 1988, the first proper set-neck Les Paul models were added to the Epi line, the Korean-made Standard and Custom – and the addition was somewhat ironic for anyone with a little knowledge of the history. Les Paul himself had begun his experiments on semi-solid electric guitars back in the 30s and 40s using Epiphone instruments, and he did some of this work at the Epiphone factory in New York City.

Anyway, more recently, many more Les Paul models have been added to the Epiphone lines, with finishes ranging from exotic and transparent to sparkle, while a seven-string version followed a fashion among hardcore rockers around the turn of the millennium. There are signature models for Ozzy's Zakk Wylde and for Slash, as well as an unbound version, the 100. The list prices range at the time of writing from about $300 to $1,400. It was this formula of copying the best-known Gibson models that has made the Epiphone line such a success to the present day, and it should be marked up as another of the smart business moves made by Gibson's present owners. As Fender has done with its Squier brand, Gibson effectively copied itself, using the benefit of cheaper overseas production – and in the process has sold and is selling an impressive number of guitars.

The name of the game is the name

During the 90s, there were two themes that seemed to be everywhere in the guitar industry. One was retro. Everyone wanted to loot the past for an old-style look. Of course, Gibson was well positioned for this, with a glorious history to draw upon. The other theme was the signature guitar. This was a model authorised by a famous player and with personal specifications or visuals – and usually a combination of the two.

Gibson was also in a good position for this trend. After all, the Les Paul model itself was the original signature electric guitar. Les Paul had endorsed the company's very first solidbody back in 1952 – but since then, no other musician's name had ever appeared alongside Mr Paul's on a production model. Fender re-popularised the idea of the signature model, starting with the Eric Clapton Stratocaster in 1988. Gibson followed by going for an equally big name among the legion of famous Les Paul players, honouring Led Zeppelin's Jimmy Page with the first signature-edition Les Paul, launched in 1995.

The Jimmy Page Les Paul was a factory model that lasted in the line until 1999. It accommodated the guitarist's request for an unusual neck shape and fret height. Visually, the guitar appeared as a basic Les Paul Standard with a lightly figured top, gold-plated hardware, and Pagey's which-way-is-up autograph logo on the pickguard. More accurate (and desirable) repros of Page's hallowed Standards would appear later: his 'Number 1' in 2004 and 'Number 2' in 2009.

An oddity of the 95 Page Les Paul was a series of switching options, apparently based on the Zep man's own modifications. The pickups were the powerful types used on the Classic, but they were combined with a push-pull switch on each of the four control knobs. Depending on your requirements, this could seem like a wonderfully expansive range of tonal possibilities ... or just too many choices.

In this way the 90s Page Les Paul neatly highlights the major advantage and disadvantage of a signature instrument – whoever the artist, whatever the manufacturer. The advantage for a fan is that if you like the player concerned, you might feel a little closer to his style by owning one of these guitars. The disadvantage for a musician is that it's unlikely that one player's specific requirements will match your own. It goes back to Les Paul himself constantly modifying the guitars that Gibson sent to him. Players adapt instruments to suit themselves, quite rightly oblivious to what anyone else might like.

More signature Les Pauls followed the Page. Aerosmith's Joe Perry saw his moody 'blackburst' arrive in 1996, at first in a limited Custom Shop run and then in a factory version, and the following year there were models for Ace Frehley of Kiss and Slash of Guns N'Roses, both with suitable graphics on the instrument. Ozzy Osbourne's guitar wiz Zakk Wylde saw his Les Paul go to market in 1999, unmistakeable with its circular 'bullseye' finish, although there was briefly a plain Rough Top alternative.

Wylde explained how the distinctive finish came about. "Originally, I had a Les Paul that had a cream colour, which looked way cool. But when I got in Ozzy's band I decided that I wanted to have something on my guitar that made me stand out, like the way Randy Rhoads did with the polka dots.

"So a friend of mine did a paint job on it, with the idea that it would look like the poster for the movie *Vertigo* – only it came out looking more like a bullseye. When I saw it, I started laughing; to me, it made perfect sense. Joining Ozzy's band and trying to fill Randy's shoes – I might as well give the fans something to aim at!"[11]

In recent years it has seemed as if almost everyone is concerned with environmental issues, and the use and abuse of timber is often high on the list of those who lobby for changes in the way that we all exploit the earth's natural resources. In the past, wood was largely considered as something that was simply available for the taking. No one much considered the consequences of such an attitude, or at least not so publicly as they do today. Over-cutting and deforestation – in other words the stripping of forests from the

It's difficult to imagine that Gibson did not consider the growing success of PRS – a US-based company making double-cutaway figured-carved-top guitars with strong Gibson influences – and aim the new Les Paul DC lines of 1997 and '98 at a similar audience. This **1997 DC Pro** (main guitar, below) was one of three models, alongside the DC Studio and DC Standard. Signature guitars continued, with this **Japanese ad** (right) selling models for Zakk Wylde, Slash, and Tony Iommi. And luxury instruments still appeared from the Custom Shop, such as this **1997 Elegant** (above), in the same series as the Catalina and Ultima, with top-quality flame maple and abalone fingerboard markers.

AGING GRACEFULLY 1997–99

James Dean Bradfield (above) seen on-stage with The Manic Street Preachers and his white Custom. Tom Murphy worked for Gibson until he set up his own firm in 1994, developing techniques for the aging of guitar finishes. Gibson was aware of Fender's successful aged Relic guitars, launched in 1995, and began in 1999 to have Murphy age various Les Paul models. This **1999 Standard 59 Flametop Aged** (above) shows how authentic the result can be.

ground – are worrying modern trends, especially in tropical regions, and illegal trade in 'banned' woods is rife.

Some guitar-makers too have become concerned with the ecological impact of their business. Others take the view that guitar-making barely dents world timber stocks and they simply carry on regardless. For small, independent craft makers turning out a handful of custom instruments, probably only a few trees would ever need to be cut down to provide them with enough raw materials to last their entire career. With the big guitar makers, however, it's arguable that their consumption of wood is of greater significance.

Some of the scarcer guitar-making woods have already been outlawed from use. Most famously, in 1992 Brazilian rosewood – the hallowed fingerboard timber and acoustic-guitar material used in countless old vintage gems – was banned from international trade. Pre-1992 stocks are occasionally available for expensive instruments, but most guitars and most makers, Gibson included, now use rosewood from other sources as well as the various alternatives. In truth, Brazilian rosewood represents more of an emotional loss than a practical hindrance in the guitar world.

In 1996, Gibson claimed to be the first guitar manufacturer to "craft a cost-effective model composed entirely of certified Smartwood". Smartwood is the Rainforest Alliance's name for its scheme to produce regular quantities of certified exotic woods in a way that strengthens the forests that supplied them – whether the end products are guitars, flooring, cabinets, picture frames, or paper. The Rainforest Alliance is an international non-profit conservation organisation that aims to promote responsible timber use.

Gibson produced a shortlived $3,399 Les Paul Smartwood Standard. It had a maple top harvested by Menominee Tribal Enterprises in Wisconsin, USA, and for its back and neck used chetchen, one of those rosewood alternatives – this one harvested by a co-operative in Mexico. (A number of other makers investigated the idea, and the Martin company produced its SWD Smartwood acoustic models a few years later, mainly using spruce, cherry, and katalox woods.)

Gibson publicised the Smartwood idea when Sting – who else? – was given the company's Les Paul Award at the 15th Annual Technical Excellence & Creativity Awards in New York City in January 2000. Les Paul himself and Gibson boss Henry Juszkiewicz presented Sting with a suitably inscribed Les Paul Smartwood Standard.

Gibson went further in its use of Smartwood with a line of six more Les Pauls, the Smartwood Exotic models, also shortlived, which retailed at about $1,500 and were launched during 1998. These Smartwoods had certified mahogany backs and curupay fingerboards, while the tops were made from rare and beautiful tropical woods harvested from a sustainable forest in Paraguay. A portion of revenue from the Exotics was donated to the Rainforest Alliance.

Meanwhile in the 90s, PRS Guitars, started by Paul Reed Smith during the previous decade, had shaken up the solidbody electric guitar market. Its most famous player Carlos Santana spearheaded an increasing number of PRS devotees. Smith's instruments clearly revealed his love of early Gibson Les Paul and Fender Stratocaster designs, melding a Standard-like carved, figured maple top and humbuckers with Strat-style offset cutaways and through-body stringing. Gradually, PRS was attracting some players who previously might naturally have opted for a Les Paul or a Strat.

When Gibson's new double-cutaway Les Paul DC Pro and DC Studio appeared in 1997, it seemed that the growing demand for a double-cutaway carved-top guitar had been noticed in Nashville. The DC line started with a Custom Shop model, the Pro, effectively merging the late-50s Junior and Special double-cut shape with the Standard's carved top – which Gibson had done before, with limited success, in the 80s, for the Double-Cutaway XPL model.

In another of Gibson's weight-saving exercises, the new DC's mahogany back was hollowed out to leave a central 'block', with a carved maple cap added on top. Matthew Klein in the Custom Shop was responsible for the Pro. "If you took a regular single-cut Les Paul, went to the bandsaw, and cut out a different horn area, you'd have the DC," he said. "The top carving is exactly the same, but the outside shape gives a little more fret access."[12]

Adding to the feeling that the DC was a reaction to PRS offerings, the Pro came with 24 frets, a straight-string-pull headstock design, and a two-knobs-and-selector control layout, as well as options of a longer scale-length and wrapover bridge – all features of Smith's instruments. But, of course, this one had the Gibson name and the Les Paul logo on the headstock.

Gibson soon realised that the DC model could be a viable production model manufactured in the main plant. The DC Studio was born later in 1997, retailing at $1,400, and it lasted in the line until recently (plus a fancier version called the Standard Lite). It retained the construction of the Pro but with a standard headstock, plain top, unbound body, and 'short'-scale only. A higher-end production version, the DC Standard, debuted in 1998, effectively halting sales of the $3,200 Pro, which was dropped soon afterward.

So, the 90s had certainly been a better decade than the 80s for Gibson. The Custom Shop's reissue models now had a clear direction and had improved dramatically since the earlier attempts, and USA factory models such as the Classic showed the way to absorb vintage flavours and attributes into the regular line.

Signature guitars provided a glittering shop window to attract old hands and new fans to the brand, and the turn of the millennium surely promised more and better Les Pauls from the now solidly Nashville-based operation.

the noughties

"Just because they designed a guitar 700 years ago doesn't mean it can't feel dead right now."

Ben Wells, Black Stone Cherry ▶

Gibson Les Pauls continued to attract guitarists at all levels through the 90s and into the 2000s. But the picture now is less clear-cut than in earlier decades, when it was easier to identify certain players as firm fans of the Les Paul, often to the exclusion of other models. It's much more common today for a player to shift around from model to model and brand to brand. If anything, this is because there are now so many viable alternatives. Simply, there are more good guitars to choose from today, and for some players it doesn't make much sense to keep still for too long.

The PRS company has continued to make good guitars that compete with Gibson's Les Paul models, among others. Paul Reed Smith's clever distillation of Gibson and Fender features into a double-cutaway carved-top design of his own even led Gibson to retaliate directly with the double-cut DC models of the late 90s, which stayed on the catalogue in various guises until 2008. PRS also managed to steal some publicity thunder when it used ex-Gibson boss Ted McCarty as a consultant and in advertising.

A further irony came with PRS's launch of its Singlecut model in 2000. The ad copy for the new guitar left little doubt about the intention: "Ted McCarty introduced the single cutaway, carved-top solidbody to the world in 1952. We learned a lot from Ted while we were working on ours." Gibson brought legal action against the Singlecut, but in 2005, after a long, complicated, and no doubt expensive battle, PRS won.

Beyond legalities and courtrooms, some players found Gibson's available guitar finishes conservative, summed up most obviously by the supreme old-fashioned look: a guitar with a sunburst top and extreme flame-figured maple showing through. To aficionados, of course, this is the classic Les Paul look; to some other (mostly younger) observers it reeks of everything that is musty and behind the times. Some kinds of retro, went the thinking, are just not cool.

So, every now and then, Gibson has tried to offer various Les Paul models in some 'new' finishes. In 2000, it was sparkle finishes for the Standard, available in diamond, blue, or green. Gibson said sparkle flake was embedded into the guitar's lacquer and claimed it would therefore add "a silky sustain to the tone". That's quite a claim.

Another striking finish came along the following year when the Les Paul Studio was offered in a special blue teal 'flip flop' finish. This was a good one: as you moved the guitar at different angles, the colours changed, in the case of blue teal going through various shades of greens into blues. It was based on something grandly named Variocrom-effect pigment technology, developed by BASF, a company better known to musicians for recording media.

Gibson's July 2001 pricelist showed 16 basic Les Pauls: Junior Lite $998; Junior $1,152; Special $1,229; Smartwood $1,537; Junior Special Plus $1,614; Studio $1,691; Studio Gothic $1,922; Standard Double Cut Plus $2,152; Studio Plus $2,383; Classic $2,537; Standard Raw Power $2,845; Deluxe $2,922; Gary Moore $2,922; Standard $3,075; Standard Plus $3,614; Custom $3,998. The Custom Shop list had three basic aged reissues: Goldtop 58 $3,880; Standard Figuredtop 58 $5,895; Custom 68 $3,900; plus 19 basic reissues: Junior 57 single or double cut $2,080; Special 60 single or double cut $3,348; SG/Les Paul Standard $4,159; Custom 54 $4,671; Custom 57 $4,525; Goldtop 52 $4,279; Goldtop 54 $4,517; Goldtop 56 $4,517; Goldtop 57 $4,582; Goldtop 57 Darkback $4,582; Custom 57 $4,671; SG/Les Paul Custom $4,938; Oxblood 54 $5,084; Standard Figuredtop 58 $5,700; Standard 59 Flametop $7,500; Standard 60 Flametop $7,500; Goldtop 56 Aged $7,680; Goldtop 57 Aged $7,706; Standard 59 Flametop Aged $10,155; and nine other basic models: Mahogany Classic $4,568; Zakk Wylde Bullseye $4,900; Class 5 $4,925; X-Men Wolverine $5,000; Custom 68 Figuredtop $5,062; Acoustic $5,350; Elegant Quilt $5,778; Peter Frampton 'Custom' $5,802; Dickey Betts Goldtop 57 $8,866.

The Custom division was still housed separately, a few doors along from the main factory in Nashville, and some interesting new models appeared from there during 2001. The Class 5 was a variant on the reissue models produced at the Custom Shop, this one with some of the flavour of a 1960 Standard. The hollowbody Les Paul Acoustic, which lasted a few years from 2001, was an immediately striking guitar. Imagine a flamed-maple Les Paul body with nothing on it at all. That's right – nothing. No pickups, no metal bridge, no controls, no pickguard … just the strings stretching across from the neck to a seemingly invisible anchor point in the midst of the maple. You have just visualised the Les Paul Acoustic. Remember that prophecy by Les Paul in 1971 about a piezo-like pickup?

Of course, the Acoustic model really did have a bridge, and there was a pickup, but both were carefully hidden within the overall maple look, and the controls were on the side of the body. It was developed in the Custom Shop by Mickey McGuire, who has a good pedigree in guitar-making: he's the son of Mike McGuire, who founded the custom guitar-maker Valley Arts in the 70s.

McGuire Jr's idea was to take a hollowed-out Les Paul's mahogany rear and add a maple cap, flat underneath and carved on top like a regular Les Paul except for an area around the bridge. The maple remaining there was hand-shaped into a kind of four-sided pyramid, rounded off a little to make a bridge, with a Baggs 'acoustic' piezo pickup worked in. The result was a Les Paul intended to provide the sound of maple with a cutting acoustic-like tonality.

Hard at work in the Custom Shop, Gibson's guitar-makers were as usual gently tweaking the Les Paul reissues to bring them closer than ever to the original instruments of the 50s and 60s. No detail was too small for attention. Take the serial number, for example, which on original-period Pauls is ink-stamped on to the rear of the headstock. As any Les Paul forger will tell you, it is very hard to get close to the typeface and style and ink-colour of the original numerals. Gibson faced the same problem. Reissue guru Tom Murphy took up the story. "At first, in the early 90s, I'd asked our normal stamp supplier for a smaller typeface, because we'd had odd-shaped, bulky numbers through the 80s," said Murphy.

"We ended up realising that the original-style number was not produced any more, so we went 'below' it: smaller, with a more aesthetically pleasing look, in the right style but

Joe Perry (right) of Aerosmith is another long-standing Les Paul fan. He's played a few different Pauls through the years, but probably none quite so conspicuously different as this Stars & Stripes Custom. But he had chosen carefully. The event at which he's pictured was the 'United We Stand: What More Can I Give' concert in Washington DC in October 2001, a tribute to victims of the 9/11 attacks on the USA. Other performers at the special concert included Michael Jackson, Al Green, P. Diddy, and Carole King.

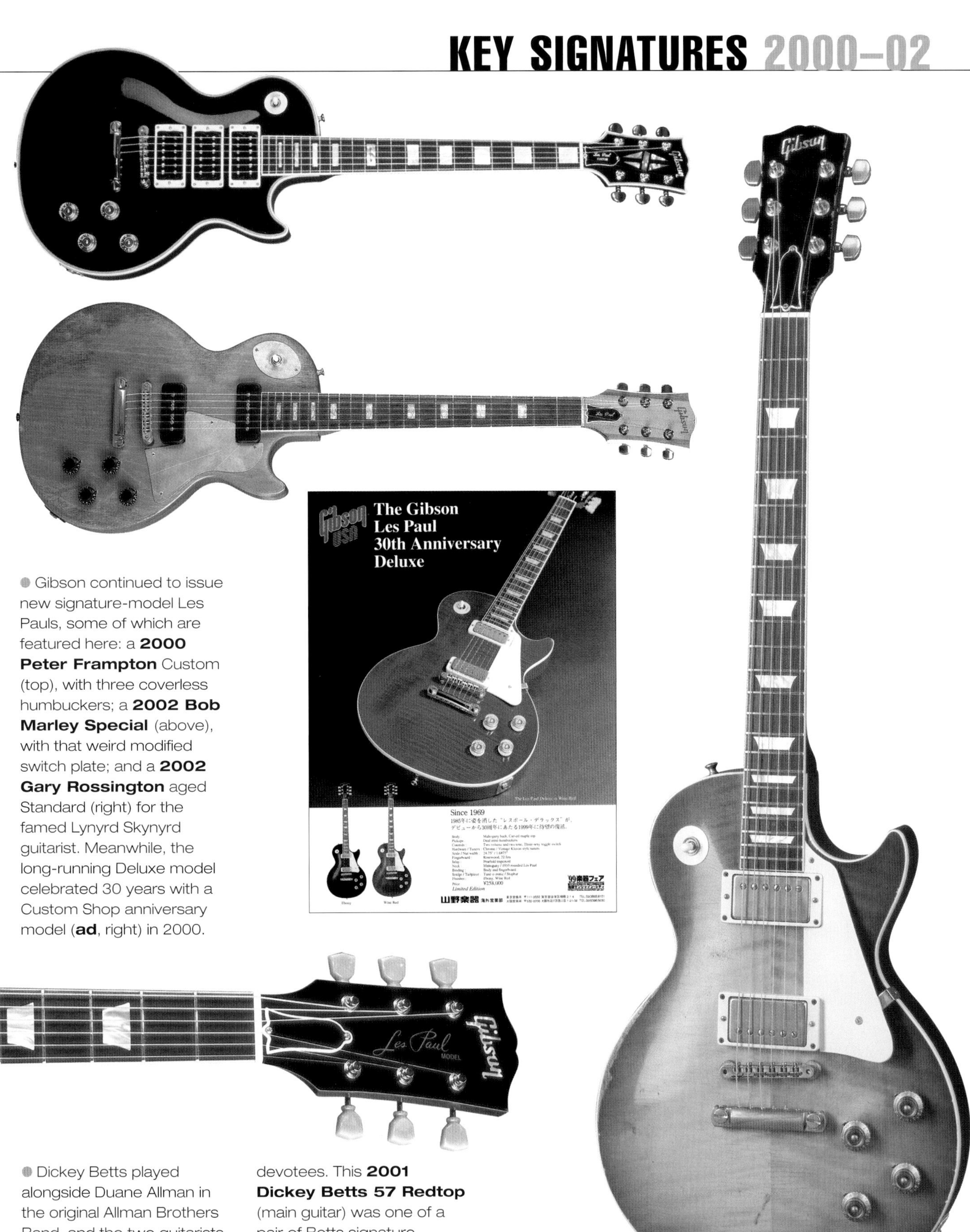

Gibson continued to issue new signature-model Les Pauls, some of which are featured here: a **2000 Peter Frampton** Custom (top), with three coverless humbuckers; a **2002 Bob Marley Special** (above), with that weird modified switch plate; and a **2002 Gary Rossington** aged Standard (right) for the famed Lynyrd Skynyrd guitarist. Meanwhile, the long-running Deluxe model celebrated 30 years with a Custom Shop anniversary model (**ad**, right) in 2000.

Dickey Betts played alongside Duane Allman in the original Allman Brothers Band, and the two guitarists were confirmed and accomplished Les Paul devotees. This **2001 Dickey Betts 57 Redtop** (main guitar) was one of a pair of Betts signature models: the other was the Dickey Betts 57 Goldtop.

not the right size," he continued. "That wasn't received greatly by the real buffs. So now we've fixed that. We stumbled on a way to put those numbers on a stamp, in another configuration. So from 1999 the number style changed again, and we're very happy with it. It's not exactly perfect, but it's now the right font, in the right height and width."

And how old are you?

Murphy had left Gibson in 1994 to set up his Guitar Preservation company, and today combines that with work for Gibson as a freelance. At his own workshop he has built on his speciality for refinishing and restoring old guitars. Gradually, he found that it was natural to 'age' the finished job, blending in the new areas to sit more comfortably with the original worn guitar. He found customers at Guitar Preservation who welcomed this, and also several at Gibson's Custom Shop.

Murphy wasn't alone in developing this technique, of course. Many guitar repairers now include aging techniques in their set of skills. But why has it become so much in demand today? He thought it's down to the scarcity now of vintage guitars. Years ago there was a good supply of original instruments about. "If a guitar was refinished because of someone's ignorance, like I did many times, or attempted as part of a repair, it denigrated the guitar. But back then there was an alterative," Murphy said. In those days there would be an original instrument available at a reasonable price.

He was talking about a time when a particular original vintage model might have sold for, shall we say, $400, while a refinished one was maybe just $100. Then, it was an easy and relatively cheap decision to go for the original. Even when the original became $2,000 and the refinished one $800, you'd probably still want to buy the original.

"But as the availability of the original instruments diminished and the prices skyrocketed," said Murphy, "the viability and the option of restoring an old one became more necessary, out of practicality. And now it's more accepted, because we've all had to say, well, it's not that big a deal if the paint has been redone on a Strat body or whatever. I'm a purist as much as anyone else. I'd rather they were all original guitars. But you can't always have that now."[1]

Murphy developed his ability to make a repaired or restored guitar 'look right' by using aging techniques. Fender had introduced its aged Relic series in 1995 after Keith Richards complained that replicas made for him by Fender's Custom Shop for a Stones tour would look better if, as he put it, they "bashed them up a bit". There followed a line of new Strats and Teles with wear-and-tear distress marks added to the finish and the hardware, intended to make the guitars look as if they'd been knocked around on stage and on the road for years. The success of Fender's Relic scheme was noted at Gibson HQ in Nashville; a few years later, Murphy was doing the same thing to selected models in the Les Paul reissue line. He preferred to call it a broken-in feel rather than an aged look.

The first reissue to benefit was the Standard 59 Aged model, which officially started life as part of the Custom Shop line in 1999. The paint colours were made to appear faded, the nickel parts on the instrument, such as the pickup covers, were realistically tarnished, and the lacquer 'skin' was cracked and effectively dulled. Remarkably, the guitar really did look old and worn.

Like Fender and its Relics, Gibson aimed to recreate that almost indefinable appeal of a vintage guitar, but in a new instrument – and at a stiff price, of course. Gibson has, as usual, used a variety of different names over the years for its aged finish, including Custom Authentic, but at the time of writing it was known as Vintage Original Spec, or VOS. Gibson describes it like this: "All VOS series guitars will use a proprietary process that includes unique steps for staining, wet-sanding, and hand-rubbing; subsequently the guitars reflect what a well-cared-for 40-year-old guitar looks like. The result is a remarkable patina that will delight even the most discriminating enthusiast."[2]

The Standard 59 reissue with VOS finish listed at $8,033 in 2009. That same year, most of the reissue Les Pauls were offered on what the Custom Shop calls its core list with VOS finish, including Custom 54, Custom 57, Custom 68, Goldtop 54, Goldtop 56, Goldtop 57, Junior 57, Junior 58, SG/Les Paul Custom, SG/Les Paul Standard, Special single-cut, Special 60, Standard 59, and Standard 60. The Shop's non-core list includes many of those models with regular un-aged finish, generally known as a gloss finish, with the implication that aged finish is now the standard for Gibson reissues.

Murphy said that the aged reissues profit from a combination of techniques that he arrived at to simulate wear on small areas of the guitar. So what's the secret of achieving the aged look? "I can't tell you that," he laughed. "I can tell you it's done by hand, though – but that's only because it's the only way it can be done. I swear that if we could do it with a laser, then we'd have the laser version and the hand-done version. But we can't. And it would be great if we had a magic box to put them in, a time machine or something where we could just switch it on to, let's say, winter in Minnesota, 1959. But we can't do that."[3] Not yet, anyway.

At the start of the 21st century, the Gibson group of companies enjoyed annual revenues of around $200 million and had 1,200 employees. And there was an important anniversary. The year 2002 marked 50 years since the introduction of the Gibson Les Paul. Gibson staged a number of celebrations, notably issuing some special 50th Anniversary models. An early manifestation came in August 2001 with an event at the Iridium jazz club in New York City, where Les Paul himself, well into his 80s, was joined by two seasoned Paul players, Slash and Al Di Meola.

At the Iridium event, Gibson CEO Henry Juszkiewicz presented Les with a Custom Shop Goldtop 52 reissue, specially engraved with this message: "Celebrate the legend. Revel in the legacy. Gibson pays tribute to the one and only Les Paul."

Les also received a proclamation from New York City declaring August 13th to be 2001's Les Paul Day. Juszkiewicz said: "Les Paul is not only America's most popular guitar player. He is a leading innovator in guitar and electronic design. He has been experimenting with electric guitars for as long as there have been electric guitars." Perhaps

● This **2003 Duane Allman** (above) is a Cusrtom Shop signature model for the great Allman Brothers guitarist, based on Duane's 'Hot 'Lanta' Burst that he acquired in 1971 – not too long before his tragic early death in October that year. Edge of U2 announced the Music Rising fundraising campaign in 2005 following the devastation of New Orleans and the US Gulf Coast by Hurricane Katrina. This **2005 Music Rising** Standard (below) was sold only through Guitar Center stores, with all proceeds benefitting Music Rising.

● At the time of writing, the Supreme was the USA factory's most lavish Les Paul. This **2003 Supreme** (main guitar, below) shows the model's remarkable flame top, seven-ply binding, and other luxurious features.

Tom Morello (above) of Rage Against The Machine and Audioslave might be better known for playing Fender and Ibanez, but he relies on this Standard for songs with altered tunings. Jimmy Page, on the other hand, is an out-and-out Les Paul aficionado and has played his 'Number 1' Burst since he acquired it from Joe Walsh in 1969. Gibson's Custom Shop issued this **2004 Jimmy Page** (right) as an exact copy of 'Number 1', down to the coverless bridge humbucker, Grover tuners, and an aged and faded finish. Gibson offered another Page replica in 2009 when the Custom Shop duplicated the guitarist's lesser-known 'Number 2'.

Les still had this last thought echoing in his ears when he got home and installed low-impedance pickups and a side-mounted mic jack on the brand new 52.

The mighty sunburst Standard enjoyed its own 50th anniversary, this time a three-year affair beginning in 2008. The Custom Shop obliged with some wonderful anniversary reissues, as well as a spectacular run of signature models, including replicas of famous Bursts played by Michael Bloomfield, Jimmy Page, Billy Gibbons, and others.

Back in the USA factory, the Standard came in for a change in 2008 when the existing model was effectively stopped and replaced with two 'new' models, the Traditional and the 2008 Standard. The slightly more expensive 2008 Standard has an asymmetrical neck shape, a chambered body base, better pots, strap-locks, and locking bridge, tailpiece, jack, and tuners, while the Traditional has none of these new features – hence the name.

Digital distractions

In 2006, Gibson began shipping its long-promised digital guitar, the HD.6X-Pro, a Les Paul with extra hex pickup that allowed the player to feed various combinations of strings to a computer, for use with recording software or similar programs. The next tech step came in 2007 with a series of Robot guitars. Various regular Gibsons – mainly Les Pauls and SG models – were offered with a clever self-tuning system using powered tuning pegs. The system had standard tuning plus six programmable tunings.

A further development in 2008 was the Dark Fire, a Les Paul that linked an improved Robot system with some of the digital guitar's features and potential. These hi-tech Dark Fires have yet to catch on in a big way with players, who (to generalise) tend to a conservative and sceptical outlook when it comes to apparently complex new technology.

Gibson's pricelist in April 2009 revealed an erratic looking line-up of ten basic USA factory models: Junior single-cut $1,199; Billie Joe Armstrong Junior $1,799; Studio $1,799; Studio Raw Power $1,858; Gary Moore BFG $2,149; Traditional $3,449; Dark Fire $3,499; 2008 Standard $3,899; Robot Studio $3,999; Supreme $5,190.

The Custom Shop list had a strong set of reissues: Junior 57 single-cut $3,527; Junior 58 double-cut $3,527; Special single-cut $3,527; Special 60 double-cut $3,527; SG/Les Paul Standard $4,421; Goldtop 54 VOS $5,174; Goldtop 56 VOS $5,174; Goldtop 57 VOS $5,174; Standard 58 VOS $5,174; Standard 58 Plaintop VOS $5,174; SG/Les Paul Custom $5,880; Custom 68 Figuredtop $5,974; Custom 54 VOS $6,351; Custom 57 two-pickup VOS $6,351; Custom 57 three-pickup VOS $6,351; Standard 59 VOS $8,033; Standard 60 VOS $8,033; Standard 59 50th Anniversary $8,504.

That 2009 Custom Shop list also featured a line of signature models – Steve Jones Custom $5,504; Warren Haynes Standard $6,115; Peter Frampton Custom $6,680; Slash Standard $6,680; Zakk Wylde Bullseye $6,680; Joe Bonamassa $6,941; Mick Jones Custom $7,998; Jeff Beck 1954 Oxblood $8,235; Michael Bloomfield 1959 Standard $14,115 – plus a handful of what we'll have to call 'others': Axcess Standard $5,292; Custom $5,504; 50th Anniversary Korina Tribute $10,588.

Gibson divides its electric guitar production into three levels: Gibson Custom Shop (more accurately the Custom/Art/Historic division), which provides limited-run instruments and high-end production models; Gibson USA, effectively the normal factory, for regular production; and the Epiphone brand for less expensive versions of Gibson classics (as well as original Epiphone models). Gibson is offering a Les Paul for every kind of player, runs the company's argument.

There is sometimes movement across these barriers. The Slash signature Les Paul, for example, began as a limited-run Custom model, then moved to Gibson USA after the initial run had sold out, and is also offered in an Epiphone version. This is logical, says Gibson. But there was little logic apparent when they named a new-for-2001 model the Les Paul Junior Special Plus. A potential buyer with a modicum of historical awareness – which I hope includes you – might well argue that a Junior is a Junior is a one-pickup Junior and a Special is a Special is a two-pickup Special. The Junior Special Plus turned out to be a Special … and a Special with humbuckers. It lasted only a few years in the line. Maybe Gibson's thinking is that young players don't care about history? I doubt it. History is continuing at this very moment, even as you read this.

One fashion that seems here to stay, right now, is the signature guitar – an instrument authorised by a famous player, carefully made to their individual specifications, and then offered for sale. The anti-hero stance of many 90s grunge players seems like a distant memory as legendary guitarists line up to have their name on a personalised instrument.

Gary Moore was the first musician to be honoured with a Les Paul signature model as we entered the 2000s. Known for his early work with Thin Lizzy in the 70s but more recently revered for some blistering blues revivals, Moore was much envied among Les Paul fanciers as the owner of Peter Green's original Standard, which he acquired from the Fleetwood Mac hero many years ago. Moore even underlined the debt with a personal tribute record, *Blues For Greenie*. Since then, in 2006, Moore has sold the Green instrument.

For his signature model, which Gibson launched in 2000, Moore opted for a workmanlike, player's instrument that had some echoes of the Green guitar: it was an unbound Standard, but it had coverless humbuckers and no pickguard. Further signature Les Pauls have been added to the line since then, including models for Duane Allman, Billie Joe Armstrong, Dickey Betts, Joe Bonamassa, Peter Frampton, Bob Marley, Gary Rossington, Neal Schon, Pete Townshend, and others.

Pat Foley is an Entertainment Relations representative at Gibson, which means he manages relationships with artists and arranges signature editions and personal instruments. I asked him in 2009 about the way this works. Foley was in Texas when we spoke, meeting with Billy Gibbons to discuss details of the replica of the ZZ Top guitarist's hallowed 'Pearly Gates' Standard.

Many of Gibson's signature models are designed to stay in the catalogue for some time – the Joe Perry guitars, for example, or the Peter Frampton Custom – and are produced variously by the Custom Shop, the USA factory, and sometimes Epiphone. But, Foley

Gibson's stripped-down BFG Les Paul was about as rough and ready as they come. This **2007 BFG** (above) in trans ink blue reveals the model's unsanded top with router 'furrows' still visible.

● Let's not forget a superb pair of rock'n'roll workhorses, Gibson's Les Paul Junior and Special models. **Billie Joe Armstrong** of Green Day (opposite) plays his signature Junior, while The Shins frontman **James Mercer** (above) digs into his doulbe-cut Special. Three **Gibson ads** (right) highlight a trio of new-for-2006 Les Paul models: the Goddess (top), here in violet burst and evidently aimed at the ladies, the GT (centre), with coil-split humbuckers, and a fancy-top Studio Premium Plus.

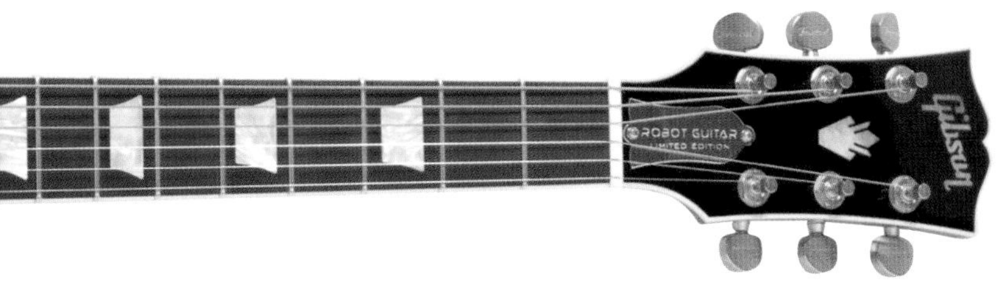

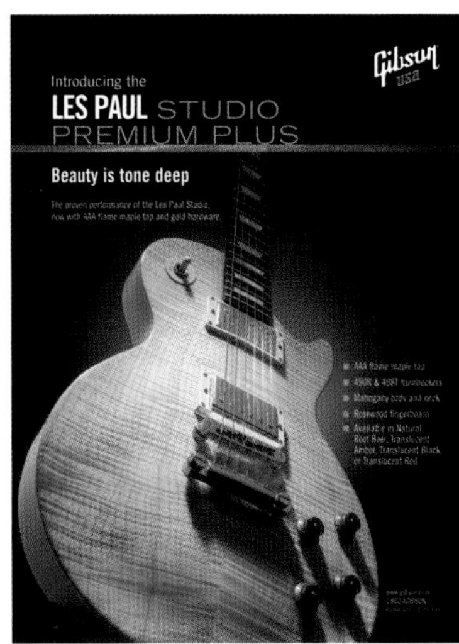

● In search of a digital guitar that appealed to musicians, Gibson has launched several 'electronic' Les Paul models in recent years, including this **2007 Robot Ltd** (main guitar). And among a few Who-related replicas was this **2006 Pete Townshend Deluxe #1** (above).

explained, the Custom Shop also makes what it calls 'Inspired By' models. These are short-run editions of one-off get-it-while-you-can instruments (and generally they are too shortlived even to show up on Gibson's regular pricelist).

Jeff Beck's 1954 'Oxblood' Les Paul is a good example, said Foley. "In recent times Jeff is more a Fender player, but he did some of his best work on a Les Paul. So the Inspired By programme is a great vehicle for approaching somebody like that, with the idea of a limited run that pays tribute to the work he did on a Les Paul and his association with a particular instrument, in his case the Oxblood guitar." This is the refinished and humbucker'd 50s Goldtop that Beck acquired in the early 70s and used for some of his classic jazz-rock album *Blow By Blow*. The original, colourfully described now by Gibson as "a guitar from the heart of tone history", is illustrated elsewhere in this book.

"We get asked about the Oxblood guitar all the time," said Foley. "People want it, but we've never been able to do an official model. Now, under the umbrella of the Inspired By programme, we were able to approach Jeff about acknowledging and paying tribute to his use of a Les Paul. The beauty of the Inspired By series is that for guys who for one reason or another don't want to commit to a long-term arrangement, they really respond to the idea of a limited-edition model."

How does Gibson decide which artists to work with and which iconic guitars to replicate? Foley described the internal meetings that take place at the company, where they focus on musicians they consider to be potential candidates with important guitars for inclusion in the programme. "It has to be an instrument that, obviously, we think would sell, and that production-wise is something we could reproduce. There are some guitars that are so heavily modified we'd think twice about it. You could boil it down to something that we feel is going to be a good quality instrument and something that the market is going to embrace."

So, meetings take place, and – ideally – artist and Gibson agree that they'd like to make an exactly-as-is copy of a famous Les Paul. Where to from there? Naturally, Gibson needs to take a close look at the original. Usually, some combination of Pat Foley, Edwin Wilson, and Matt Klein will examine the instrument in almost microscopic detail. Ideally, the guitar will go to Gibson HQ, but very often, for reasons related to practicality and security, the team travels to the guitar. Foley reported that they now use a portable digital scanning unit, a distinct improvement upon the old method using callipers and a mimic gauge to measure the neck. The neck is the part of the instrument that requires the most exacting physical replication when it comes to conjuring up the precise feel of a particular guitar.

"Now, we've got it down to a science," said Foley, "and we'll get very accurate measurements. Overall, the things that you're trying to reproduce are the look and feel and sounds of the guitar. So that means documenting it with photographs to get the wear marks, the cigarette burns, that kind of thing. We have to get neck dimensions. We weigh the guitar. Sometimes pickups have been changed or rewound, so we measure the output levels of the guitar. We try to note any idiosyncrasies. It's great for us when the guitar does have minor modifications, because these are the things that make it really distinctive." Steve Jones's white Custom with girlie decals comes to mind, or Zakk Wylde's striking bullseye finish, both targets of the Custom Shop's signature efforts.

Next in the process, Gibson makes a prototype based on all the gathered intelligence. The artist takes a look at this prototype, has a play, and usually offers some feedback, so a second prototype is made. Sometimes the team gets it right first time, more often the second. When I spoke to Foley, he was going busily back and forth with Jimmy Page on the electrics for the reproduction of Page's 'Number 2' Standard, due for release later in 2009.

"Jimmy Page is the high-water mark," Foley explained. "Everything we do with Jimmy, because of his status, is done to the nth degree. He is the benchmark for what these programmes should be. I think that the 2004 Jimmy Page Les Paul – the reproduction of his 'Number 1' Standard – changed the guitar market, and our competition had to rethink everything they were doing. It showed the world that there really was a demand for repros of these guitars, and that the real collectors are concerned more with accuracy and having a collector's piece, while the cost of it is secondary."

Once the prototype is approved, the Custom Shop goes into production on the model. The prices can be a worry for the faint-hearted. "But those guitars do more than sell for a high dollar," said Foley. "I think they epitomise what Gibson is all about, which is producing the highest-quality guitar possible. I don't think anyone can touch us on that stuff."

As part of a Gibson limited edition, there will often be a small number of artist-signed guitars. "In the case of Jeff Beck and the Oxblood guitar, we took them to our London office," Foley explained. "He went through and gave each one a little strum. And we usually take more than is needed; in the case of Jeff it was 55 or 56 guitars. We know in advance that they're all right, but just in case he feels something's a bit funny, we'll pull that one aside, and we'll end up with 50 that he'll sign. The artist almost always keeps number one, the first of the run, as his own personal guitar, and in most cases he would also keep the prototype. We would have a production prototype that we keep to base them all on, and then when we're done with that the prototype generally goes to the artist's collection."

Looking down the list of names that Gibson has honoured over the years with a signature model, there are still a few players you might expect to see in there but are missing. Who would Gibson still like to see represented with a signature Les Paul? Keith Richards is certainly one, said Foley. That's understandable: he was the first 'name' guitarist ever to be seen publicly playing the now-revered sunburst Standard model, back in 1964.

"In a lot of these cases, the people around them are protective and trying to keep outsiders at arm's length," Foley reported. "When you get to the artist directly, they are generally open to the idea. But getting to Keith Richards has proved problematic. I've always felt if I could get an introduction and sit down and talk about it, he'd say hell yeah, man … why not?"

In fact, Mr Richards does not own the guitar in question any more. But that isn't necessarily a problem, said Foley. "Quite a few times, we don't have the actual guitar to

● Gibson has celebrated the 50th anniversary of the most important Les Paul models, the original 1958–60 Bursts. This **2008 Standard 58 50th Anniversary** (main guitar) was aged by Tom Murphy and carries a special logo on the pickguard.

● Michael Bloomfield is one of the latest to be honoured by Gibson's special series of Custom Shop replicas of distinctive Bursts. This **2009 Michael Bloomfield 1959 Standard** (below) goes to great lengths to duplicate his guitar exactly – even though the original instrument was not available for study. It was lost following Bloomfield's untimely death in 1981.

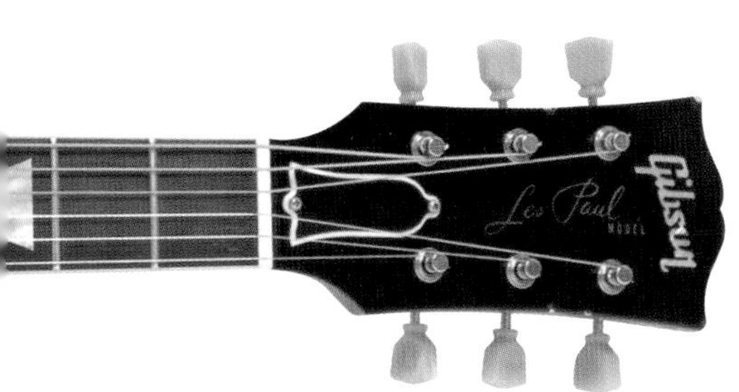

Gibson split the long-running Standard into two models in 2008. Shown here are a **2008 Standard** (centre; the model name includes the '2008') and a **2008 Traditional** (bottom of page). The two mixed old and new features to offer a choice of Standard.

Joe Bonamassa, blues-rock guitar star and Les Paul addict, pictured (above) with a reissue Burst. Gibson issued a Bonamassa Goldtop in 2008. And so the maker–musician exchange continues – well beyond Gibson's first signature electric guitar, the Les Paul Model of 1952.

look at, as with the Michael Bloomfield Standard, for example. So you work from photographs; you work from memories; you get in touch with guitar techs that were there; sometimes you find a repair guy that worked on the guitar and knows it well. You gather as much information as you can. There can be a lot of research that goes into those instruments," said Foley.

Another important Les Paul man who has so far eluded the Gibson reissue schemes is Neil Young. "He has an aversion to corporate endorsements," said Foley. "Part of the job is to communicate to the artist how important this is to a lot of people: we realise that to him it may simply be a tool with which he produces his music, but that tool helps create the art, and therefore is valid and important. Given the opportunity, I think Neil Young would probably support the idea."

What kind of reward does the artist get for his involvement in these reissue programmes? "In most cases the artist receives guitars," Foley explained, "usually the prototype and number one. That's kind of standard. Because they're such limited runs, there's not a tremendous amount of royalties generated, but in a lot of cases we make donations to their charity of choice as a goodwill gesture. Often that is an important aspect: not only to generate funds for their charity, but to help shed some light on the charities they support."[4]

Bonamassa's basket case

The fine blues guitarist Joe Bonamassa benefited from a Gibson signature Les Paul in 2008 when his Inspired By Goldtop appeared from the Custom Shop. He drew inspiration from a wrecked and otherwise unwanted 54 Goldtop that his dad picked up at a guitar show for $1,000 back in the early 90s, with black plasticware, a black-painted back to hide repairs, and a crazed and dinged finish.

"In fact, a complete basket case," laughed Bonamassa. "But it was one of the best playing and sounding guitars. It was such a lesson in the collectable guitar market. The ones that are museum pieces are normally the ones that are shit. No one's ever wanted them. The one's that were beat up and completely trashed are the ones everyone plays, because they were and are the best. I want the Joe Bonamassa Les Paul to be a played Les Paul."[5]

Beyond the signature models, the modern Gibson company not only aims to offer every kind of guitar, but also appears to aspire to that dreadful modern invention, the 'lifestyle' company. Gibson's Beale Street Showcase in Memphis was a step in that direction, aiming to be a customer-friendly retail, performance, restaurant, and manufacturing facility. In 2002, the manufacturing section was made part of Gibson's Custom division, and today it produces the company's ES semi-hollowbody electric models. A few years later Gibson teamed up with Universal Studios in California to revitalise the newly-named Gibson Amphitheatre venue.

Back with the guitars, the Gibson Les Paul is just about the longest-running solidbody electric guitar still in production today, beaten only by the Fender Telecaster, which is some two years older. A lot has changed in those 50-plus years. And yet, in some ways, nothing has changed. When I spoke to Les Paul in 2008, the 93-year-old guitarist still seemed as fascinated with the Gibson Les Paul as he was all those years ago. "I can't wait to get up and get out of bed, to get to my guitar and play it," he told me. "I love it so much. It's so personal. And yet it defies explanation. It makes a fella who's playing the guitar work like hell – because you can get better, but it's not easy. There are so many ways of expressing your feeling. It's an awesome instrument."[6]

The best new Gibson Les Pauls still stand out, and still they can be awesome instruments that make you want to play on into the small hours. It must be apparent to Gibson that, among today's big diverse guitar market, it is uniquely placed to serve up its own true, traditional flavour – and with all the improvements of modern manufacturing. As we've seen throughout this book, that tradition can be a hindrance, too, when Gibson asks players to accept new designs or hi-tech twists.

But, without a doubt, the story continues. And the Gibson Les Paul looks set for many new adventures in the hands of succeeding generations of musicians and in the care of its present owners.

FOOTNOTES

the fifties

1 Author's interview March 1 1989
2 Author's interview March 1 1989
3 *Melody Maker* May 19 1951
4 Author's interview October 27 1992
5 *The Music Trades* February 1952
6 Author's interview October 27 1992
7 Author's interview March 1 1989
8 Author's interview October 27 1992
9 Author's interview March 16 1993
10 Author's interview October 27 1992
11 Author's interview March 16 1993
12 *The Music Trades* August 1952
13 *Melody Maker* September 13 1952
14 Author's interview March 16 1993
15 Author's interview March 16 1993
16 Author's interview October 27 1992
17 Author's interview March 16 1993
18 Author's interview October 30 1992
19 Author's interview December 12 2001
20 Author's interview October 30 1992
21 *Guitar Player* September 1973
22 *Gibson Gazette* December 1958
23 Gibson.com
24 Author's interview October 30 1992

the sixties

1 Author's interview March 16 1993
2 Wheeler *American Guitars*
3 *The Music Trades* November 1966
4 Author's interview December 10 1992
5 Author's interview January 29 1993
6 *Guitar Player* April 1985
7 *Beat Instrumental* August 1967
8 Author's interviews January 25 1984, February 12 1993, April 27 2005
9 *The Wizard Of Waukesha* (movie; 1979)
10 Author's interview April 10 2008
11 *Beat Instrumental* June 1966
12 *Beat Instrumental* August 1967
13 *Beat Instrumental* September 1967
14 Author's interview January 29 1993
15 Author's interview March 1 1989
16 Author's interview December 10 1992
17 Author's interview January 29 1993
18 *Beat Instrumental* June 1968
19 Author's interview December 10 1992
20 Author's interview December 10 1992
21 Author's interview October 27 1992
22 Author's interview March 4 1991
23 *Guitar Player* July 1977

the seventies

1 *Guitar Player* September 1971
2 Author's interview January 29 1993
3 *Guitar Player* December 1976
4 *Guitar Player* December 1976
5 *Guitar Player* January 1975
6 Bellson *Gibson Story*
7 *Guitar Player* January 1977
8 Author's interview December 10 1992
9 Author's interview December 10 1992
10 *Guitar Player* October 1972
11 *Guitar Player* October 1975
12 *Guitar Player* June 1974
13 Author's interview February 11 1993

the eighties

1 Author's interview February 11 1993
2 *Guitar Trader's Vintage Guitar Bulletin* December 1982
3 Author's interview October 29 1992
4 Author's interview April 24 2008
5 Author's interview February 11 1993
6 Author's interview October 28 1992
7 Author's interview March 3 1993
8 Author's interview January 29 1993
9 Author's interview March 15 1993
10 Author's interview March 4 1993
11 Author's interview March 3 1993
12 Author's interview March 4 1993
13 Author's interview February 11 1993
14 Author's interview March 15 1993
15 *Guitar Player* November 1989
16 *Guitar Player* April 1988
17 *Vintage Guitar* November 2005
18 *Guitar Magazine* April 1992

the nineties

1 Author's interview January 10 2002
2 Author's interview March 4 1993
3 Author's interview December 12 2001
4 Author's interview March 4 1993
5 Author's interview December 12 2001
6 Author's interview March 4 1993
7 Gibson.com
8 Author's interview March 4 1993
9 Author's interview December 12 2001
10 Author's interview January 10 2002
11 Gibson.com
12 Author's interview January 10 2002

the noughties

1 Author's interview December 12 2001
2 Gibson.com
3 Author's interview December 12 2001
4 Author's interview March 20 2009
5 Author's interview June 18 2008
6 Author's interview April 25 2008

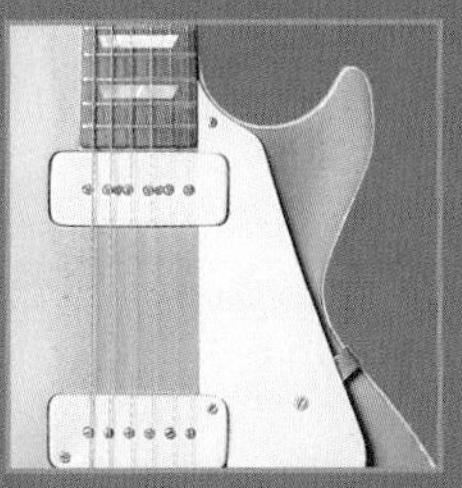

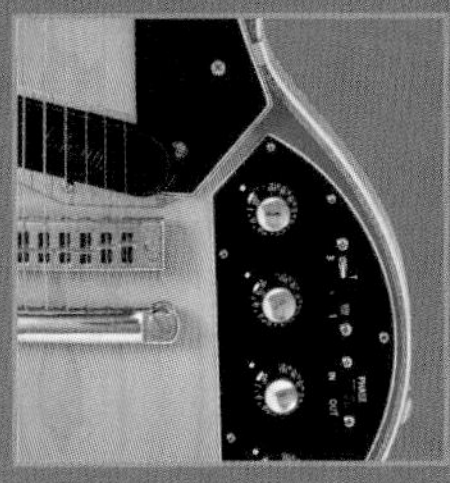

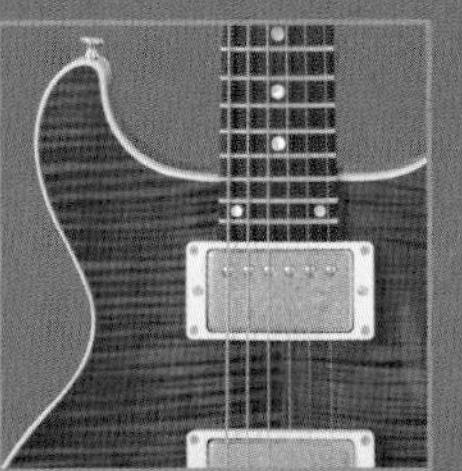

the reference section

How to use the model directory

The main model directory in this reference listing offers a simple, condensed format to give you a great deal of information about every Gibson Les Paul model. The following notes are designed to help you use this unique directory. At the end of the listing is a dating guide and model chronology.

Individual entries in the directory contain all or some of the following: model name; date or range of dates in production; brief one-sentence identification; references to other model entries where relevant; list of specification points; variations; general comments; official production totals.

At the head of each entry or group of entries is the **main model name** in bold type, listed in alphabetical order. Under this are listed a single model or a number of individual models, as appropriate.

After the model name, each entry shows a **date or range of dates** for the **production period** of the instrument. These dates, and any other dates shown within this model directory, are approximate. In many cases it's virtually impossible to pinpoint precisely the period during which a model was in production. Gibson's promotional material is often dated, but the content is usually decided far in advance and does not always reflect what was being made at any given time. Gibson's logs of the total numbers of guitars 'shipped' (in other words leaving the factory) sometimes show instruments made in years beyond the range we give for production. Where only a small quantity of guitars is shown for a model otherwise produced in reasonably substantial numbers, we assume that these are either samples made before the start of a production period or leftovers sold off after production has ceased. We have tried to list the most accurate dates possible for the production periods and changes made to Gibson's Les Paul models, but please treat them as approximate, because that is all they can be.

In italics, following the model name and production dates, is a brief **one-sentence identification** of the guitar in question. This is intended to help you recognise a specific model at a glance by noting combinations of elements unique to that particular model.

For some guitars, there may be a sentence below this reading "**Similar to … except:**" or "**As … except:**". This will take the form of a reference to another model entry. The description will list any major differences between the two models.

The list of **specification points**, where given, is separated into groups and provides details of the model's features. In the order listed, the points refer to: neck, fingerboard, headstock; body; pickups; controls; pickguard; bridge; and hardware finish.

Of course, not every model will need all seven points. And to avoid repetition in the specification points, we have considered a number of **features common to all Gibson Les Paul models**. They are, unless stated: plastic truss-rod cover; metal tuner buttons; 22 frets; scale length approximately 24.6 inches; single-cutaway body; side-mounted jack (socket); nickel or chrome-plated hardware.

Some models were made in a number of **variations**, and where this is so the variations are listed after the specification points, in italics. Other general comments are also made here.

Also at the end of each entry or group of entries we sometimes show **production figures**. For guitars made up to the end of the 70s, these figures are taken from official Gibson records logging the number of instruments shipped from the Kalamazoo factory each year. These figures in the listing should be treated with caution: the calculations were tallied by hand, and human error is very evident. The figures we've used here continue to 1979, but we could find no figures for Kalamazoo from 1980 until its closure in 1984, and no figures for any Nashville production since its opening in 1975 until the late 1980s – they are apparently lost. The current owners of Gibson are again logging production numbers, but for commercial reasons they will not release them to us. We have also indicated production numbers for relatively recent Custom Shop limited editions where we have this information.

All this detail is designed to tell you more about Gibson Les Paul guitars. By using the general information and illustrations earlier in the book, combined with the knowledge you can draw from this reference listing, you should be able to build up a very full picture of any instrument and its pedigree.

■ ACE FREHLEY

ACE FREHLEY 1997–2000 *Three white-coil pickups, Ace Frehley graphic on headstock.*

Similar to **Custom**, except:

- ■ Lightning-bolt markers; signature inlaid at 12th fret; Ace playing-card on truss-rod cover (chrome for Custom Shop run; black plastic for production version); Frehley face on headstock.
- ■ Bound carved-top body; flamed maple top cap; cherry sunburst.
- ■ Three coverless pickups with white coils.
- ■ Four controls (two volume, two tone) plus three-way selector.
- ■ *Custom Shop version (1997), production 300, numbered with ACE prefix; USA factory version (1997–2000) numbered with regular eight-digit serial.*

■ ACOUSTIC

ACOUSTIC 2001–05 *No visible pickups, acoustic-style pin bridge, figured top.*

- ■ Bound rosewood fingerboard; crown markers, pearl "Gibson" logo on headstock, plastic tuner buttons.
- ■ Bound carved-top body; figured maple top; trans blue, trans black, or tangerineburst.
- ■ Electronics from Gibson Chet Atkins SST model, piezo pickup.
- ■ Two controls (volume, tone) mounted on rim.
- ■ No pickguard.
- ■ Rosewood bridge with bridge pins.
- ■ *Custom Shop.*

■ ACTIVE

See later **Artist** *entry.*

■ ARTISAN

ARTISAN 1976–82 *Ornate fingerboard markers.*

- ■ Bound ebony fingerboard, ornate markers; script Gibson logo and ornate inlay on headstock; "Artisan" on truss-rod cover.
- ■ Bound carved-top body; sunburst, brown, black, or white.
- ■ Two or three metal-cover humbucker pickups.
- ■ Four controls (two volume, two tone) plus three-way selector.
- ■ Black laminated plastic pickguard.
- ■ Six-saddle bridge plus separate bar tailpiece (some with six fine-tuning knobs).
- ■ Gold-plated hardware.

Some without fine-tuners on tailpiece.

Production: 1976 2; 1977 1,469; 1978 641; 1979 108. Figures not available for 80s.

■ ARTIST

ARTIST 1979–81 *Block fingerboard markers, "LP" headstock inlay, three controls and three mini-switches.*

- ■ Bound ebony fingerboard, block markers; "LP" inlay on headstock; metal truss-rod cover; brass nut.
- ■ Bound carved-top body; sunbursts or black.
- ■ Two metal-cover humbucker pickups.
- ■ Three controls (volume, bass, treble) plus three-way selector, three mini-switches (brightness, expansion, compression); active circuit.
- ■ Black laminated plastic pickguard.
- ■ Six-saddle bridge plus separate bar tailpiece with six fine-tuning knobs.
- ■ Gold-plated hardware.

Also known as **Active** *model.*

Production: 1979 234. Figures not available for 1980 and 1981.

■ AXCESS

AXCESS STANDARD 2009–current *Plain truss-rod cover, contoured neck heel, contoured back.*
Similar to **Traditional**, except:
- Plain truss-rod cover, contoured neck heel.
- Contoured back with ribcage cutout; ice tea burst or gun metal grey.
- Two coverless humbucker pickups.
- Push/pull on bridge-pickup volume control for coil tap.

Custom Shop.

AXCESS STANDARD FLOYD ROSE 2008–current *Floyd Rose trem with locking nut.*
Similar to **Traditional**, except:
- Locking nut, plain truss-rod cover, contoured neck heel.
- Additional control plate in middle of back, contoured back with ribcage cutout; ice tea burst or gun metal grey.
- Two coverless humbucker pickups.
- Push/pull on bridge-pickup volume control for coil tap.
- Floyd Rose tremolo.

Custom Shop.

■ BANTAM

Early name for Elite and Florentine models; see later **Elite** *and* **Florentine** *entries.*

■ BFG

BFG 2006–08 *Unsanded top with router furrows.*
- Unbound rosewood fingerboard, no markers, no truss-rod cover.
- Unbound carved-top with router furrows, chambered mahogany back; various trans(parent) colours.
- One plastic-cover six-polepiece single-coil pickup (neck) and one coverless zebra-coil humbucker pickup (bridge).
- Three wooden controls (one tone, two volume) plus three-way selector and kill-switch toggle.
- No pickguard.
- Six-saddle bridge plus separate bar tailpiece.
- Gun metal hardware with trans cherry, distressed black chrome with black, or trans gold.

■ BILLIE JOE ARMSTRONG

BILLIE JOE ARMSTRONG JUNIOR 2006–current *50s-specification* **Junior Single-Cut** *with one plastic-cover six-polepiece stacked double-coil pickup, wrap-over bridge–tailpiece; sunburst, black, or white; signature on back of headstock.*

■ BLACK BEAUTY

See later **Custom: Reissue Models**.

■ BOB MARLEY

BOB MARLEY SPECIAL 2002–04 *Elliptical switch washer.*
Similar to **Special single-cut**, except:
- Small block fingerboard markers, wide binding on headstock.
- Aged cherry finish appears stripped.
- Elliptical switch washer.
- Aluminium pickguard.

Custom Shop; production 200.

■ BUDWEISER

BUDWEISER 2002 *Similar to* **Studio**, *except Budweiser beer graphics. Custom Shop; production 50.*

■ CATALINA

CATALINA 1996–98 *Opaque colours, pearl Custom Shop logo on headstock.*
Similar to **Standard second version**, except:
- Ebony fingerboard with compound radius; pearl crown markers; pearl Custom Shop logo inlaid on headstock.
- Semi-hollow body; black, yellow, red, or turquoise.
- *Custom Shop.*

■ CLASS 5

CLASS-5 2001–08 *Similar to* **Standard 59 reissue**, *except weight relief holes (not tone chambers) to lighten weight (not visible); non-traditional finishes (amber, cranberry, tangerineburst, trans blue, trans black). Custom Shop.*

■ CLASSIC

CLASSIC 1990–2008 *"Classic" on truss-rod cover.*
- Bound rosewood fingerboard, crown markers; "Les Paul Model" on headstock; "Classic" on truss-rod cover; plastic tuner buttons.
- Bound carved-top body; sunbursts or colours (gold only in 1998).
- Two coverless humbuckers.
- Four controls (two volume, two tone) plus three-way selector.
- Cream plastic pickguard with "1960" logo.
- Six-saddle bridge plus separate bar tailpiece.

Vintage-style inked five or six-digit serial number, with first digit or first two digits corresponding to year of manufacture.
Also Guitar Of The Week models 2007, production 400 each: Fireburst finish; Ripple-effect finish designed by artist Tom Morgan; Antiqued appointments, H-90 pickups (stacked double-coil), iced tea sunburst; Antiqued appointments, zebra wood body; Mahogany top, antiqued appointments, faded cherry; Mahogany top, antiqued appointments, scroll logo, vintage sunburst.

CLASSIC ANTIQUE 2007–08 *Figured top, 'crown' headstock inlay (does not say "Les Paul"), antiqued parts, honeyburst or vintage sunburst.*

CLASSIC CELEBRITY 1992 *"Celebrity" on pickguard.*
Similar to **Classic**, except:
- Bound ebony fingerboard.
- Black only.
- Two coverless humbuckers.
- White plastic pickguard with "Celebrity" logo.
- Gold-plated hardware.

Production 200.

CLASSIC CENTENNIAL 1994 *Goldtop; production no more than 101; four-digit serial number on tailpiece with first digit (1) in diamonds. Custom Shop.*

CLASSIC CUSTOM 2007–08 *Single-ply antiqued binding, ebony fingerboard, 'crown' headstock ornament, gold-plated hardware; ebony finish standard (silverburst or white available as Guitar Of The Week models 2007, production 400 each).*

CLASSIC CUSTOM P-90 2007 *Guitar Of The Week model 2007; two plastic-cover six-polepiece single-coil pickups; antique ebony. Production 400.*

CLASSIC CUSTOM 3-PICKUP 2007 *Guitar Of The Week model 2007; three DiMarzio coverless humbucker pickups with double-white coils, gold-plated hardware; cherry sunburst. Production 400.*

CLASSIC DC 2003–05 *Carved-top double-cutaway, "Classic" on truss-rod cover, two metal-covered humbuckers, two controls, aged inlays; gold top.*

CLASSIC MAHOGANY 2000–07 *Mahogany top cap, zebra-coil pickups (one black coil, one white)*
Similar to **Classic**, except:
- Mahogany top cap; natural, trans red, or sunbursts.
- 'Zebra' pickup coils (one black, one white coil).

Also Guitar Of The Week models 2007, production 400 each: Antiqued appointments, faded cherry; Antiqued appointments, scroll logo, vintage sunburst.

CLASSIC/MIII 1991–92 *Additional central single-coil pickup; bound fingerboard.*
Similar to **Classic**, except:
- Sunburst only.
- Two coverless humbuckers plus one central six-polepiece single-coil pickup.
- Two controls (volume, tone) plus five-way selector and mini-switch.
- No pickguard.

CLASSIC BIRDSEYE 1993
CLASSIC PLUS 1992–95, 1999–2000
CLASSIC PREMIUM BIRDSEYE 1993
CLASSIC PREMIUM PLUS 1993–97
CLASSIC QUILT TOP 1998
All similar to **Classic**, except:
- Varying grades of figured maple carved-top (Premium Plus better than Plus, Premium Birdseye better than Birdseye). Some Premium Plus models made in Custom Shop.
- No pickguard on earliest, then pickguard with inscribed "1960" included in case but not mounted, then pickguard mounted.

CORVETTE

See later **50th Anniversary** *entry.*

CRAZY HORSE

CRAZY HORSE 2003 *Similar to* **Standard second version**, *except unbound fingerboard; features from customized Ford Bronco vehicle, including tyre tread. Custom Shop; production 25.*

CUSTOM

CUSTOM: ORIGINAL MODELS
chronological order

CUSTOM first version 1954–57 *Block fingerboard markers, split-diamond headstock inlay, "Les Paul Custom" on truss-rod cover, two plastic-cover pickups.*
- Bound ebony fingerboard, block markers; split-diamond inlay on headstock; "Les Paul Custom" on truss-rod cover.
- Bound carved-top all-mahogany body; black only.
- Two plastic-cover six-polepiece single-coil pickups (neck unit with oblong polepieces; bridge unit with round polepieces).
- Four controls (two volume, two tone) plus three-way selector.
- Black laminated plastic pickguard.
- Six-saddle bridge plus separate bar tailpiece.
- Gold-plated hardware.

Production: 1954 94; 1955 355; 1956 489; 1957 283 (includes some Custom second version models).

CUSTOM second version 1957–61 *Three humbucker pickups.*
Similar to **Custom first version**, except:
- Three metal-cover humbucker pickups.

Some with two humbucker pickups. Shape changed in 1961: see later **SG/Les Paul Custom** *entry. Also 35th Anniversary version with appropriate inlay on headstock (1989–90): see later* **35th Anniversary** *entry. Production: 1957 283 (includes some Custom first version models); 1958 256; 1959 246; 1960 189; 1961 513 (includes some SG/Les Paul Custom models).*

CUSTOM third version 1968–current *Two humbuckers.*
Similar to **Custom second version**, except:
- Maple top cap (53 made with Brazilian rosewood top, 1975–76), mahogany back; sunbursts, natural, or colours.
- Two metal-cover humbucker pickups.

Also: three-humbucker version (various periods); versions with nickel-plated hardware (1976–83, 1996) or chrome-plated hardware (1983–87); maple fingerboard version (1975–81). Production: Kalamazoo-made: 1968 433; 1969 2,353; 1970 2,612; 1971 3,201; 1972 4,002; 1973 7,232; 1974 7,563; 1975 7,448; 1976 4,323; 1977 3,133; 1978 10,744; 1979 1,624. Figures not available for large Nashville production started 1975 and continuing to current.
At the time of writing (2009) this is a Custom Shop model.

CUSTOM: 54 REISSUE MODELS
chronological order

CUSTOM 54 LTD EDITION 1972–73 *Reissue based on* **Custom first version**, *identifiable by serial number prefixed with LE. Production: 1972 60; 1973 1090; 1975 3; 1977 1.*

CUSTOM 54 reissue 1991–current *Reissue based on* **Custom first version**. *Optional Bigsby. "R4" stamped in control cavity from 1993. Known by various names through the years, including* Black Beauty 54. *Aged versions available, known as* VOS *Vintage Original Spec (2006–current). Custom Shop.*

CUSTOM: 57 REISSUE MODELS chronological order

CUSTOM 57 two-pickup reissue 1991–current *Reissue based on rare two-humbucker* **Custom second version**. *Optional Bigsby. "R7" stamped in control cavity from 1993. Known by various names through the years, including* 1957 Les Paul Custom Black Beauty *(1998–2005)* and 1957 Les Paul Custom 2-Pickup *(2006–current). Aged versions available, known as* Aged, *optional faded cherry finish (2002–05) and* VOS *Vintage Original Spec (2006–current). Custom Shop.*

CUSTOM 57 three-pickup reissue 1991–current *Reissue based on* **Custom second version**. *Optional Bigsby. "R7" stamped in control cavity from 1993. Known by various names through the years, including* 1957 Les Paul Custom Black Beauty 3-Pickup *(1998–2005)* and 1957 Les Paul Custom 3-Pickup *(2006–current). Aged version available, known as* VOS *Vintage Original Spec (2006–current). Also with optional control layout of three volume, one master tone (1999–2005). Custom Shop.*

CUSTOM 57 CENTENNIAL three-pickup reissue 1994 *Similar to* **Custom 57 three-pickup reissue**, *except four-digit serial number on tailpiece and first digit (1) of diamonds. Custom Shop.*

CUSTOM: 68 REISSUE MODELS chronological order

CUSTOM 68 FIGUREDTOP 2000–current *Similar to* **Custom second version**, *except figured maple top; antique natural, butterscotch, heritage cherry sunburst, or triburst (only offered in ebony or vintage white; VOS Vintage Original Spec aging treatment, 2009–current). Aged version available, known as* Custom Authentic *(2002–05). Custom Shop.*

CUSTOM 68 CHAMBERED 2007–08 *Chambered body; pelham blue aged to green. Custom Shop.*

CUSTOM: OTHER MODELS alphabetical order

ACE FREHLEY *See earlier* **Ace Frehley** *entry.*

CUSTOM BLACK BEAUTY 82 1982–83 *Combines features of Custom and Standard, multi-ply body binding, unbound ebony fingerboard with crown inlay, gold-plated hardware.*

CUSTOM LITE 1987–89 *Contoured, thinner body; block fingerboard markers.*

- Bound ebony fingerboard, block markers; split-diamond inlay on headstock.
- Bound carved-top thinner body with contoured back; sunburst, black, or pink.
- Two metal-cover humbucker pickups.
- Three controls (two volumes, one tone) plus three-way selector (two controls plus three-way selector 1989) and mini-switch.
- Black laminated plastic pickguard.
- Six-saddle bridge, separate bar tailpiece (locking vibrato option).
- Gold-plated hardware (black-plated 1989).

CUSTOM LITE SHOWCASE EDITION 1988 *Similar to* **Custom Lite**, *except plastic-cover EMG pickups, active electronics, gold top, gold-plated hardware. Production 250.*

CUSTOM PLUS 1991–96 *Similar to* **Custom third version**, *except fancier grade of figured maple carved-top; sunbursts; no pickguard.*

CUSTOM SHOWCASE EDITION 1988 *Guitar Of The Month series, EMG pickups; ruby finish. Custom Shop; production 200 for US distribution, 50 for overseas.*

CUSTOM 20th ANNIVERSARY 1974 *Anniversary model based on* **Custom third version** *but with "Twentieth Anniversary" inlaid into position marker at 15th fret. Sunburst or colours.*

CUSTOM 25th ANNIVERSARY 1977 *Anniversary model based on* **Custom third version** *– even though 1977 was 25th anniversary of Les Paul Standard – but with "25th Anniversary" engraved on tailpiece, "Les Paul" signature on pickguard, chrome-plated hardware, metallic silver.*

CUSTOM/400 1991–92 *Split-block fingerboard markers, Custom Shop Edition logo on rear of headstock.*
Similar to **Custom third version**, except:

- Bound ebony fingerboard, split-block markers; "Custom Shop Edition" logo on rear of headstock.
- Bound carved-top body; black only.
- Gold-plated hardware.

Name derives from Custom-style appointments and Gibson Super 400-style fingerboard markers. Custom Shop.

JIMMY PAGE CUSTOM *See later* **Jimmy Page** *entry.*

JOHN SYKES CUSTOM *See later* **John Sykes** *entry.*

LE (LIMITED EDITION) CUSTOM SILVERBURST 2007–08 *Silverburst finish.*

MAHOGANY CUSTOM 1998 *Similar to* **Custom second version**, *except one-piece mahogany body (no top cap); faded cherry finish; three metal-cover humbucker pickups.*

MICK JONES CUSTOM *See later* **Mick Jones** *entry.*

PETER FRAMPTON *See earlier* **Peter Frampton** *entry.*

STEVE JONES CUSTOM *See later* **Steve Jones** *entry.*

SUPER CUSTOM (1984 prototypes, 2007 production) *Curly maple top, back, and side veneers, one covered humbucker and one coverless humbucker, slashed-block markers.*

ZAKK WYLDE BULLSEYE *See later* **Zakk Wylde** *entry.*

35th ANNIVERSARY CUSTOM 1989–90 *Anniversary model based on* **Custom second version**, *but with "35th Anniversary" in bar of split-diamond inlay on headstock.*

CUSTOM AUTHENTIC
Hand aging of finish and hardware with mild abrasive, available 2001–05.

CUSTOM SHOP
Special one-off custom orders were available from Gibson's original factory in Kalamazoo from its earliest days, but a bona fide Custom Department wasn't officially established until the 60s. There has been a Custom Shop at the current Nashville factory from 1983 until 1988 and then again since 1992. The Custom Shop's purpose is to manufacture special models, custom-order one-of-a-kinds, and limited-edition production runs in relatively small quantities, including the reissue series and signature models, as well as exclusive guitars for dealers and others. Custom Shop guitars sometimes carry an identifying logo visible on the back of the headstock.

■ CUSTOM 25

CUSTOM 25 2008 *Flame-maple headstock veneer, no headstock ornament.*
- Bound ebony fingerboard, slashed-block markers, flame-maple headstock overlay.
- Bound carved-top body; sunburst.
- Two metal-cover humbucker pickups.
- Four controls (two volume, two tone) plus three-way selector and mini-switch.
- Flame maple pickguard.
- Six-saddle bridge, fine-tune tailpiece.
- Gold-plated hardware.

■ DALE EARNHARDT

DALE EARNHARDT 1999–2001 *Signature on fingerboard, automotive hood pins and lug nuts*
- Bound ebony fingerboard, signature inlay.
- Flat-top body; single-cutaway; graphic overlay by artist Sam Bass; ebony finish.
- Two metal-cover humbucker pickups.
- Four lug-nut knobs (two volume, two tone), three-way selector.
- No pickguard.
- Six-saddle bridge plus separate bar tailpiece.
- *Custom Shop; production 333.*

DALE EARNHARDT: THE INTIMIDATOR 2000–01 *Silver finish with black drawings and red trim, "The Intimidator" on fingerboard, "3" on headstock. Production 333.*

DALE EARNHARDT JR. 2001 *Top graphic features #8 race car, signature, and Bud logo; signature on fingerboard; Earnhardt red finish. Production 333.*

■ DARK FIRE

DARK FIRE 2008–current *Robot auto-tuners, "Dark Fire" on truss-rod cover.*
- Unbound ebony fingerboard, small block carbon-fibre markers, "Dark Fire" on truss-rod cover, 'flowerpot' headstock inlay, does not say "Les Paul".
- Dark-bound carved-top, Robot-style master tone knob with LED lights (controls effects), chambered mahogany body, gloss top finish, satin back,
- One covered six-polepiece single-coil pickup (neck), one covered humbucker pickup (bridge), carbon-fiber pickup covers, piezo bridge pickup.
- Four knobs (two volume, one tone, one multi-purpose with LED lights), rotary pickup selector switch.
- Transparent pickguard.
- Six-saddle bridge plus separate flat-plate tailpiece.
- Brushed chrome hardware.

■ DC

DC PRO 1997–98 *Double-cutaway carved-top body, non-standard headstock with straight string-pull (no "Les Paul" on headstock or truss-rod cover).*
- Unbound ebony fingerboard, dot markers; 24 3/4–inch scale-length (25 1/2–inch scale optional); headstock with straight string-pull.
- Bound carved-top body with shape of **Special double-cut**; flamed maple top; sunbursts or translucents.
- Optional pickup and bridge configurations: two plastic-cover single-coil pickups with wrap-over bridge, two metal-cover humbucker pickups with wrap-over bridge or with separate bridge and tailpiece.
- Two controls (volume, tone) plus three-way selector.
- Nickel-plated hardware.

Custom Shop.

DC STANDARD 1998–2007 *Double-cutaway carved-top body, crown markers, standard Gibson headstock (no "Les Paul" on headstock or truss-rod cover).*
- Bound rosewood fingerboard, crown markers; 24 3/4–inch scale-length; standard Gibson headstock shape.
- Unbound carved-top body with shape of **Special double-cut**; maple top (flamed from 2001); sunbursts or colours (sparkle finishes only in 2000, trans finishes only from 2001).

- Two metal-cover humbucker pickups.
- Two knobs (tone, volume) plus selector switch
- Wrap-over tailpiece.
- Chrome-plated hardware (in 2000, hardware was chrome with lemonburst, or gold with tangerineburst; from 2001, hardware was gold-plated).

Listed as **Standard Double Cut Plus** *from 2001.*

DC STUDIO 1997–98, 2006–08 *Unbound double-cutaway carved-top body, dot markers, chrome hardware.*

- Unbound rosewood fingerboard, dot markers; 24 3/4-inch scale-length; standard Gibson headstock shape.
- Unbound carved-top body with shape of **Special double-cut**; sunbursts or colours.
- Two metal-cover humbucker pickups.
- Two knobs (tone, volume) plus selector switch
- Wrap-over tailpiece (separate bridge and tailpiece from 1998).
- Chrome-plated hardware.

For a similar guitar with gold-plated hardware and crown markers, see **Standard Lite**.

DELUXE

DELUXE 1969–84, 1992–97, 1999–2008 *"Deluxe" on truss-rod cover.*

- Bound rosewood fingerboard, crown markers; "Les Paul Model" on headstock; "Deluxe" on truss-rod cover; plastic tuner buttons (later metal).
- Bound carved-top body; sunbursts, natural, or colours.
- Two mini-sized metal-cover humbucker pickups.
- Four controls (two volume, two tone) plus three-way selector.
- Cream plastic pickguard.
- Six-saddle bridge plus separate bar tailpiece.

Earliest examples with plastic-cover six-polepiece single-coil pickups.
Some mini-humbucker-equipped examples with extra plastic ring around pickup covers.
Also 30th Anniversary version (2000): see **30th Anniversary** *entry here.*
Also Guitar Of The Week model 2007, goldtop finish with antiqued binding.
Production: Kalamazoo-made: 1971 4,466; 1972 5,194; 1973 10,484; 1974 7,367; 1975 2,561; 1976 172; 1977 413; 1978 4,450; 1979 413. Figures not available for 1969, 1970, and 80s, nor for any Nashville production.

DELUXE HALL OF FAME EDITION 1991 *Similar to* **Deluxe**, *except gold finish all around (sides, back, back of neck). Custom Shop.*

PETE TOWNSHEND DELUXE *models, see later* **Pete Townshend** *entry.*

30th ANNIVERSARY DELUXE 2000 *Ebony, wine red, or bullion gold. Custom Shop.*

DICKEY BETTS

DICKEY BETTS 57 GOLDTOP 2001 *Similar to* **Goldtop 57 reissue**, *except aged by Tom Murphy; replica Dickey Betts strap and faux alligator hardshell case included. Custom Shop; production 114, numbered with DB prefix.*

DICKEY BETTS 57 REDTOP 2002–03 *Similar to* **Goldtop 57 reissue**, *except red top. Custom Shop; production 55, numbered with DBR prefix.*

DOUBLE CUTAWAY XPL
See later **XPL** *entry.*

DUANE ALLMAN

DUANE ALLMAN 2003 *"DUANE" on back.*
Similar to **Standard 59 reissue**, except:

- Finish aged by Tom Murphy.
- Grover Rotomatic tuners.
- 'Ribbon' flame on maple top; "DUANE" spelled out in fretwire on body back.

Numbered with DALLMAN prefix. Custom Shop.

ELEGANT

ELEGANT 1996–2000 *Abalone crown markers, figured top.*

- Bound ebony fingerboard with compound radius, abalone pearl crown markers, pearl "Gibson" logo on headstock, metal tuner buttons.
- Bound semi-hollow carved-top body; figured maple top; natural, stains, or sunbursts.
- Two covered six-polepiece humbucker pickups.
- Four controls (two volumes, two tones) plus three-way selector.
- No pickguard.
- Six-saddle bridge plus separate bar tailpiece.
- *Custom Shop.*

ELEGANT DOUBLE QUILT 1997
ELEGANT QUILT 1997–98, 2001–05
ELEGANT SUPER DOUBLE QUILT 1997
Progressively heavier quilt figure in maple top: Quilt; Double Quilt; Super Double Quilt. Custom Shop.

ELITE DIAMOND SPARKLE

ELITE DIAMOND SPARKLE 1995–97 *Diamond soundholes.*

- Bound ebony fingerboard, pearl rectangular markers, split-diamond headstock inlay.
- Bound carved-top body, diamond soundholes, sparkles.
- Two metal-cover humbucker pickups.
- Four knobs (two tone, two volume) plus selector switch.
- Six-saddle bridge plus separate tailpiece.
- Gold-plated hardware.

Early examples known as **Bantam Elite**. *Custom Shop.*

EPIPHONE
Gibson acquired the Epiphone brandname in 1957 and started making Epiphone guitars in 1959. Production of Epiphones in the USA stopped in 1970, while production had started around 1968 in Japan. In the late 80s, these were succeeded by Epiphones made in Korea (and, for the Japanese market, Orville-branded Japanese-made guitars). Epiphone introduced a Korean-built Les Paul Standard in 1988, adding some Japanese-made models in 1998. At the time of writing, the line of Epiphone Les Paul models included: Black Beauty, Custom, Custom Zakk Wylde (Bullseye, Buzzsaw, Camo), Goldtop 56, Prophecy Custom (24 frets, blade markers), Slash (Goldtop, Standard), Special II, Standard (also Plus-Top, Plain-Top, Ultra, and Ultra-II versions), Studio, and 100 (no binding, dot markers).

■ FADED DOUBLE CUTAWAY
See later entry in **Special Double-Cutaway: Other Models**.

■ FIGURED
See later entry for **Supreme**.

FIREBRAND
See later entries for **The Paul Standard** and for **The Paul Deluxe**.

■ FLORENTINE
FLORENTINE PLUS 1995–98 *Similar to* **Florentine Standard** *(below), except flamed maple top, trans colours (earliest named Bantam Elite Plus). Some with 'diamond' soundholes, sparkle finish. Custom Shop.*

FLORENTINE STANDARD 1995–98 *F-holes in top.*
- Bound ebony fingerboard, pearl rectangular markers, split-diamond headstock inlay.
- Bound semi-hollow carved-top body, f-holes, sunburst.
- Two metal-cover humbucker pickups.
- Four knobs (two tone, two volume) plus selector switch.
- Six-saddle bridge plus separate tailpiece.
- Gold-plated hardware.

Early examples known as **Bantam Elite**. *Some without f-holes. Custom Shop.*

■ GARY MOORE
GARY MOORE 2000–current *Zebra-coil neck pickup, black-coil bridge pickup, "Gary Moore" on truss-rod cover.*
Similar to **Standard second version**, except:
- Unbound carved-top of figured maple; lemonburst.
- Unbound rosewood fingerboard; "Gary Moore" on truss-rod cover.
- Two coverless humbucker pickups (black-white coils in neck position, black coils in bridge position).
- No pickguard.

■ **GARY MOORE SIGNATURE BFG** 2009–current *Similar to* **BFG**, *except two 60s knobs, one 50s knob, distressed hardware; satin lemonburst.*

■ GARY ROSSINGTON
GARY ROSSINGTON 2002 *Screws in headstock simulating broken headstock repair.*
Similar to **Standard 59 reissue**, except:
- Two screws in headstock, Schaller tuners (with holes from original Klusons).
- Finish wear aged by Tom Murphy, including large wear spot on back; aged sunburst.
- Aged nickel-plated hardware.

Numbered with GR prefix. Custom Shop; production 250.

■ GODDESS
GODDESS 2006–08 *Two coverless pickups with clear bobbins.*
- Bound ebony fingerboard, crown markers, "Goddess" on truss-rod cover, decal logo.
- Bound carved-top; violet burst, sky burst, rose burst, ice burst, ebony.
- Two coverless humbucker pickups with clear bobbins.
- One volume, one tone, three-way selector.
- No pickguard.
- Wrap-over bar bridge/tailpiece.

■ GOLDTOP

GOLDTOP: ORIGINAL MODELS
chronological order

GOLDTOP first version 1952–53 *Crown fingerboard markers, two plastic-cover pickups, bridge/tailpiece on long 'trapeze' anchor.*
- Bound rosewood fingerboard, crown markers; "Les Paul Model" on headstock; plastic tuner buttons.
- Bound carved-top body; gold only.
- Two plastic-cover six-polepiece single-coil pickups.
- Four controls (two volume, two tone) plus three-way selector.
- Cream plastic pickguard.
- Wrap-under bar bridge/tailpiece on long 'trapeze' anchor.

Some early examples do not have a bound fingerboard and/or have a bridge pickup with fixing screws at two corners rather than among polepiece screws.
Examples from 1952 have no serial number.
Some with all-gold body (rather than normal gold top with brown back and sides) and gold back of neck.
Production: 1952 1,716; 1953 2,245 (includes some Goldtop second version models).

GOLDTOP second version 1953–55 *Angled one-piece bridge/tailpiece.*
Similar to **Goldtop first version**, except:
- Wrap-over bar bridge/tailpiece.

Some with all-gold body and back of neck.
Production: 1953 2,245 (includes some Goldtop first version

models); 1954 1,504; 1955 862 (includes some Goldtop third version models).

GOLDTOP third version 1955–57 *Six-saddle bridge plus separate bar tailpiece, two plastic-cover pickups.*
Similar to **Goldtop second version**, except:
■ Six-saddle bridge plus separate bar tailpiece.
Production: 1955 862 (includes some Goldtop second version models); 1956 920; 1957 598 (includes some Goldtop fourth version models).

GOLDTOP fourth version 1957–58 *Two humbuckers, six-saddle bridge plus separate bar tailpiece.*
Similar to **Goldtop third version**, except:
■ Two metal-cover humbucker pickups.
Finish changed to sunburst in 1958: see later **Standard first version** *entry.*
Production: 1957 598 (includes some Goldtop third version models); 1958 434 (includes some sunburst Standard models).

GOLDTOP fifth version 1968–69 *Based on* **Goldtop third version** *(bridge and separate tailpiece), but wide binding in cutaway. Confusingly referred to in Gibson literature as "Standard" model. Production: 1968 1,224; 1969 2,751.*

GOLDTOP sixth version 1971–72 *Based on* **Goldtop second version** *(one-piece bridge/tailpiece), but with Gibson logo on pickups. Some examples with extra plastic ring around pickup covers. Also referred to in literature as "Standard 58". Production: 1971 25; 1972 1,046; 1973 4; 1974 1.*

GOLDTOP: REISSUE MODELS
original-model year order

GOLDTOP 52 reissue 1999–2005 *Based on* **Goldtop first version**. *"R2" stamped in control cavity. Known by various names through the years. Aged version available, known as* Aged *(2002, production 50). Custom Shop.*

GOLDTOP 54 reissue 1997–current *Based on* **Goldtop second version**. *"R4" stamped in control cavity. Known by various names through the years. Aged version available, known as* VOS *Vintage Original Spec (2006–current). Custom Shop.*

GOLDTOP 56 reissue 1990–current *Based on* **Goldtop third version,** *except plastic-covered humbucker pickups (visually identical to single-coils) through 1996, then single-coils. "R6" stamped in control cavity from 1993. Known by various names through the years, including* Goldtop Reissue *(1990). Aged versions available, known as* Custom Authentic *(2001) and* VOS *Vintage Original Spec (2006–current). Custom Shop.*

GOLDTOP 57 reissue 1983–90, 1993–current *Based on* **Goldtop fourth version**. *"R7" stamped in control cavity from 1993. Known by various names through the years, including* Goldtop Reissue *(1983–90). Aged versions available, known as* Aged, *with optional reissue case and amplifier (2001),* Custom Authentic *(2002), and* VOS *Vintage Original Spec (2006–current). Also with optional dark-stained back, known as* Goldtop 57 Darkback *(2000–current); aged version available, known as* VOS *Vintage Original Spec (2006–current). Custom Shop.*

GOLDTOP: OTHER MODELS
alphabetical order

DICKEY BETTS 57 GOLDTOP/REDTOP *See earlier* **Dickey Betts** *entry.*

GOLDTOP 30th ANNIVERSARY 1982–83 *Anniversary model based on* **Goldtop fourth version** *but with "Thirtieth Anniversary" inlaid into position marker at 19th fret, gold finish all-around. Numbered with prefix A, B, or C.*

GOLDTOP 57 MARY FORD 1997 *Based on* **Goldtop fourth version**, *except gold-stencilled leaves on pickguard, custom armrest. Custom Shop.*

JOE BONAMASSA *See later* **Joe Bonamassa** *entry.*

40th ANNIVERSARY GOLDTOP 1992–93
Similar to **Goldtop third version**, except:
■ Ebony fingerboard; "40th Anniversary" inlaid into position marker at 12th fret and on rear of headstock.
■ Black finish.
■ Pickups, although visually similar to single-coils, are actually humbuckers.
■ Gold-plated hardware.
Custom Shop.

50th ANNIVERSARY STANDARD GOLDTOP 2007–08 *All-gold finish, gold pickguard, gold-plated head-plate with etched crown. "50th" serial numbered with 57S prefix. Custom Shop; production 157.*

50th ANNIVERSARY 1958 MURPHY-AGED GOLDTOP 2007–08 *50th Anniversary banner on pickguard, gold-top; aged by Tom Murphy. Custom Shop; production 100.*

■ GT

GT 2006 *Monochrome finish with flames.*
■ Bound ebony fingerboard, mirror crown markers, "GT" on truss-rod cover, locking tuners, pearl logo.
■ Bound carved-top, mahogany back, extended strap buttons; finishes with flame graphic (also fire engine red finish with no flame graphic, 2007 Guitar Of The Week, production 400).
■ Two metal-cover humbucker pickups.
■ Four push/pull knobs, high-pass tone filter, coil taps on both pickups, three-way selector.
■ No pickguard.
■ Six-saddle bridge plus separate bar tailpiece.

■ HD.6X-PRO

HD.6X-PRO 2006 *No fingerboard inlays; oblong black pickup between bridge-position pickup and bridge.*
- Unbound ebony fingerboard; carbon-fiber block markers, pearl "Gibson" logo on headstock, knurled metal cylinder tuner knobs.
- Silver-bound carved-top body; blue metallic top.
- Two metal-cover humbucking pickups and one hex-output pickup; standard quarter-inch jack plus microphone input jack and ethernet output jack; onboard digital converter requires BOB (breakout box).
- Four controls (two volume, two tone) plus three-way selector.
- No pickguard.
- Six-saddle bridge plus separate bar tailpiece.
- Platinum-plated hardware.

■ HERITAGE

HERITAGE STANDARD 80 1980–82 *"Heritage Series Standard-80" on truss-rod cover; extra four-figure number on back of headstock.*
- Bound rosewood fingerboard, crown markers; "Les Paul Model" on headstock; "Heritage Series Standard-80" on truss-rod cover.
- Bound carved-top body; sunbursts.
- Two metal-cover humbucker pickups.
- Four controls (two volume, two tone) plus three-way selector.
- Cream plastic pickguard.
- Six-saddle bridge plus separate bar tailpiece.

Four-figure series number on back of headstock in addition to regular serial.

HERITAGE STANDARD 80 AWARD 1981 *Pearl crown markers, gold-plated hardware*
Similar to **Heritage Standard 80**, except:
- Bound ebony fingerboard.
- Gold-plated hardware.

Limited edition; oval pearl medallion on back of headstock has three-digit edition number.

HERITAGE STANDARD 80 ELITE 1980–82 *"Heritage Series Standard-80 Elite" on truss-rod cover; additional four-figure serial number on back of headstock.*
Similar to **Heritage Standard 80**, except:
- Bound ebony fingerboard; "Heritage Series Standard-80 Elite" on truss-rod cover.
- Quilted maple carved-top.

■ JEFF BECK

JEFF BECK 1954 OXBLOOD 2009 *Brown finish, cream backplates.*
Similar to **Goldtop 54 reissue**, except:
- No "Les Paul Model" on headstock, metal tuner buttons.
- Cream control plates on back; chocolate brown finish all over body.
- Two coverless humbucker pickups.

Custom Shop; production 50 custom-aged and signed; 100 with Vintage Original Spec aging treatment.
See also later **54 Oxblood** *entry.*

■ JIM BEAM

JIM BEAM 2000–03 *Ornamentation motif from Jim Beam whiskey.*
Similar to **Studio**, except:
- Unbound ebony fingerboard; medal graphic with letter B on headstock.
- Top overlay with "Jim Beam" and medal graphic.

Custom Shop.

■ JIMMY PAGE

JIMMY PAGE Standard first version 1995–99 *Flamed top, signature on pickguard*
Based on **Standard second version**, except:
- Push/pull knobs for phasing and coil-tapping (no visible difference)
- Faded cherry sunburst.
- Locking nut added to bridge-height adjustment after first 500.
- Page signature on pickguard.
- Gold-plated hardware.

JIMMY PAGE Standard second version 2004–08 *Metal-cover humbucker pickup (neck), coverless humbucker (bridge); 'Page' burst.*
Custom Shop replica of Page's 'Number 1'; production: 25 signed, hand-numbered 1–25; 150 aged by Tom Murphy and numbered with PAGE prefix; unlimited with Custom Authentic aging, numbered with JPP prefix.

JIMMY PAGE CUSTOM 2008 *Similar to 1960-period* **Custom second version**, *with three pickups, '60s-style thin neck profile, push/pull tone pot for bridge-pickup coil split; option of separate bar or Bigsby tailpiece; Vintage Original Spec aging treatment. Custom Shop; production 500.*

■ JOE BONAMASSA

JOE BONAMASSA 2008–current *"Bonamassa" on truss-rod cover.*
Similar to **Goldtop 57 reissue**, except:
- "Bonamassa" on truss-rod cover; Grover tuners with kidney-bean buttons.
- Antique gold finish.
- Black pickup surrounds, pickguard, and switch washer.
- Two amber knobs, two metal-capped knobs.

Custom Shop.

■ JOE PERRY

JOE PERRY 1996–2000 *Black stain finish on flamed top; white pearloid pickguard.*
Similar to **Standard second version**, except:
- Unbound rosewood fingerboard; Custom Shop run has "Joe Perry" pearloid inlay on headstock (production version has "Les Paul Model").
- Unbound carved figured-maple top; production version has

"Joe Perry" logo near bridge; blackburst.
- Two coverless humbucker pickups; four controls (two volume, two tone; push/pull tone knob to activate mid-boost on production version) plus selector.
- White pearloid pickguard.
- Black hardware.

Limited-edition Custom Shop run (1996) numbered with JP prefix. Production version (1996–2000) with regular eight-digit serial.

JOE PERRY BONEYARD 2003–08 *"Joe Perry" on truss-rod cover, Boneyard logo on headstock.*
Similar to **Standard second version**, except:
- Aged fingerboard markers, "Joe Perry" on truss-rod cover, Boneyard (hot sauce) logo on headstock.
- Flamed top, weight-relieved body, no pickguard; green tiger finish with Custom Authentic aging.
- Six-saddle bridge; separate bar or Bigsby tailpiece.
- Aged nickel-plated hardware.

Early examples are numbered as "Pilot Run"; later examples are numbered with BONE prefix.
Custom Shop.

JOHN LENNON

JOHN LENNON 2007 *Dog-eared P-90 and Charlie Christian pickups.*
Similar to **Junior single-cut**, except:
- "Custom" on truss-rod cover.
- Natural mahogany finish.
- Plastic-cover six-polepiece single-coil pickup (bridge), 'Charlie Christian' bar pickup (neck).
- Two controls (tone and volume) plus three-way selector.
- Six-saddle bridge with two thumbwheels on treble side; separate bar tailpiece.
- Aged chrome-plated hardware.

Custom Shop.

JOHN SYKES

JOHN SYKES CUSTOM 2007 *Mirror pickguard, chrome pickup frames.*
Similar to 1978-period **Custom third version**, except:
- Brass nut.
- Ebony finish (aged or gloss).
- Two coverless humbucker pickups with chrome mounting frames.
- Mirror-finish pickguard.
- Bridge-pickup tone control disabled.
- *Custom Shop.*

JUMBO

JUMBO 1970–71 *Round soundhole.*
- Rosewood fingerboard, dot markers; "Les Paul Jumbo" on truss-rod cover.
- Bound single-cutaway Jumbo acoustic body; natural.
- One round-end plastic-cover low-impedance humbucker pickup.
- Four controls (volume, treble, bass, 'Decade') plus bypass switch.
- Black plastic pickguard.
- Height-adjustable one-piece bridge with string-anchor pins in wooden surround.

Requires special cord with built-in impedance-matching transformer to match normal amplification impedance. Production: 1971 43; 1972 3; 1973 3. Figures not available for 1970.

JUNIOR SINGLE-CUTAWAY

JUNIOR SINGLE-CUTAWAY: ORIGINAL MODELS chronological order

JUNIOR single-cut 1954–58, 2008–current *Slab single-cutaway body, one pickup.*
- Unbound rosewood fingerboard, dot markers; "Les Paul Junior" on headstock ("Les Paul Model" on headstock, "Junior" on truss-rod cover, 2008–current); plastic tuner buttons.
- Unbound slab body; sunburst. (For beige examples, see later **TV single-cut** entry.)
- One plastic-cover six-polepiece single-coil pickup.
- Two controls (volume, tone).
- Black or tortoiseshell plastic pickguard.
- Wrap-over bar bridge/tailpiece.

Production: 1954 823; 1955 2,939; 1956 3,129; 1957 2,959; 1958 2,408 (includes some Junior double-cut models). Figures not available for later years.

JUNIOR single-cut three-quarter 1956–58 *Shorter 19–fret neck.*
Similar to **Junior single-cut**, except:
- Shorter neck (with 19 frets) and scale-length (two inches less than normal).

Production: 1956 18; 1957 222; 1958 181 (includes some Junior double-cut three-quarter models).

JUNIOR SINGLE-CUTAWAY: OTHER MODELS alphabetical order

BILLIE JOE ARMSTRONG JUNIOR *See earlier* **Billie Joe Armstrong** *entry.*

JOHN LENNON *See earlier* **John Lennon** *entry.*

JUNIOR (JR.) SPECIAL *See later entry in* **Special Single-Cutaway: Other Models**.

JUNIOR (JR.) SPECIAL HUM (or HB) *See later entry in* **Special Single-Cutaway: Other Models**.

JUNIOR (JR.) SPECIAL PLUS *See later entry in* **Special Single-Cutaway: Other Models**.

JUNIOR II *See later entry in* **Special Single-Cutaway: Other Models**.

JUNIOR 54 single-cut reissue 1986–92 *Based on* **Junior single-cut** *but six-saddle bridge plus separate bar tailpiece; sunburst, cherry, or white.*

JUNIOR 57 single-cut reissue 1998-current *Based on* **Junior single-cut** *but six-saddle bridge plus separate bar tailpiece; sunburst, cherry, or TV yellow. Optional VOS Vintage Original Spec aging treatment (2006–current). Custom Shop.*

■ JUNIOR DOUBLE-CUTAWAY

JUNIOR DOUBLE-CUTAWAY: ORIGINAL MODELS chronological order

JUNIOR double-cut 1958–61, 1997–98 *Slab double-cutaway body, one pickup.*
- Unbound rosewood fingerboard, dot markers; "Les Paul Junior" on headstock; plastic tuner buttons.
- Unbound slab double-cutaway body; cherry. (For yellow examples, see later **TV double-cut** entry.)
- One plastic-cover six-polepiece single-coil pickup.
- Two controls (volume, tone).
- Black or tortoiseshell plastic pickguard.
- Wrap-over bar bridge/tailpiece.

Shape changed in 1961: see later **SG/Les Paul Junior** *entry.*
Some examples in sunburst.
Production: 1958 2,408 (includes some Junior single-cut models); 1959 4,364; 1960 2,513; 1961 2,151 (includes some SG/Les Paul Junior models). Figures not available for later years.
Also Guitar Of The Week version, 2007, with satin white finish, wrap-over bridge, floral pattern (J-200 acoustic style) on pickguard; production 400.

JUNIOR double-cut three-quarter 1958–61 *Shorter 19-fret neck.*
Similar to **Junior double-cut**, except:
- Shorter neck (with 19 frets) and scale-length (two inches less than normal).

Production: 1958 181 (includes some Junior single-cut three-quarter models); 1959 199; 1960 96; 1961 71.

JUNIOR DOUBLE-CUTAWAY: OTHER MODELS alphabetical order

JUNIOR LITE *see later* **Special Double-Cutaway: Other Models**.

JUNIOR 58 double-cut reissue 1987–95, 1998–current *Based on* **Junior double-cut** *but six-saddle bridge plus separate bar tailpiece; nickel-plated hardware and plastic cover humbucker pickup (appears identical to single-coil) 1990–92 only. Optional VOS Vintage Original Spec aging treatment (2006–current). Custom Shop.*

■ KEITH RICHARDS

KEITH RICHARDS STANDARD 2007 *Aged sunburst finish, Bigsby.*
Similar to **Standard 58 reissue**, except:
- Finish aged by Tom Murphy, Bigsby tailpiece.
- Aged nickel-plated hardware.

Custom Shop; production 25, made for Vintage World (US dealer).

■ KM

KM 1979 *"Les Paul KM" on truss-rod cover.*
Similar to **Standard second version**, except:
- "Les Paul KM" on truss-rod cover.
- Sunbursts or natural.
- Two coverless cream-coil humbucker pickups.
- Larger rectangular six-saddle bridge plus separate bar tailpiece.

Made in Kalamazoo (hence KM) after Les Paul production moved to Nashville.
Early examples with "Custom Made" plastic plate on body face below tailpiece.
Production 1,052.

■ KORINA

KORINA 1996 *Korina (wood type) back and neck.*
Similar to **Standard second version**, except:
- Figured maple top, korina back and neck.
- *Custom Shop.*

■ K-II

K-II 1980 *Carved-top double-cutaway body, two humbucker pickups, "K-II" on truss-rod cover.*

■ LP XR

LP XRI 1981–82 *"XR-I" on truss-rod cover.*
- Unbound rosewood fingerboard, dot markers; "Les Paul Model" on headstock; and with "XR I" on truss-rod cover.
- Unbound carved-top body; sunbursts.
- Two coverless humbucker pickups.
- Four controls (two volume, two tone) plus three-way selector and mini-switch.
- No pickguard.
- Six-saddle bridge plus separate bar tailpiece.

LP XRII 1981–82 *"XR-II" on truss-rod cover.*
Similar to **LP XRI**, except:
- "XR II" on truss-rod cover.
- Bound slab body; sunbursts or natural.
- Two mini-sized metal-cover humbucker pickups.

LP XRIII 1982 *"XR-III" on truss-rod cover.*
Similar to **LP XRI**, except:
- "XR III" on truss-rod cover.
- Possibly only red-finish body.

No other information available for this model.

■ LP-295 GOLDTOP

LP-295 GOLDTOP 2008 *Wider and more pointed cutaway than regular Les Paul shape, floral pickguard, Bigsby vibrato, double-parallelogram markers, bound headstock, crown headstock ornament (does not say "Les Paul" anywhere), goldtop finish; production 1,000.*

■ MELODY MAKER

LES PAUL MELODY MAKER 2007–08 *Single-cut, narrow headstock, one P-90*
- ■ Unbound rosewood fingerboard, dot markers, narrow headstock, decal logo, no "Les Paul" on headstock.
- ■ Unbound slab mahogany body, single cutaway; satin yellow, satin ebony, satin cherry.
- ■ One black dog-eared P-90 pickup with non-adjustable polepieces.
- ■ One volume, one tone.
- ■ No pickguard.
- ■ Six-saddle bridge plus separate bar tailpiece (earliest with wrap-over bar bridge/tailpiece).

Gibson's earliest publicity for the original Melody Maker model, which was launched in 1959, called it a "Les Paul Melody Maker", but otherwise there is no connection. This modern model, which reactivated the long name, was shortlived.

■ MENACE

MENACE 2006–08 *Fist inlay on fingerboard*
- ■ Unbound ebony fingerboard, brass fist inlay at fifth fret (no other markers), brass frets, custom multi-colour logo on headstock.
- ■ Carved top with 'tribal' routs, mahogany back; black.
- ■ Two coverless humbucker pickups with brass stud poles.
- ■ Four controls (two volume, two tone) plus three-way selector.
- ■ No pickguard.
- ■ Six-saddle bridge plus separate bar tailpiece.
- ■ Black-plated hardware.

■ MICHAEL BLOOMFIELD

MICHAEL BLOOMFIELD 1959 STANDARD 2009 *Grover tuners, two holes in top.*
Similar to **Standard 59 reissue**, except:
- ■ Grover Rotomatic tuners with metal kidney-bean buttons; "Les Paul" on truss-rod cover.
- ■ Two holes in top below bridge; 'Bloomfield burst' finish.
- ■ Neck-pickup volume control with metal cap.

Custom Shop; production: 100 custom aged; 200 with Vintage Original Spec aging treatment.

■ MICK JONES

MICK JONES CUSTOM 2008–current *Two mini switches between standard control knobs.*
Similar to **Custom third version**, except:
- ■ Aged ebony.
- ■ Schaller tuners.
- ■ Schaller strap-lock buttons, black metal jackplate.
- ■ Two coverless humbucker pickups.
- ■ Two mini switches for pickup on/off selection.

Custom Shop.

■ MILLER GENUINE

MILLER GENUINE 1992 *Similar to* **Studio**, *except Miller Genuine beer logo. Custom Shop; production approximately 20.*

MURPHY-AGED

Vintage aging treatment by Tom Murphy, Gibson employee who finished the first "R9" reissues in 1993 and later became an independent contractor specialising in aged finishing. See specific models.

■ MUSIC RISING

MUSIC RISING 2005 *Hand-painted multi-colour top.*
Similar to **Standard second version**, except:
- ■ Top hand-painted in Mardi Gras colours.
- ■ All plastic parts replaced by wood parts.
- ■ Music Rising logo on pickguard.

Custom Shop; production less than 300, sold at Guitar Center retail stores.

■ NEAL SCHON

NEAL SCHON 2005–08 *Double-slashed-diamond fingerboard markers.*
- ■ Bound ebony fingerboard, pearl diamond markers with double slash, six-piece slashed-diamond headstock inlay, locking nut, sculpted heel.
- ■ Multiple-bound carved-top mahogany body; green gold, alpine white, or ebony.
- ■ One coverless poleless humbucker pickup (neck) and one covered humbucker (bridge).
- ■ Four controls (two tone, two volume), two mini-switches (on/off for neck pickup, octave effect), three-way selector.
- ■ Floyd Rose vibrato.
- ■ *Custom Shop.*

■ NORTH STAR

NORTH STAR 1978 *Star inlay on headstock.*
Similar to **Standard second version**, except:
- ■ Multi-layer (Custom-style) body binding.
- ■ "North Star" on truss-rod cover, star inlaid in headstock.

■ OLD HICKORY

OLD HICKORY 1998 *"Old Hickory" on fingerboard*
- ■ Bound hickory fingerboard; "Old Hickory" fingerboard inlay; image of President Andrew Jackson ("Old Hickory") on headstock.
- ■ Bound, carved-top tulip poplar body from tree felled by 1998 tornado in Nashville.
- ■ Two metal-cover humbucker pickups.

Custom Shop.

ORVILLE

The forename of the founder of the American company was used by Gibson on a line of Japanese-made guitars that officially 'copied' Gibson's most famous designs, launched in 1988 and lasting until about 1998 (when Gibson began making some Epiphone-branded guitars in Japan). While the cheaper models carried the Orville logo, the higher-priced versions were branded Orville By Gibson. The 'By Gibsons' bore the Les Paul logo when appropriate, and models included Custom, Standard, and Junior, equipped with US-made Gibson pickups. Both Orville brands were high-quality accurate repros sold only on the Japanese market.

PERSONAL

PERSONAL 1969–72 *Two angled pickups, block markers, gold hardware.*

- Bound ebony fingerboard, block markers; split-diamond inlay on headstock.
- Bound carved-top body; brown.
- Two angled round-end plastic-cover low-impedance humbucker pickups.
- Five controls (volume, bass, treble, Decade, microphone volume) plus three-way selector, all on body; phase slide switch and tone selector on small panel. Microphone input socket on upper left side of body.
- Black laminated plastic pickguard.
- Gold-plated hardware.

Requires special cord with built-in impedance-matching transformer to match regular amplification impedance. Production: 1971 95; 1972 49; 1973 2. Figures not available for 1969 and 1970.

PETE TOWNSHEND

PETE TOWNSHEND DELUXE #9 2006 *"9" on top.*
Similar to 70s-period **Deluxe**, except:

- "9" decal on top below bridge; heritage cherry sunburst.
- Two metal-cover mini-humbuckers and one coverless DiMarzio humbucker.
- Four knobs (three volume, one master tone), three-way selector, two mini toggles (phase and tap for DiMarzio).

Numbered with PETE prefix. Custom Shop; production 75.

PETE TOWNSHEND DELUXE #1 2006 *Similar to* **Pete Townshend Deluxe #9**, *except numeral "1" decal on front; wine red. Custom Shop.*

PETE TOWNSHEND DELUXE GOLDTOP 2006 *Similar to* **Pete Townshend Deluxe #9**, *except numeral "3" decal on front; gold top. Custom Shop.*

PETER FRAMPTON

PETER FRAMPTON 'CUSTOM' 2000–current *Three coverless humbucker pickups, "Peter Frampton" on 12th fret marker.*
Similar to **Custom third version**, except:

- "Peter Frampton" on 12th fret marker.
- Three coverless humbucker pickups.
- Custom-wired selector switch (no visible difference).
- No pickguard.
- Strap-locking endpin.

Numbered with PF prefix. Custom Shop.

PETER FRAMPTON 'SPECIAL' 2006 *Three plastic-cover six-polepiece single-coil pickups, "Peter Frampton" on truss-rod cover.*

- Bound ebony fingerboard, dot markers, "Peter Frampton" on truss-rod cover, Grover tuners with gold-plated kidney-bean buttons, thin neck profile.
- Unbound slab all-mahogany body; sunburst.
- Three plastic-cover six-polepiece single-coil pickups.
- Four controls (three volume, one tone) plus three-way selector.
- Red tortoiseshell plastic pickguard.
- Six-saddle bridge plus separate bar tailpiece.
- Strap-locking endpin.

Numbered with PF prefix. Custom Shop.

PRO DELUXE

PRO DELUXE 1976–82 *Bound ebony fingerboard with crown markers.*

- Bound ebony fingerboard, crown markers; "Les Paul Model" on headstock; "Pro" on truss-rod cover.
- Bound carved-top body; sunbursts or colours.
- Two plastic-cover six-polepiece single-coil pickups.
- Four controls (two volume, two tone) plus three-way selector.
- Cream plastic pickguard.
- Six-saddle bridge plus separate bar tailpiece.

PRO SHOWCASE EDITION

PRO SHOWCASE EDITION 1988 *Goldtop. Custom Shop; production 250.*

PROFESSIONAL

PROFESSIONAL 1969–71 *Two angled pickups, crown markers, nickel-plated hardware.*

- Bound rosewood fingerboard, crown markers.
- Bound carved-top body; brown.
- Two angled round-end plastic-cover low-impedance humbucker pickups.
- Four controls (volume, bass, treble, Decade) plus three-way selector, all on body; phase slide switch and tone selector on small panel.
- Black laminated plastic pickguard.

Requires special cord with built-in impedance-matching transformer to match normal amplification impedance. Production: 1971 116; 1973 2; 1977 11; 1978 1,399 (probably a misprint); 1979 6. Figures not available for 1969 and 1970.

PUSH TONE

PUSH TONE 2008 *Maple crown fingerboard markers*
Similar to **Standard second version**, except:

- Unbound ebony fingerboard, maple crown markers, metal truss-rod cover, locking grover tuners.

- Antique natural.
- Interchangeable pickups (comes with two Burstbuckers and two P-94s), no pickup frames.

Guitar Of The Month model 2008; Custom Shop; production 1,000.

RECORDING

RECORDING first version 1971–77 *"Les Paul Recording" on truss-rod cover; all controls on panel.*

- Bound rosewood fingerboard, block markers; split-diamond inlay on headstock; "Les Paul Recording" on truss-rod cover.
- Bound carved-top body; sunburst, brown, or white.
- Two angled round-end plastic-cover low-impedance humbucker pickups.
- Four controls (volume, bass, treble, Decade) plus three-way selector, tone selector, phase slide switch, low/high impedance slide switch, and jack socket, all on laminated black plastic panel; built-in impedance-matching transformer.
- Black laminated plastic pickguard.
- Six-saddle bridge plus separate bar tailpiece.

Production: Kalamazoo-made: 1971 236; 1972 1,314; 1973 1,759; 1974 915; 1975 204; 1976 352. Figures not available for any Nashville production.

RECORDING second version 1977–79 *"Les Paul Recording" on truss-rod cover; selector by neck pickup.*

Similar to **Recording first version**, except:

- Sunburst, brown, white, or black.
- Bound ebony fingerboard.
- Four controls (volume, bass, treble, Decade) plus phase slide switch and tone selector, all on laminated black plastic panel; three-way selector on body; one jack socket on side of body for normal high-impedance output, plus second jack socket on body face for low-impedance output.

Production: Kalamazoo-made: 1977 362; 1978 180; 1979 78. Figures not available for any Nashville production.

RICHARD PETTY

RICHARD PETTY 2003 *Similar to* **Studio** *but with graphics related to stock-car driver Richard Petty on top and back, "The King" on fingerboard. Custom Shop; production 43.*

ROBOT

The Robot name describes an auto-tune system available on the models noted here. See also **Dark Fire** *entry.*

ROBOT LTD 2007–08 *White knob with LED light in neck tone control, metal tuner buttons, bound fingerboard. Some numbered with RG prefix.*

ROBOT STUDIO 2007–current *White knob with LED light in neck tone-control, metal tuner buttons, unbound fingerboard.*

SG/LES PAUL CUSTOM

SG/LES PAUL CUSTOM 1961–63 *Bevelled-edge two-cutaway body; three pickups.*

- Bound ebony fingerboard, block markers; split-diamond inlay on headstock; "Custom" on truss-rod cover.
- Bevelled-edge two-cutaway body; white only.
- Three metal-cover humbucker pickups.
- Four controls (two volume, two tone) plus three-way selector; jack socket on body face.
- White laminated plastic pickguard, plus small white plastic plate reading "Les Paul Custom".
- Six-saddle bridge plus separate sideways-action vibrato tailpiece.
- Gold-plated hardware.

Some examples with standard-action vibrato tailpieces, some of which have inlaid decorative block in body face masking holes intended for sideways-action vibrato unit.

Production: 1961 513 (includes some Les Paul Custom models); 1962 298; 1963 264 (includes some SG Custom models).

SG/LES PAUL CUSTOM reissue 1987–90, 1998–current *Reissue based on original version, but with six-saddle bridge plus separate bar tailpiece; optional Maestro vibrato (long cover but not side-pull). Also available (2006–current) with VOS Vintage Original Spec aging treatment.*

SG/LES PAUL CUSTOM 30th ANNIVERSARY 1991–92 *Anniversary model based on* **SG/Les Paul Custom Reissue** *but split-diamond inlay on headstock has "30th Anniversary" in bar and "1961, 1991" in diamond sections. Yellow finish. Custom Shop.*

SG/LES PAUL JUNIOR

SG/LES PAUL JUNIOR 1961–63 *Bevelled-edge two-cutaway body; one pickup.*

- Unbound rosewood fingerboard, dot markers; "Les Paul Junior" on headstock; plastic tuner buttons.
- Bevelled-edge two-cutaway body; cherry.
- One plastic-cover six-polepiece single-coil pickup.
- Two controls (volume, tone); jack socket on body face.
- Black laminated plastic pickguard.
- Wrap-over bar bridge/tailpiece; optional separate vibrato tailpiece.

Production: 1961 2,151 (includes some Les Paul Junior models); 1962 2,395; 1963 2,318 (includes some SG Junior models).

SG/LES PAUL SPECIAL

SG/LES PAUL SPECIAL 2000–03 *Based on 1961–63 SG Special, two black soapbar P-90 pickups, bound fingerboard, dot inlay.*

- Bound rosewood fingerboard, pearl dot inlays, pearl logo (does not say "Les Paul" on headstock or truss rod cover).
- Bevelled-edge two-cutaway body; faded cherry, classic white, or TV yellow.
- Two black plastic-covered single-coil pickups.
- Four controls (two volume, two tone) plus three-way selector; jack socket on body face.
- Black laminated plastic pickguard.

■ Wraparound bridge or Maestro vibrola.
Despite Gibson's name for this model, the 1961–63 version was never called or labelled "Les Paul". The model continued after 2003 as the more accurately named SG Special Reissue.

■ SG/LES PAUL STANDARD

SG/LES PAUL STANDARD 1961–63 *Bevelled-edge two-cutaway body; two humbucker pickups.*

- Bound rosewood fingerboard, crown markers; 'thistle'-style inlay on headstock; "Les Paul" on truss-rod cover; plastic tuner buttons.
- Bevelled-edge two-cutaway body; cherry.
- Two metal-cover humbucker pickups.
- Four controls (two volume, two tone) plus three-way selector; jack socket on body face.
- Black laminated plastic pickguard.
- Six-saddle bridge plus separate sideways-action vibrato tailpiece.

Some examples with standard-action vibrato tailpieces, some of which have inlaid decorative block in body face masking holes intended for sideways-action vibrato unit.
Some examples in white or sunburst.
Production: 1961 1,662; 1962 1,449; 1963 1,445 (includes some SG Standard models).

SG/LES PAUL STANDARD reissue 2000–current *Reissue based on original version but with optional Maestro vibrato (long cover but not side-pull); faded cherry, white, or TV yellow. Known by various names since 1986, including* 62 SG Standard, 61 SG Standard, *and* Les Paul/SG 61 Reissue *(1993–95), but the* **SG/Les Paul Standard reissue** *(2000–current) is the only one with "Les Paul" on the truss-rod cover. "Les Paul" was dropped from the model name in 2004, but the model continues in current production with "Les Paul" on the truss-rod cover. Aged versions available, known as* Custom Authentic *(2000–03),* VOS *Vintage Original Spec (2006–current). Custom Shop.*

■ SIGNATURE

SIGNATURE 1974–78 *Semi-acoustic with two f-holes and offset cutaways.*

- Bound rosewood fingerboard, crown markers; "Les Paul Signature" on headstock; plastic tuner buttons.
- Bound semi-acoustic thinline body with two f-holes and offset cutaways; gold or sunburst.
- Two rectangular plastic-cover low-impedance humbucker pickups.
- Two controls (volume, tone) plus three-position impedance rotary switch, two-way phase rotary switch, and three-way selector; one jack socket on side of body for normal high-impedance output, plus second jack socket on body face for low-impedance output; built-in impedance transformer.
- Cream plastic pickguard.
- Six-saddle bridge plus separate bar tailpiece.

Earliest examples with two round-end plastic-cover low-impedance humbucker pickups, and two side-mounted jack sockets.
Production: 1973 3; 1974 1046; 1975 118; 1976 150; 1977 123; 1978 20; 1979 3.

■ SILVER STREAK

SILVER STREAK 1982 *Similar to* **Standard second version**, *except dot markers, all silver finish.*

■ SLASH

SLASH 1997 *Slash 'snakepit' logo carved into top, snake inlay on fingerboard, cranberry finish. Custom Shop; production 50.*

SLASH LES PAUL STANDARD *See* **Slash Signature** *below.*

SLASH SIGNATURE 2004–current *Plain maple top, aged nickel-plated hardware, coverless Seymour Duncan humbuckers, Fishman Powerbridge pickup, three volume controls, one master tone, three-way pickup selector, three-way mini-toggle for bridge pickup; antique tobacco sunburst with dark walnut back; initial Pilot Run from Custom Shop, with Custom Authentic aging and numbered with SL prefix, followed by regular production version (known as* **USA Slash Les Paul Standard***) in limited run of 1,600.*

SLASH GOLDTOP 2008 *Coverless humbucking pickups, TonePro six-saddle bridge, vintage Kluson Deluxe-style tuners, Slash graphic with top hat on headstock (does not say "Les Paul"). Custom Shop; production 1,000.*

SLASH #1 STANDARD 2008 *Three-piece top, Seymour Duncan humbuckers; faded heritage cherry sunburst with* VOS *Vintage Original Spec aging treatment. Custom Shop.*

■ SM

SM 1980 *Dot markers, "SM" on truss-rod cover, coil tap.*

- Bound rosewood fingerboard, dot markers; "SM" on truss-rod cover.
- Multiple-bound carved-top body, silverburst.
- Two metal-cover humbucker pickups.
- Four controls (2 volume, 2 tone) plus selector and coil-tap switch
- Six-saddle bridge plus separate bar tailpiece.

■ SMARTWOOD

SMARTWOOD EXOTIC 1998–2002 *"Smart Wood" on truss-rod cover, thin body with carved top*
Similar to **The Paul**, except:

- Wood certified by Rainforest Alliance.
- Curupay fingerboard, dot markers, "Smart Wood" on truss-rod cover.
- Gold-plated hardware.
- Top cap of ambay guasu, banara, curupay, or peroba wood.
- Natural finish, optional 'SL' matte urethane finish.

SMARTWOOD STANDARD 1996–2000 *"Smart Wood" on truss-rod cover.*
Similar to **Standard second version**, except:

- Wood certified by Rainforest Alliance.
- Chechen fingerboard, pearl crown markers, "Smart Wood" on truss-rod cover.
- Gold-plated hardware.
- Natural finish.

SPECIAL SINGLE-CUTAWAY

SPECIAL SINGLE-CUTAWAY: ORIGINAL MODELS chronological order

SPECIAL single-cut 1955–58, 1972, 1998 *Slab single-cutaway body, two pickups.*
- Bound rosewood fingerboard (unbound on SL version 1998), dot markers (small blocks 1972); "Les Paul Special" on headstock; plastic tuner buttons.
- Unbound slab body; beige (SL urethane colours 1998 only).
- Two plastic-cover six-polepiece single-coil pickups.
- Four controls (two volume, two tone) plus three-way selector.
- Black laminated plastic pickguard.
- Wrap-over bar bridge/tailpiece.

Some early examples with brown plastic parts (knobs, pickguard, etc).
Production: 1955 373; 1956 1,345; 1957 1,452; 1958 958. Figures not available for later years.

SPECIAL SINGLE-CUTAWAY: OTHER MODELS alphabetical order

JUNIOR SPECIAL 1999–2005 *Similar to* **Special single-cut**, *except humbucker pickups (at first not visibly different from single-coils), six-saddle bridge with separate tailpiece, unbound fingerboard, half-size crown markers (dots from 2001), contoured back of body.*

JUNIOR SPECIAL HUM (or HB) 2001–08 *Similar to* **Special single-cut**, *except metal-cover humbucker pickups; six-saddle bridge with separate tailpiece; unbound fingerboard, contoured back of body.*

JUNIOR SPECIAL PLUS 2001–05 *Similar to* **Special single-cut**, *except figured maple top cap; metal-cover humbucker pickups; six-saddle bridge with separate tailpiece; selector switch on upper bass bout; unbound fingerboard; gold-plated hardware; trans amber or trans red.*

JUNIOR II 1989 *Similar to* **Special single-cut**, *except humbucker pickups (not visibly different from single-coils) and six-saddle bridge with separate tailpiece (renamed* **Special** *in 1989: see* **Special single-cut reissue**).

SPECIAL single-cut reissue 1989–current
Similar to **Special single-cut**, except:
- Metal tuner buttons (white plastic from 1998).
- Sunburst, cherry, yellow, or black (faded cherry or TV yellow from 1998).
- Pickups, although visually similar to originals, are actually humbuckers (single-coils from 1998).
- Six-saddle bridge plus separate bar tailpiece (wrap-over from 1998).

Originally and erroneously referred to in Gibson literature as Junior II. Also available (2006–current) with VOS Vintage Original Spec aging treatment.

SPECIAL SINGLE-CUTAWAY CENTENNIAL 1994 *Gold or TV yellow, four-digit serial number on tailpiece with first digit (1) in diamonds. Custom Shop; production no more than 101, promotional prototypes only.*

SPECIAL 55 1974, 1977–80 *Based on* **Special single-cut**: *earliest examples with wrap-over bar bridge/tailpiece; majority have six-saddle bridge plus separate bar tailpiece. Sunbursts or colours. Earlier examples have plastic tuner buttons.*
Production: Kalamazoo-made: 1974 1925; 1976 2; 1977 331; 1978 293; 1979 224. Figures not available for 1980 nor for any Nashville production.

SPECIAL 400 1985 *Based on* **Special single-cut**, *except one humbucker and two single-coil pickups; two knobs (master tone and master volume), three switches (on/off pickup selector), vibrato, most with ebony fingerboard.*

SPECIAL DOUBLE-CUTAWAY

SPECIAL DOUBLE-CUTAWAY: ORIGINAL MODELS chronological order

SPECIAL double-cut 1959–60, 1998 *Slab double-cutaway body, two pickups.*
- Bound rosewood fingerboard, dot markers; "Les Paul Special" on headstock; plastic tuner buttons.
- Unbound slab double-cutaway body; yellow or cherry.
- Two plastic-cover six-polepiece single-coil pickups.
- Four controls (two volume, two tone) plus three-way selector.
- Black laminated plastic pickguard.
- Wrap-over bar bridge/tailpiece.

Later '59–60 examples with neck pickup moved further down body, away from end of fingerboard, and selector moved next to bridge.
Model name changed to SG Special in 1960 when Les Paul logo removed.
Production: 1959 1,821; 1960 1,387 (includes some SG Special models). Figures not available for 1998.

SPECIAL double-cut three-quarter 1959–60 *Shorter 19-fret neck.*
Similar to **Special double-cut**, except:
- Shorter neck (with 19 frets) and scale-length (two inches less than normal).
- Cherry finish only.

Model name changed to SG Special three-quarter in 1960 when Les Paul logo removed.

Production: 1959 12; 1960 39 (includes some SG Special three-quarter models).

SPECIAL DOUBLE-CUTAWAY: OTHER MODELS alphabetical order

BOB MARLEY SPECIAL *See earlier* **Bob Marley** *entry.*

FADED DOUBLE CUTAWAY 2007–08 *Unbound fingerboard; worn cherry, worn yellow, or worn brown finish. Custom Shop.*

JUNIOR LITE 1999–2002 *Based on* **Special double-cut** *but with two 'stacked' humbucker pickups (not visibly different from single-coils), six-saddle bridge with separate tailpiece, unbound fingerboard, half-size crown markers, contoured back of body.*

SPECIAL DOUBLE-CUTAWAY CENTENNIAL 1994 *Heritage cherry finish. Custom Shop; production of no more than 101, four-digit serial number on tailpiece with first digit (1) in diamonds.*

SPECIAL DOUBLE CMT 1979 *Curly maple top. Custom Shop; production 133.*

SPECIAL 58 1976–85, 1998 *Based on* **Special double-cut** *but six-saddle bridge plus separate bar tailpiece; sunbursts or colours.*
Production: Kalamazoo-made: 1976 162; 1977 1,622; 1978 803; 1979 150. Figures not available for any Nashville production.

SPECIAL 60 double-cut reissue 1998–current *Similar to* **Special double-cut**, *except nickel-plated hardware; faded cherry or TV yellow finish (ebony, cinnamon, or natural from 2001). Also available (2006–current) with VOS Vintage Original Spec aging treatment. Custom Shop.*

STANDARD LITE *This model has the Special double-cut's body shape but with a carved-top; see* **Standard: Other Models**.

■ SPIDER-MAN

SPIDER-MAN LES PAUL 2002 *Spider-man graphic on body, crown fingerboard markers, signed by Stan Lee and Les Paul. Custom Shop; production 15.*

■ SPOTLIGHT

SPOTLIGHT SPECIAL 1983 *Contrasting wood stripe down centre of body.*
- Bound rosewood fingerboard, crown markers; "Les Paul Model" on headstock; "Custom Shop Edition" logo on rear of headstock; plastic tuner buttons (natural versions) or metal tuner buttons (sunburst versions).
- Bound carved-top body with darker contrasting wood stripe down centre; natural (ANT) or sunburst (ASB).
- Two metal-cover humbucker pickups.
- Four controls (two volume, two tone) plus three-way selector.
- Usually no pickguard.
- Six-saddle bridge plus separate bar tailpiece.
- Gold-plated hardware.

Serial number consists of "83" plus three-figure number, on back of headstock, instead of regular serial.
Custom Shop marking; production around 200 (records indicate 211).

SPOTLIGHT FLAME 2008 *Similar to* **Spotlight Special**, *except: brown binding on top and fingerboard, does not say "Les Paul" on headstock or truss-rod cover, "Gibson Custom" logo on rear of headstock, inked serial number prefixed with CS.*

■ STANDARD

STANDARD: ORIGINAL MODELS chronological order

STANDARD first version 1958–60 Similar to **Goldtop fourth version**, except:
- Body with sunburst top.

Production: 1958 434 (includes some Goldtop models); 1959 643; 1960 635.
For 50s/60s Goldtop model, sometimes referred to as Standard, see earlier **Goldtop** *entry.*
For early-60s SG-shaped version, see earlier **SG/Les Paul Standard** *entry.*

STANDARD second version 1976–2007 (continues as **2008 Standard**, see below, and **Traditional**, see later entry)
"Standard" on truss-rod cover.
- Bound rosewood fingerboard, optional '50s fat or '60s thin neck-profile from 2002, crown markers; "Les Paul Model" on headstock; "Standard" on truss-rod cover.
- Bound carved-top body; sunbursts, natural, or colours.
- Two metal-cover humbucker pickups.
- Four controls (two volume, two tone) plus three-way selector.
- Cream plastic pickguard.
- Six-saddle bridge plus separate bar tailpiece.
- Chrome-plated hardware (gold optional in many years, nickel from 2002).

Also: natural-finish version with gold-plated hardware (1991–92); antique vintage sunburst finish with '50s neck, 2007 Guitar Of The Week model, production 400.
Production: Kalamazoo-made: 1975 1; 1976 24; 1977 586; 1978 5,947; 1979 1,054. Figures not available for large Nashville production started in 70s and continuing to current.
For 80s Standard-80 models, see earlier **Heritage** *entry.*
Model changed in 2008 to **2008 Standard** *(see below) and* **Traditional** *(see later entry).*

2008 STANDARD 2008–current *Locking tuners, extended strap buttons.*
Similar to **Standard second version**, except:
- Asymmetrical neck profile, locking tuners with metal tuner buttons.
- Early examples have extended strap buttons.

STANDARD: 58 REISSUE MODELS
chronological order

STANDARD 58 PLAINTOP reissue 1994–99, 2003–current. *Similar to* Standard 58 reissue *except plain (un-figured) maple top. Aged versions available, known as* Custom Authentic *(2003–05) and* VOS *Vintage Original Spec (2006–current). Custom Shop.*

STANDARD 58 reissue 1996–99, 2001–current *Based on* **Standard first version** *from 1958 period, with figured maple top (but less figure than 59 reissues). Over the years, more 'accurate' features, eg longer neck tenon, smaller headstock. "R8" stamped in control cavity. Cherry sunburst finish; then vintage red or butterscotch finish; butterscotch only from 2001. Known by various names through the years, including* Standard 58 Figuredtop. *Aged version available, known as* Custom Authentic *(2002). Custom Shop.*

STANDARD 58 CHAMBERED VOS 2007–08 *Similar to* **Standard 58 reissue** *except 'chambered' semi-hollow body (lighter weight but no visible difference), Vintage Original Spec aging treatment. Custom Shop.*

STANDARD 58 50th ANNIVERSARY 2007–08 *Similar to* **Standard 58 reissue** *except 50th Anniversary banner on pickguard, cherry sunburst; aged by Tom Murphy. Custom Shop; production 200.*

STANDARD: 59 REISSUE MODELS
chronological order

STRINGS & THINGS reissue 1975–78 *Reissue based on 1959-period original; special order by Strings & Things store in Memphis, TN; production 28 (four of which destroyed).*

JIMMY WALLACE reissue 1978–97 *Reissue based on 1959-period original; special order by Arnold & Morgan store in Dallas, TX (1978–81), then by Sound Southwest store in Sunnyvale, TX; "Jimmy Wallace" on truss-rod cover.*

GUITAR TRADER reissue 1982–84 *Reissue based on 1959-period original; special order by Guitar Trader store in Redbank, NJ; serial number begins with 9, except for a few beginning with 0 (with thinner 1960-style neck); production around 53.*

LEO'S reissue 1982–84 *Reissue based on 1959-period original; special order by Leo's music store in Oakland, CA; serial number begins with L.*

STANDARD 59 reissue 1983–current *Based on* **Standard first version** *from 1959 period, with figured top and relatively 'fat' neck profile. Over the years, more 'accurate' features, eg longer neck tenon, smaller headstock. "R9" stamped in control cavity from 1993. Known by various names through the years, including* Standard Reissue *(1983–90),* Les Paul Reissue *(1983–93),* Standard 59 Flametop *(1991–99),* Standard 59 Figuredtop *(2000–02). Aged versions available, known as* Aged *(1999–2003),* Custom Authentic *(2004–05), and* VOS *Vintage Original Spec (2006–current). Also 50th Anniversary version (2009): see* 50th Anniversary 1959 Standard. *Custom Shop.*

STANDARD 59 PLAINTOP reissue 1999–2000 *Similar to* **Standard 59 reissue** *except plain (un-figured) maple top. Custom Shop.*

STANDARD 59 EXOTIC WOOD 2008–current *Similar to* **Standard 59 reissue** *except oak top/korina back and other wood combinations; natural finish. Custom Shop.*

STANDARD 59 50th ANNIVERSARY 2009 *Similar to* **Standard 59 reissue** *except heritage cherry burst or heritage dark burst. Custom Shop; production 500.*

STANDARD: 60 REISSUE MODELS
chronological order

STANDARD 60 reissue 1991–current *Reissue based on* **Standard first version** *from 1960 period, with figured top and relatively 'slimmer' neck profile. Over the years, more 'accurate features', eg longer neck tenon, smaller headstock. "R0" stamped in control cavity from 1993. Known by various names through the years, including* Standard 60 Flametop *(1991–99) and* Standard 60 Figuredtop *(2000–02). Aged versions available, known as* Custom Authentic *(2004–05) and* VOS *Vintage Original Spec (2006–current). Custom Shop.*

STANDARD 60 PLAINTOP reissue 2002 *Similar to* **Standard 60 reissue** *except plain (un-figured) maple top. Custom Shop; production 5, made for Guitar Center (US dealer).*

STANDARD: OTHER MODELS
alphabetical order

CUSTOM SHOP STANDARD 1997–2005 *Similar to* **Standard second version**, *except coverless pickups (one with zebra-coil, one with black-coil), vintage-style inked serial number, with first digit corresponding to year of manufacture (as with Les Paul Classic). Custom Shop.*

DUANE ALLMAN *See earlier* **Duane Allman** *entry.*

GARY MOORE *See earlier* **Gary Moore** *entry.*

GARY ROSSINGTON *See earlier* **Gary Rossington** *entry.*

KEITH RICHARDS STANDARD *See earlier* **Keith Richards** *entry.*

JIMMY PAGE *See earlier* **Jimmy Page** *entry.*

JOE PERRY *See earlier* **Joe Perry** *entry.*

MICHAEL BLOOMFIELD 1959 REISSUE *See earlier* **Michael Bloomfield** *entry.*

SLASH STANDARD *See earlier* **Slash** *entry.*

STANDARD BIRDSEYE 1993–96 *Similar to* **Standard second version**, *except special figured maple top.*

STANDARD CENTENNIAL 1994 *Similar to* **Standard second version**, *except brown sunburst, four-digit serial number on tailpiece, first digit (1) in diamonds. Custom Shop.*

STANDARD CMT 1986–89 *Similar to* **Standard 59 reissue** *except wide binding in cutaway, metal jack-socket plate. CMT stands for curly maple top.*

STANDARD DOUBLE-CUT PLUS *See earlier* **DC Standard** *entry.*

STANDARD DOUBLE-CUT W/ P-90s 2003–05 *Two plastic-covered 'soapbar' single-coil pickups.*

STANDARD FADED 2007–08 *Coverless zebra-coil humbuckers, no "Les Paul Model" on headstock, 50s neck; satin heritage cherry sunburst, tobacco sunburst, or honey burst. Custom Shop.*

STANDARD KORINA QUILT 2001 *Quilt maple top, korina back and neck. Custom Shop.*

STANDARD LITE 1999–2000 *Unbound double-cutaway carved-top body, crown markers, gold-plated hardware.*
- Unbound rosewood fingerboard, three-quarter-size crown markers; 24 3/4-inch scale-length; standard Gibson headstock shape.
- Unbound carved-top body with shape of **Special double-cut**; maple top cap; sunbursts or colours.
- Two metal-cover humbucker pickups.
- Two knobs (tone, volume) plus selector switch
- Wrap-over tailpiece.
- Gold-plated hardware.

For a similar guitar with chrome-plated hardware and dot markers, see **DC Studio**.

STANDARD MAHOGANY 1993 *Similar to* **Standard second version**, *except solid mahogany body (no top cap), plastic-covered single-coil pickups.*

STANDARD P-100 1989 *Two P-100 stacked humbucker pickups with 'soapbar' covers; gold top. Custom Shop.*

STANDARD PLUS 1995–99 *Similar to* **Standard second version**, *except figured maple top.*

STANDARD PREMIUM PLUS 2007 *Highly figured top.*

STANDARD RAW POWER 2000–01 *Similar to* **Standard second version**, *except plain top, chrome-plated hardware, natural satin finish.*

STANDARD SHOWCASE EDITION 1988 *Similar to* **Standard second version**, *except black-cover poleless EMG pickups, silverburst.*

STANDARD SILVERBURST 2008–09 *Silverburst finish, made for Sweetwater (US dealer).*

STANDARD SPECIAL 1983 *Similar to* **Standard second version**, *except ebony fingerboard, pearl inlay, gold-plated hardware, cardinal red finish.*

STANDARD TIE DYE 1996, 2002 *Similar to* **Standard second version**, *except simulated tie-dye top finish (each instrument unique); 1996 production around 100.*

STANDARD UN-BURST 2007 *Natural finish, double-white pickup coils.*
Similar to **Standard second version**, except:
- Natural finish.
- Two coverless DiMarzio humbuckers with double-white coils.

Guitar Of The Week model 2007, production 400.

STANDARD 82 1982 *Reissue made in Kalamazoo, "Standard 82" on truss-rod cover.*

STANDARD 83 1983 *PAF Reissue pickups, pearl crown markers, nickel-plated hardware, natural and sunbursts.*

WARREN HAYNES *See later* **Warren Haynes** *entry.*

STARS AND STRIPES

STARS AND STRIPES 2001–08 *US flag in metallic finish on top, '60s neck profile, pearl crown markers. Custom Shop.*

STEVE JONES

STEVE JONES CUSTOM 2008–current *Two girlie decals on top.*
Similar to **Custom third version**, except:
- Carved maple top, decals of girl sitting on vinyl LP and girl playing uke; white finish aged to ivory.
- Two coverless humbucker pickups.
- Late-'60s style 'witch hat' knobs.
- Aged hardware.

Custom Shop.

STINGER SERIES

STINGER SERIES 2003 *Custom-ordered by Music Machine retailer, similar to 1954 and 1956–60 reissues except for: back of headstock painted black with 'stinger' point, additional serial number prefixed MM; various neck sizes and finish colours. Custom Shop.*

STUDIO

STUDIO: ORIGINAL MODEL

STUDIO 1983–current *"Studio" on truss-rod cover.*

- Unbound rosewood fingerboard (rosewood or ebony 1987–98, rosewood 1999–current), dot markers (crown markers 1990–98, three-quarter-size crown markers 1999–2000, full-size crown markers 2001–current); "Les Paul Model" on headstock; "Studio" on truss-rod cover.
- Unbound carved-top body; sunburst, natural, or colours.
- Two metal-cover humbucker pickups.
- Four controls (two volume, two tone) plus three-way selector.
- Cream or laminated black plastic pickguard.
- Six-saddle bridge plus separate bar tailpiece; optional bridge/vibrato unit.
- Optional gold-plated hardware (from 1986).

Also: version with P-90 pickups, white finish, gold-plated, 1997 only; Platinum version (2003–04) with 'monochrome' look, ebony fingerboard with no markers, silver-colour pickguard. Guitar Of The Week version with EMG pickups, satin ebony finish, 2007; production 400.

STUDIO: OTHER MODELS alphabetical order

SMARTWOOD STUDIO 2003–08 *Carved top, green 'leaf' on truss-rod cover*

- Unbound muirapiranga fingerboard, dot markers, green 'leaf' on truss-rod cover.
- Unbound carved-top of certified muirapiranga wood, mahogany back; natural.
- Two metal-cover humbucker pickups.
- Four controls (two volume, two tone) plus three-way selector.
- No pickguard.
- Gold-plated hardware.

STUDIO BARITONE 2004–05 *28-inch scale, unbound fingerboard, dot markers; sunrise orange, pewter metallic, or black.*

STUDIO BFG 2007 *Guitar Of The Week, plastic-cover six-polepiece single-coil pickup (neck) and zebra-coil humbucker (bridge), three knobs, three-way selector, kill-switch toggle; ebony; production 400.*

STUDIO CUSTOM 1984–85 *Similar to* **Studio**, *except gold-plated hardware.*

STUDIO FADED MAPLE TOP 2007–08 *Faded heritage cherry sunburst.*

STUDIO GEM 1996–97
Similar to **Studio**, except:

- Single-coil pickups with cream plastic covers.
- Gold-plated hardware.
- Rosewood fingerboard, crown markers.
- Gemstone finishes.

STUDIO GOTHIC 2000–01
Similar to **Studio**, except:

- Ebony fingerboard, moon-and-star marker at 12th fret.
- Black hardware.
- Flat black finish.

STUDIO MAHOGANY *See* **Vintage Mahogany** *entry.*

STUDIO PLUS 2001–05 *Similar to* **Studio**, *except figured top, translucent red or desert burst (brown) finish; gold-plated hardware.*

STUDIO PREMIUM PLUS 2006–08 *Figured maple top, gold-plated hardware, cream truss-rod cover, transparent finishes.*

STUDIO RAW POWER 2009–current *Unbound maple fingerboard, three-piece maple neck, dot inlays except for crown inlay at 12th fret, solid maple body, metal-covered humbuckers, chrome or gold-plated hardware.*

STUDIO STANDARD 1984–87 *Similar to* **Studio**, *except bound rosewood fingerboard, bound carved-top body.*

STUDIO SYNTHESIZER 1985 *Similar to* **Studio**, *except Roland 700 synthesizer system.*

SWAMP ASH STUDIO 2003–08 *Swamp ash body, no binding, rosewood fingerboard, dot markers, natural finish.*

VINTAGE MAHOGANY 2007–08 *Carved mahogany top, nickel-plated hardware, worn brown or worn cherry. Also known as* **Studio Mahogany**.

STUDIO LITE

STUDIO LITE first version 1988–90 *Unbound ebony fingerboard, dot markers.*

- Unbound ebony fingerboard, dot markers; 'thistle'-style inlay on headstock.
- Unbound carved-top thinner body with contoured back; sunbursts or colours.
- Two plastic-cover humbucker pickups.
- Two controls (volume, tone) plus three-way selector and mini-switch.
- No pickguard.
- Six-saddle bridge plus separate bar tailpiece; optional bridge/vibrato unit (1988–89).
- Black-plated or gold-plated hardware.

STUDIO LITE second version 1990–98 *Unbound ebony fingerboard, crown markers.*
Similar to **Studio Lite first version**, except:

- Crown markers.
- "Les Paul Model" on headstock.

■ Lightweight carved-top flat-back body.
■ Two coverless humbucker pickups.
■ Four controls (two volume, two tone) plus three-way selector.
Also version with three-piece figured maple top, amber or red finish (1991).

STUDIO LITE/MIII 1992–94
Similar to **Studio Lite second version**, except:
■ Two coverless humbuckers plus one central six-polepiece single-coil pickup.
■ Two controls (volume, tone) plus five-way selector and mini-switch.

■ SUPREME

SUPREME 2003–current *Globe on headstock.*
■ Bound ebony fingerboard, pearl split-block markers, headstock inlay of "Supreme" around globe; trans black, desert burst, trans amber, heritage cherry sunburst, root beer, autumn burst (Guitar Of The Week model 2007), goldtop (Guitar Of The Week model 2007).
■ Bound carved-top, chambered mahogany body covered entirely with curly maple veneer, no back coverplates.
■ Two metal-cover humbucker pickups.
■ Four controls (two volume, two tone) plus three-way selector.
■ No pickguard.
■ Six-saddle bridge plus separate bar tailpiece.
• Gold-plated hardware.
Also known as **Les Paul Figured**.
See also later **90th Anniversary** *entry.*

■ THE LES PAUL

THE LES PAUL 1976–79 *"The Les Paul" on truss-rod cover.*
■ Bound ebony fingerboard, block markers; split-diamond inlay on headstock; "The Les Paul" on truss-rod cover.
■ Bound carved-top body; natural or wine red.
■ Two metal-cover humbucker pickups.
■ Four controls (two volume, two tone) plus three-way selector.
■ Wooden pickguard.
■ Six-saddle bridge plus separate bar tailpiece.
■ Gold-plated hardware.
Some examples with fine-tuning tailpiece.
Most examples have carved wooden components (pickup surrounds, pickguard, knobs, etc) rather than plastic.
Production: 1976 33; 1977 10; 1979 11. Total not available for 1978.

■ THE PAUL

THE PAUL STANDARD 1978–81 *Thin carved walnut body.*
■ Unbound ebony fingerboard, dot markers, decal logo ('Firebrand' logo, routed but with no pearl inlay, from mid 1981).
■ Unbound single-cutaway walnut body; natural.
■ Two coverless humbucker pickups.
■ Four controls (two volume, two tone) plus three-way selector.
■ No pickguard.
■ Six-saddle bridge plus separate tailpiece.

THE PAUL DELUXE 1980–85 *Mahogany body, "Firebrand" on truss-rod cover, decal logo.*

THE PAUL II 1996 *Three-piece mahogany body.*

THE PAUL SL 1998 *Same as the Paul II except satin finish ('Sans Lacquer') but some with lacquer finish.*

THE PAUL SMARTWOOD EXOTIC 1998–2002 *Top cap of exotic wood, two knobs.*

■ TONY IOMMI

TONY IOMMI SIGNATURE LES PAUL SG 1998, 2001–05
Horizontal cross markers of sterling silver; does not say "Les Paul" anywhere.
■ Bound ebony fingerboard, 24 frets, horizontal cross markers of sterling silver.
■ Bevelled-edge two-cutaway body with pointed horns (SG); black.
■ Two metal-covered poleless humbucker pickups.
■ Four knobs (two volume, two tone) plus three-way selector.
■ Six-saddle bridge plus separate bar tailpiece.
Numbered with TI prefix.
There is no obvious reason why Gibson chose to include "Les Paul" in the name of this model as it has nothing to do with any Les Paul models.

■ TRADITIONAL

TRADITIONAL 2008–current *"Traditional" on truss-rod cover.*
Similar to **Standard second version**, except:
■ Single-ring tuner buttons, '50s rounded-neck profile, "Traditional" on truss-rod cover.
■ 'Plus' figured top, weight-relieved body, antiqued binding.
■ Low-profile 'speed' control knobs.
See also **Standard: Original Models**.

■ TV

TV single-cut 1955–58 *Slab single-cutaway body, one pickup, beige finish, "Les Paul TV Model" on headstock.*
■ Unbound rosewood fingerboard, dot markers; "Les Paul TV Model" on headstock; plastic tuner buttons.
■ Unbound slab body; beige.
■ One plastic-cover six-polepiece single-coil pickup.
■ Two controls (volume, tone).
■ Black or tortoiseshell plastic pickguard.
■ Wrap-over bar bridge/tailpiece.
A 'three-quarter' short-scale version of this model has been documented.
Production: 1954 5; 1955 230; 1956 511; 1957 552; 1958 429 (includes some TV double-cut models).

TV double-cut 1958–59 *Slab double-cutaway body, one pickup, yellow finish, "Les Paul TV Model" on headstock.*
■ Unbound rosewood fingerboard, dot markers; "Les Paul TV Model" on headstock; plastic tuner buttons.
■ Unbound slab double-cutaway body; yellow.

- One plastic-cover six-polepiece single-coil pickup.
- Two controls (volume, tone).
- Black or tortoiseshell plastic pickguard.
- Wrap-over bar bridge/tailpiece.

Name changed to SG TV in 1959 when Les Paul logo removed. Production: 1958 429 (includes some TV single-cut models); 1959 543 (includes some SG TV models).

ULTIMA

ULTIMA 1996–2000 *Abalone top border, fancy fingerboard inlay.*
- Bound ebony fingerboard, four optional inlay patterns: flame, tree of life, harp, butterfly; Custom Shop logo inlaid on headstock; pearl tuner buttons.
- Bound semi-hollow carved-top body with abalone pearl border; flamed maple top; natural, stains, or sunbursts.
- Two covered six-polepiece humbucker pickups.
- Four controls (two volumes, two tones) plus three-way selector.
- No pickguard.
- Six-saddle bridge plus separate bar tailpiece, optional trapeze tailpiece.
- Gold-plated hardware.

Custom Shop.

VINTAGE MAHOGANY

See earlier entry under **Studio**.

VIXEN

VIXEN 2006–08 *"Vixen" on truss-rod cover.*
- Unbound rosewood fingerboard, small diamond markers, "Les Paul Model" on headstock, decal logo.
- Unbound carved-top thin mahogany body with rib-cage scarf on back; opaque colours.
- Two covered humbucker pickups.
- Two controls (tone and volume) plus three-way selector.
- No pickguard.
- Wrap-over bar bridge/tailpiece.

VOODOO

VOODOO 2002–04 *Voodoo-doll inlay at fifth fret.*
- Unbound ebony fingerboard, voodoo-doll inlay at fifth fret, white-outline headstock logo.
- Unbound carved-top swamp ash body; 'juju' finish (black with red wood filler).
- Two coverless humbucker pickups with red and black coils.
- Four controls (two volume, two tone) plus three-way selector.
- No pickguard.
- Six-saddle bridge plus separate bar tailpiece.
- Black-plated hardware.

VOS

Vintage Original Spec – aging of finish and hardware with a chemical application.

WARREN HAYNES

WARREN HAYNES STANDARD 2006–current *Mini-switch between tone controls.*
Similar to **Standard 58 reissue**, except:
- Plain-top finish.
- Schaller extended strap buttons; faded 'Haynes' burst.
- Mini-switch between tone controls for pre-amp control.
- Tone Pro locking bridge.

Custom Shop.

XPL

DOUBLE-CUTAWAY XPL 1984–86 *Carved-top, double cutaway, headstock with six tuners on bass side.*
- Bound ebony fingerboard, dot markers, 'scimitar' headstock with six tuners on bass side, decal logo.
- Bound carved-top body, double-cutaway; heritage cherry sunburst or heritage dark sunburst.
- Two humbucker pickups.
- Four controls (two volume, two tone) plus three-way selector.
- Six-saddle bridge or Gibson/Kahler vibrato.

DOUBLE-CUTAWAY XPL/400 1984 *Two knobs and three mini-switches.*
Similar to **Double-Cutaway XPL**, except:
- One coverless humbucker pickup and two single-coil pickups.
- Two knobs (master tone and master volume/coil-tap) and three mini switches.

XPL 1984 *Similar to* **Standard second version**, *with regular single-cut Les Paul shape, except 'scimitar' headstock with six tuners on bass side.*

ZAKK WYLDE

ZAKK WYLDE BULLSEYE 1999–current *Bull's-eye finish.*
Based on **Custom second version**, except:
- Unfinished maple neck; engraved gold-plated truss-rod cover; Zakk Wylde decal on back of headstock
- Two plastic-covered poleless EMG pickups.
- Black/white bullseye (concentric circles) top finish; white finish on back of body and headstock.
- No pickguard.

Numbered with ZW prefix. Custom Shop.

ZAKK WYLDE CAMO BULLSEYE 2004–current *Camouflage bullseye, maple fingerboard. Custom Shop; first 25 labelled "Pilot Run", numbered with ZPW prefix.*

ZAKK WYLDE ROUGH TOP 1999–2000 *Rough maple top (very little sanding), crown markers, nickel-plated hardware, natural finish; numbered with ZW prefix. Custom Shop.*

3D

3D 2003–04 *Similar to* **Standard second version**, *except relief carving on top, executed with CNC router (diamond pattern or flame pattern).*

■ 20th ANNIVERSARY
See earlier entry in **Custom: Other Models**.

■ 25th ANNIVERSARY
See earlier entry in **Custom: Other Models**.

■ 25/50 ANNIVERSARY
25/50 ANNIVERSARY 1978–79 *"25 50" inlay on headstock.*
- Bound ebony fingerboard, split-block markers; "Les Paul 25 50" on headstock; "Les Paul Anniversary" on gold-plated metal truss-rod cover; brass nut; four-figure number on back of headstock in addition to normal serial number.
- Bound carved-top body; sunburst, natural, red, or black.
- Two metal-cover humbucker pickups.
- Four controls (two volume, two tone) plus three-way selector and mini-switch.
- Black laminated plastic pickguard.
- Six-saddle bridge plus separate bar tailpiece with six fine-tuning knobs.
- Gold-/chrome-plated hardware.

Production: 1978 1,106; 1979 2,305.

■ 30th ANNIVERSARY
See earlier entries in **Goldtop: Other Models**, **SG/Les Paul Custom**, *and* **Deluxe**.

■ 35th ANNIVERSARY
See earlier entry in **Custom: Other Models**.

■ 40th ANNIVERSARY
See earlier entry in **Goldtop: Other Models**.

■ 50th ANNIVERSARY
50th ANNIVERSARY CORVETTE 2003 *Les Paul Special double-cutaway body with scoop in top.*
- Ebony fingerboard with script "Corvette" inlay, pearl headstock logo.
- Double-cutaway slab body, scoop carved into top, 50th anniversary logo on top; 'Corvette 50th Anniversary red' finish.
- Two plastic-cover six-polepiece single-coil pickups.
- Two control knobs (one volume, one tone).
- Six-saddle bridge; strings anchor through body.

Custom Shop; production 50.

50th ANNIVERSARY KORINA TRIBUTE 2009 *Offset-V headstock shape.*
Similar to **Standard 59 reissue**, except:
- Korina neck, unbound fingerboard, dot markers, moulded plastic logo, offset-V headstock shape.
- Korina body.
- Three humbucker pickups.
- Four controls (three in line and one offset), slotted selector switch.

Custom Shop.
See also 50th Anniversary entries in earlier **Goldtop: Other Models** *and* **Standard: Reissue Models**.

■ 54 OXBLOOD
54 OXBLOOD 1997–2008 *Similar to* **Goldtop 54 reissue**, *except oxblood finish, coverless humbucker pickups. Custom Shop. See also earlier* **Jeff Beck** *entry.*

■ 60 CORVETTE
60 CORVETTE 1995–97 *Similar to* **Standard second version**, *except top scooped out to simulate 1960 Chevrolet Corvette car body, Corvette-related appointments, automotive colours. Custom Shop.*

■ 90th ANNIVERSARY
90th ANNIVERSARY SUPREME 2005 *Signed by Les Paul under final lacquer coat. Custom Shop; production 90.*

■ 2008 STANDARD
See entry in **Standard: Original Models**.

Dating Les Pauls

How to date Gibson Les Pauls
In this book we're dealing with a specific selection of guitars from the range of instruments produced by the Gibson company during more than 50 years. Gibson made surprisingly few changes during much of this time that will now help a Les Paul owner easily and accurately put a date to an instrument.

It's worth stressing that no single method provides foolproof and totally accurate dating. Gibson, like all mass-manufacturers of instruments, made numerous changes to production procedures, construction technicalities, and component styles. But many were introduced over a period of time rather than instantaneously. Often, Gibson would continue to use existing parts, sometimes in combination with revised methods or new features, creating a variety of 'transitional' guitars. Such instruments tend to cause confusion and blur the chronological picture. However, if you use the following information carefully you should be able to date most Gibson Les Pauls to a relatively narrow time slot.

Vintage verification

Instruments from Fender and other makers are often easier to date than those from Gibson, which show fewer obvious clues. Many of Gibson's pointers require direct comparison between two or more instruments, or involve technical measuring equipment or specialised knowledge of the construction and workings of the company's electric guitars. It's essential to have a keen, trained eye, plus a very good memory, as some of the data relating to the age of Les Pauls is complex and confusing.

Just as with Fender and other high-profile US-made guitars, many Gibson instruments occupy prime spots in the vintage market. Certain Les Pauls are among the most desirable of all and therefore reside at the very top of the big-money league. Other Les Paul models too command much interest and high values, and the year of manufacture has a great bearing on this. Sometimes a guitar's vintage can seem more important than the inherent quality and playability of an individual guitar. Conversely, there are other Les Pauls that have little appeal among players and collectors, mostly thanks to the low esteem in which a particular production period is held – and here, determining age can help you to know what to avoid. Or how to fly in the face of fashion. Your choice.

Specific changes made to various Les Pauls have been included in the relevant entries in the main reference listing, and those details provide an accurate timescale for individual models. But there are a number of more general indicators of age. Of course, these are only of use if they are original to the instrument concerned. With so many broad similarities between groups of Les Paul models, even the replacement of something as apparently innocent as a truss-rod cover can give the impression that one model is actually another, even on relatively recent guitars. As ever, please beware of modifications made to mislead.

In the info that follows, note that a 'c' in front of a date stands for circa, which means 'about'.

Gibson headstock logo

The Gibson brandname is proudly displayed on the headstock of all Les Pauls. The style and method of lettering has been modified in various small ways over the years, and these mods can be related to certain periods. While many are extremely minor and can be very hard to spot or determine accurately, some are less subtle and of more immediate help.

- From c1952 to c1968, the dot of the i in Gibson was not joined to the G, and the b and o were not continuously solid.
- From c1968, the i lost its dot and the b and o became continuously solid.
- In 1972, the dotted i appeared again, but then it came and went with confusing irregularity until c1981.
- From 1981, the o and n were linked at the top, and not at the bottom as usual. However, the usual style was soon reintroduced, and both versions have been used since.

Headstock angle

From 1965 to 1973, the 'tilt-back' angle of the headstock in relation to the neck was altered from the previously standardised 17 degrees to 14 degrees. In 1973, the angle of 17 degrees was reintroduced, and both have been employed since. Direct comparison between two instruments is necessary to determine the rather subtle difference of three degrees.

Headstock volute

A volute is a carved 'heel' situated at the transition point between the rear of the neck and the angled headstock. The extra timber of the volute was intended to provide reinforcement in this potentially weak area. Gibson introduced the feature c1970 and kept it until c1981.

Made In USA headstock logo

From 1970 to 1975, "Made In USA" was stamped into the rear of the headstock. A version of this logo on a decal (transfer) was applied from 1975 to 1977, but in 1977 Gibson reintroduced the stamping method and has continued this since that date.

Gibson pickup logo

Plastic-covered P-90 and metal-covered humbucker pickups bore the Gibson logo from c1970 to c1972.

Control knobs

Gibson has used four distinct types of control knob on the Les Paul models over the years, and these do help to indicate production periods, although certain versions have of course been reintroduced in more recent years. The dates shown below refer to the original periods of use.

- Speed Knob: Smooth-side barrel shape, internal numbers, clear/coloured all-plastic. First used c1952 to c1955.
- Bell Knob: Smooth-side bell shape, internal numbers, clear/coloured all-plastic. First used c1955 to c1960.
- Metal-Top Knob: Smooth-side larger bell shape, internal numbers, clear/coloured plastic with "Volume" or "Tone" inset on large metal top. First used c1960 to c1967.
- Witch-Hat Knob: Ribbed-side conical shape, numbered skirt, black plastic with "Volume" or "Tone" on small metal top. First used c1967 to c1975.

Control pot codes

Removing the control plate on the rear of a Les Paul's body will reveal the metal casings of the control potentiometers, usually called pots. Some American-made pot casings carry code numbers that, when translated, can provide a useful confirmation of the instrument's age – although bear in mind that the pots may have been changed since the guitar was made.

On pots used in Les Pauls from 1952 to 1995, the code consists of six or seven digits. The first three identify the manufacturer and can be ignored. The next one or two digits show the year: one shows the last digit of 195X; a pair indicates any year thereafter. The final two digits signify the week of the appropriate year.

In 1995, Gibson began using a new code consisting of a pair of alpha-numeric figures, followed by the numbers 440, followed by a hyphen and four final numbers. The first figure corresponds to the month (1 to 9 for January to September; letters X, Y and

Z for October, November, and December, respectively). The second figure corresponds to the last digit of the year.

Bridge

Gibson has used various types of bridges on Les Paul models since 1952. Some have been reintroduced, but the dates shown below refer to the original periods of use.

- Wrap-Under, aka Trapeze: Combination unit with two long rod 'anchors', as on the very first Les Paul Goldtops. First used 1952 to 1953.
- Wrap-Over, aka Stopbar: Stud-mounted successor to the above. First used 1953 to c1962.
- Ridged Wrap-Over: As the previous unit, but with a staggered, moulded ridge on the top. First used c1962 to c1971.
- Tune-O-Matic: A bridge with six saddles, individually adjustable for length. First used c1954 to c1961.
- Tune-O-Matic Retainer: As above, but with a bridge-saddle retaining wire. First used c1961 to c1971.
- Tune-O-Matic Nylon: As above, but with white nylon bridge saddles replacing the metal type of the other versions. First used c1961 to c1971.
- New Tune-O-Matic: A heavier-duty version with no bridge-saddle retaining wire. Introduced c1971 and still in use.
- Rectangular Tune-O-Matic: A large rectangular bridge (sometimes known as the Nashville Tune-O-Matic) with six long-travel metal saddles. First used c1971 to c1982.
- Nashville Wide-Travel Tune-O-Matic: Similar to earlier Tune-O-Matics but with wider adjustability for saddles. First used 1977.
- TP-6: Six fine-tuner adjustments at bridge. First used 1978.

SERIAL NUMBERS

Gibson has changed its system for serial-numbering of instruments several times. Logical and orderly sequences exist only during certain periods, and in those instances it's easy to give a guitar an accurate production date once the system is understood. However, the company has been guilty of using numbers that apparently have little basis in logic, often applied out of sequence or, worse still, duplicated once or more. Such numbers provide confusion and very little else, and they should be disregarded for dating purposes – except perhaps to confirm a broad period otherwise indicated by clues from construction styles and component types.

The serial-number systems

The earliest Les Paul Goldtops from **1952** had no serial numbers. As production increased, they were provided with a three-digit number stamped on the top edge of the headstock. However, in **1953**, Gibson started a serial-numbering system specifically for its new solidbody guitars.

At first, this consisted of a five-digit number, ink-stamped on to the rear of the headstock. The first digit was slightly apart from the other four and indicated the year of manufacture. In **1955**, Gibson's increased output required the addition of a sixth digit to some sequences, effectively in the 'second' position, between the 'date code' digit and the rest of the number. In both styles, the first digit always provides the date: 3 = 1953; 4 = 1954; 5 = 1955; 6 = 1956; 7 = 1957; 8 = 1958; 9 = 1959; 0 = 1960; 1 = 1961. For example:

3 0786 indicates 1953 (first digit 3)
010955 indicates 1960 (first digit 0)

During **1961**, inked-on numbering was replaced by a method using numbers physically stamped into the back of the headstock. At this time, Gibson introduced a new serialisation system for all instruments. The numbers were supposed to be allocated in a strict sequence, but this didn't happen in practice – and the fun started. During the **60s**, many serial numbers were duplicated on more than one instrument, not only twice but sometimes as many as six or seven times on different guitars.

Similar problems afflicted manufacture during the first five years of the **70s**, with numerous duplications of sequences that had already been used. Beginning in **1970**, Gibson stamped "MADE IN USA" on the back of the headstock, so 70s numbers can be isolated from 60s numbers by the presence of that stamp. It's difficult to provide a useful table of the numbers used during this 15-year period, from **1961 to 1975**, as it provides only an approximate guide while illustrating perfectly some of the duplicated permutations. But we've compiled our best information here for you (see table overleaf, on page 166).

In **1975**, Gibson at last replaced this haphazard system with a simpler scheme that ran for three years. Instead of stamping serials into the back of the headstock, Gibson made those from this series part of a decal (transfer) that also included the model name and "Made In USA". The scheme used eight digits, the first two of which formed a coded date prefix: 99 = 1975; 00 = 1976; 06 = 1977. For example:

00129986 indicates 1976 (first two digits 00)

In **1977**, Gibson reverted to stamping the serial number into the rear of the headstock and again changed the system. The number remained at eight digits (although some old-style six-digit numbers were in use at Kalamazoo until the end of the 70s for various special Les Paul models). With the new eight-digit scheme, the first and fifth numbers indicated the last two digits of the year of production. For example:

93291369 indicates 1991 (first digit 9 + fifth digit 1)
01933306 indicates 2003 (first digit 0 + fifth digit 3).

For **1994 only**, Gibson's Nashville plant (but not the Custom Division) changed the system to one in which the first two digits were always 94, to indicate the year of manufacture. In **1995**, Gibson returned to the system in which the first and fifth digits indicate the year. This system is successful and reliable and is still in operation at the time of writing.

In July **2005**, Gibson added a digit to the previous eight-digit system. Digits one and five still denote the year. For example:

029090389 indicates 2009 (first digit 0 + fifth digit 9)

Serial Numbers 1961–1975

Numbers	Approximate period
100 to 61,000s	1961–62
61,000s to 70,000s	1962–64
71,000s to 99,000s	1962–64
000,000s	1967, 1973–75
100,000s	1963–65, 1970–75
100,000s to 144,000s	1963–64, 1967
147,000s to 199,000s	1963–65
200,000s to 290,000s	1964–65, 1973–75
300,000s	1965–68, 1974–75
301,000s to 305,000s	1965
306,000s to 307,000s	1965, 1967
309,000s to 310,000s	1965, 1967
311,000s to 326,000s	1965, 1967
328,000s to 329,000s	1965
329,000s to 332,000s	1965, 1967–68
332,000s to 368,000s	1965–66
348,000s to 349,000s	1965–66
368,000s to 370,000s	1966–67
380,000s to 385,000s	1966
390,000s	1967
400,000s	1965–68, 1974–75
401,000s to 409,000s	1966
420,000s to 438,000s	1966
500,000s	1965–66, 1968–69, 1974–75
501,000s to 503,000s	1965
501,000s to 530,000s	1968
530,000s	1966
530,000s to 545,000s	1969
540,000s	1966
550,000s to 556,000s	1966
558,000s to 567,000s	1969
570,000s	1966
580,000s	1969
600,000s	1966–69, 1970–72, 1974–75
601,000s	1969
605,000s to 606,000s	1969
700,000s	1966–67, 1970–72
750,000s	1968–69
800,000s	1966–69, 1973–75
801,000s to 812,000s	1966, 1969
812,000s to 814,000s	1969
817,000s to 819,000s	1969
820,000s to 823,000s	1966
820,000s	1969
824,000s	1969
828,000s to 847,000s	1966, 1969
847,000s to 858,000s	1966
859,000s to 880,000s	1967
893,000s to 897,000s	1967
895,000s to 896,000s	1968
897,000s to 898,000s	1967
899,000s to 920,000s	1968
900,000s	1968, 1970–72
940,000s to 943,000s	1968
945,000s	1968
947,000s to 966,000s	1968
959,000s to 960,000s	1968
970,000s to 972,000s	1968
A + 6 digits	1973–75
B, C, D, E or F + 6 digits	1974–75

Modern reissues of 50s Les Paul models have a five-digit number with a space after the first digit, or a six-digit number. In either case, the first digit corresponds to the final digit of the year style being reissued and the second digit to the final digit of the year of manufacture. For example:

8 8411 indicates a 1958 reissue made in 2008 (first digit 8 + second digit 8)

Modern reissues of 60s Les Paul models have a six or seven-digit number. The first two digits correspond to the final two digits of the year of manufacture, and the final digit to the year style being reissued. For example:

0710348 indicates a 1968 reissue made in 2007 (last digit 8 + first two digits 07)

The **Les Paul Classic models** have a four, five, or six-digit vintage-style number. Four and five-digit numbers were used between 1989 and 1999, with the first digit corresponding to the final digit of the year of manufacture. For example:

9 612 indicates 1989 (first digit 9; four-digit numbers used 1989 only)
9 3031 indicates 1999 (first digit 9; five-digit number)

With Classic six-digit numbers, used from 2000 to 2008, the first and second digits correspond to the final digits of the year of manufacture. For example:

072983 indicates 2007 (first two digits 07)

Production models from the Custom Shop (as opposed to the Shop's reissues, signature models etc) have a serial number beginning with CS. The digit immediately after CS corresponds to the last digit of the year of manufacture. For example:

CS10229 indicates 2001 (first digit 1 after CS)

The various methods and systems of serial numbering explained here cover almost all Gibson Les Pauls issued between 1952 and 2009. Some individual models, for example special Custom Shop guitars and especially signature models, have a one-off style of numbering, and we've noted these, where we have data, in the earlier model directory.

On some older instruments made by Gibson, a separate stamped '2' can be seen, usually below the serial number, which indicates a factory second. This is an instrument officially identified at some point in its production as having some cosmetic defect, usually minor and often very hard to detect.

Model chronology

(*...) = also available earlier during year(s) shown

1952–53 **GOLDTOP first version**

1953–55 **GOLDTOP second version**

1954–57 **CUSTOM first version**
1954–58, 2008–current **JUNIOR single-cut**

1955–57 **GOLDTOP third version**
1955–58, 1972, 1998 **SPECIAL single-cut**
1955–58 **TV single-cut**

1956–58 **JUNIOR single-cut three-quarter**

1957–61 **CUSTOM second version**
1957–58 **GOLDTOP fourth version**

1958–61, 1997–98 **JUNIOR double-cut**
1958–61 **JUNIOR double-cut three-quarter**
1958–60 **STANDARD first version**
1958–59 **TV double-cut**

1959–60, 1998 **SPECIAL double-cut**
1959–60 **SPECIAL double-cut three-quarter**

1961–63 **SG/LES PAUL CUSTOM**
1961–63 **SG/LES PAUL JUNIOR**
1961–63 **SG/LES PAUL STANDARD**

1968–current **CUSTOM third version**
1968–69 **GOLDTOP fifth version**

1969–84, 1992–97, 1999–2008 **DELUXE**
1969–72 **PERSONAL**
1969–71 **PROFESSIONAL**

1970–71 **JUMBO**

1971–72 **GOLDTOP sixth version**
1971–77 **RECORDING first version**

1972–73 **CUSTOM 54 LTD EDITION**
1972, 1998 **SPECIAL single-cut** (* 55–58)

1974 **CUSTOM 20th ANNIVERSARY**
1974–78 **SIGNATURE**
1974, 1977–80 **SPECIAL 55**

1975–78 **STRING & THINGS reissue**

1976–82 **ARTISAN**
1976–82 **PRO DELUXE**
1976–85, 1998 **SPECIAL 58**
1976–2007 **STANDARD second version**
1976–79 **THE LES PAUL**

1977 **CUSTOM 25th ANNIVERSARY**
1977–79 **RECORDING second version**
1977–80 **SPECIAL 55** (* 74)

1978–97 **JIMMY WALLACE reissue**
1978 **NORTH STAR**
1978–81 **THE PAUL STANDARD**
1978–79 **25/50 ANNIVERSARY**

1979–81 **ARTIST**
1979 **KM**
1979 **SPECIAL DOUBLE CMT**

1980–82 **HERITAGE STANDARD 80**
1980–82 **HERITAGE STANDARD 80 ELITE**
1980 **K-II**
1980 **SM**
1980–85 T**HE PAUL DELUXE**

1981 **HERITAGE STANDARD 80 AWARD**
1981–82 **LP XRI**
1981–82 **LP XRII**

1982–83 **CUSTOM BLACK BEAUTY 82**
1982–83 **GOLDTOP 30th ANNIVERSARY**
1982–84 **GUITAR TRADER reissue**
1982–84 **LEO'S reissue**
1982 **LP XRIII**
1982 **SILVER STREAK**
1982 **STANDARD 82**

1983–90, 1993–current **GOLDTOP 57 reissue**
1983 **SPOTLIGHT SPECIAL**
1983–current **STANDARD 59 reissue**
1983 **STANDARD SPECIAL**
1983 **STANDARD 83**
1983–current **STUDIO**

1984–86 **DOUBLE-CUTAWAY XPL**
1984–86 **DOUBLE-CUTAWAY XPL/400**
1984–85 **STUDIO CUSTOM**
1984–87 **STUDIO STANDARD**
1984 **XPL**

1985 **SPECIAL 400**
1985 **STUDIO SYNTHESIZER**

1986–92 **JUNIOR 54 single-cut reissue**
1986–89 **STANDARD CMT**

1987–89 **CUSTOM LITE**
1987–95, 1998–current **JUNIOR 58 double-cut reissue**
1987–90, 1998–current **SG/LES PAUL CUSTOM reissue**

1988 **CUSTOM LITE SHOWCASE EDITION**
1988 **CUSTOM SHOWCASE EDITION**
1988 **PRO SHOWCASE EDITION**
1988 **STANDARD SHOWCASE EDITION**
1988–90 **STUDIO LITE first version**

1989 **JUNIOR II**
1989–current **SPECIAL single-cut reissue**
1989 **STANDARD P-100**
1989–90 **35th ANNIVERSARY**

1990–2008 **CLASSIC**
1990–current **GOLDTOP 56 reissue**
1990–98 **STUDIO LITE second version**

1991–92 **CLASSIC/MIII**
1991–current **CUSTOM 54 reissue**
1991–current **CUSTOM 57 two-pickup reissue**
1991–current **CUSTOM 57 three-pickup reissue**
1991–96 **CUSTOM PLUS**
1991–92 **CUSTOM/400**
1991 **DELUXE HALL OF FAME EDITION**
1991–92 **SG/LES PAUL CUSTOM 30th ANNIVERSARY**
1991–current **STANDARD 60 reissue**

1992 **CLASSIC CELEBRITY**
1992–95, 1999–2000 **CLASSIC PLUS**
1992–97, 1999–2008 **DELUXE** (* 69–84)
1992 **MILLER GENUINE**
1992–94 **STUDIO LITE/MIII**
1992–93 **40th ANNIVERSARY GOLDTOP**

1993 **CLASSIC BIRDSEYE**
1993 **CLASSIC PREMIUM BIRDSEYE**
1993–97 **CLASSIC PREMIUM PLUS**
1993–current **GOLDTOP 57 reissue** (* 83–90)
1993–96 **STANDARD BIRDSEYE**
1993 **STANDARD MAHOGANY**

1994 **CLASSIC CENTENNIAL**
1994 **CUSTOM 57 CENTENNIAL three-pickup reissue**
1994 **SPECIAL DOUBLE-CUTAWAY CENTENNIAL**
1994 **SPECIAL SINGLE-CUTAWAY CENTENNIAL**
1994 **STANDARD CENTENNIAL**
1994–99, 2003–current **STANDARD 58 PLAINTOP reissue**

1995–97 **ELITE DIAMOND SPARKLE**
1995–98 **FLORENTINE PLUS**
1995–98 **FLORENTINE STANDARD**
1995–99 **JIMMY PAGE Standard first version**
1995–99 **STANDARD PLUS**

1995–97 **60 CORVETTE**

1996–98 **CATALINA**
1996–2000 **ELEGANT**
1996–2000 **JOE PERRY**
1996 **KORINA**
1996–2000 **SMARTWOOD STANDARD**
1996, 2002 **STANDARD TIE DYE**
1996–99, 2001–current **STANDARD 58 reissue**
1996–97 **STUDIO GEM**
1996 **THE PAUL II**
1996–2000 **ULTIMA**

1997–2000 **ACE FREHLEY**
1997–2005 **CUSTOM SHOP STANDARD**
1997–98 **DC PRO**
1997–98, 2006–08 **DC STUDIO**
1997 **ELEGANT DOUBLE QUILT**
1997–98, 2001–05 **ELEGANT QUILT**
1997 **ELEGANT SUPER DOUBLE QUILT**
1997–current **GOLDTOP 54 reissue**
1997 **GOLDTOP 57 MARY FORD**
1997–98 **JUNIOR double-cut** (* 58–61)
1997 **SLASH**
1997–2008 **54 OXBLOOD**

1998 **CLASSIC QUILT TOP**
1998–2007 **DC STANDARD**
1998–current **JUNIOR 57 single-cut reissue**
1998–current **JUNIOR 58 double-cut reissue** (* 87–95)
1998 **MAHOGANY CUSTOM**
1998 **OLD HICKORY**
1998–current **SG/LES PAUL CUSTOM reissue** (* 87–90)
1998–2002 **SMARTWOOD EXOTIC**
1998 **SPECIAL single-cut** (* 55–58, 72)
1998 **SPECIAL double-cut**
1998 **SPECIAL 58** (* 76–85)
1998–current **SPECIAL 60 double-cut reissue**
1998 **THE PAUL SL**
1998–2002 **THE PAUL SMARTWOOD EXOTIC**
1998, 2001–05 **TONY IOMMI LES PAUL SG**

1999–2000 **CLASSIC PLUS** (* 92–95)
1999–2001 **DALE EARNHARDT**
1999–2008 **DELUXE** (* 69–84, 92–97)
1999–2005 **GOLDTOP 52 reissue**
1999–2002 **JUNIOR LITE**
1999–2005 **JUNIOR SPECIAL**
1999–2000 **STANDARD LITE**
1999–2000 **STANDARD 59 PLAINTOP reissue**
1999–current **ZAKK WYLDE BULLSEYE**
1999–2000 **ZAKK WYLDE ROUGH TOP**

2000–07 **CLASSIC MAHOGANY**
2000–current **CUSTOM 68 FIGUREDTOP**
2000–01 **DALE EARNHARDT: THE INTIMIDATOR**
2000–current **GARY MOORE**
2000–current **GOLDTOP 57 DARKBACK reissue**
2000–03 **JIM BEAM**
2000–current **PETER FRAMPTON 'CUSTOM'**
2000–03 **SG/LES PAUL SPECIAL**
2000–current **SG/LES PAUL STANDARD reissue**
2000–01 **STANDARD RAW POWER**
2000–01 **STUDIO GOTHIC**
2000 **30th ANNIVERSARY DELUXE**

2001–05 **ACOUSTIC**
2001–08 **CLASS 5**
2001 **DALE EARNHARDT JR.**
2001 **DICKEY BETTS 57 GOLDTOP**
2001–05 **ELEGANT QUILT** (* 97–98)
2001–current **GOLDTOP 57 REISSUE AGED**
2001–08 **JUNIOR SPECIAL HUM/HB**
2001–05 **JUNIOR SPECIAL PLUS**
2001–current **SG/LES PAUL STANDARD reissue**
2001 **STANDARD KORINA QUILT**
2001–08 **STARS AND STRIPES**
2001–05 **STUDIO PLUS**
2001–05 **TONY IOMMI LES PAUL SG** (* 98)

2002–04 **BOB MARLEY SPECIAL**
2002 **BUDWEISER**
2002–03 **DICKEY BETTS 57 REDTOP**
2002 **GARY ROSSINGTON**
2002 **SPIDER-MAN LES PAUL**
2002 **STANDARD TIE DYE** (* 96)
2002 **STANDARD 60 PLAINTOP reissue**
2002–04 **VOODOO**

2003–05 **CLASSIC DC**
2003 **CRAZY HORSE**
2003 **DUANE ALLMAN**
2003–08 **JOE PERRY BONEYARD**
2003–08 **SMARTWOOD STUDIO**
2003 **RICHARD PETTY**
2003–05 **STANDARD DOUBLE-CUT W/ P-90s**
2003–current **STANDARD 58 PLAINTOP reissue** (*94–99)
2003 **STINGER SERIES**
2003–current **SUPREME**
2003–08 **SWAMP ASH STUDIO**
2003–04 **3D**
2003 50th **ANNIVERSARY CORVETTE**

2004–08 **JIMMY PAGE Standard second version**
2004–current **SLASH SIGNATURE**

2004–05 **STUDIO BARITONE**
2004–current **ZAKK WYLDE CAMO BULLSEYE**

2005 **MUSIC RISING**
2005–08 **NEAL SCHON**
2005 90th **ANNIVERSARY SUPREME**

2006–08 **BFG**
2006–current **BILLIE JOE ARMSTRONG JUNIOR**
2006–08 **DC STUDIO** (* 97–98)
2006 **GT**
2006–08 **GODDESS**
2006 **HD.6X-PRO**
2006–08 **MENACE**
2006 **PETE TOWNSHEND DELUXE GOLDTOP**
2006 **PETE TOWNSHEND DELUXE #1**
2006 **PETE TOWNSHEND DELUXE #9**
2006 **PETER FRAMPTON 'SPECIAL'**
2006–08 **STUDIO PREMIUM PLUS**
2006–08 **VIXEN**
2006–current **WARREN HAYNES**

2007–08 **CLASSIC ANTIQUE**
2007–08 **CLASSIC CUSTOM**
2007 **CLASSIC CUSTOM P-90**
2007 **CLASSIC CUSTOM 3-PICKUP**
2007–08 **CUSTOM 68 CHAMBERED**
2007–08 **FADED DOUBLE CUTAWAY**
2007 **JOHN LENNON**
2007 **JOHN SYKES CUSTOM**
2007 **KEITH RICHARDS STANDARD**
2007–08 **LE CUSTOM SILVERBURST**
2007–08 **LES PAUL MELODY MAKER**
2007–08 **ROBOT LTD**
2007–current **ROBOT STUDIO**
2007–08 **STANDARD FADED**
2007 **STANDARD PREMIUM PLUS**
2007 **STANDARD UN-BURST**
2007–08 **STANDARD 58 CHAMBERED VOS**
2007–08 **STANDARD 58 50th ANNIVERSARY**
2007 **STUDIO BFG**
2007–08 **STUDIO FADED MAPLE TOP**
2007 **SUPER CUSTOM**
2007–08 **VINTAGE MAHOGANY**
2007-08 **50th ANNIVERSARY STANDARD GOLDTOP**
2007-08 **50th ANNIVERSARY 1958 MURPHY-AGED GOLDTOP**

2008–current **AXCESS STANDARD FLOYD ROSE**
2008 **CUSTOM 25**
2008–current **DARK FIRE**
2008 **JIMMY PAGE CUSTOM**
2008–current **JOE BONAMASSA**
2008–current **JUNIOR single-cut** (* 54–58)
2008 **LP-295 GOLDTOP**
2008–current **MICK JONES CUSTOM**
2008 **PUSH TONE**
2008 **SLASH GOLDTOP**
2008 **SLASH #1 STANDARD**
2008 **SPOTLIGHT FLAME**
2008–09 **STANDARD SILVERBURST**
2008–current **STANDARD 59 EXOTIC WOOD**
2008–current **STEVE JONES CUSTOM**
2008–current **TRADITIONAL**
2008–current **2008 STANDARD**

2009–current **AXCESS STANDARD**
2009–current **GARY MOORE SIGNATURE BFG**
2009 **JEFF BECK 1954 OXBLOOD**
2009 **MICHAEL BLOOMFIELD 1959 STANDARD**
2009 **STANDARD 59 50th ANNIVERSARY**
2009–current **STUDIO RAW POWER**
2009 **50th ANNIVERSARY KORINA TRIBUTE**

Index

Signature models are indexed by the artist's forename; in other words, the Duane Allman model is listed here under D for Duane and not A for Allman. Page numbers in *italics* indicate illustrations. Page numbers from 141 to 163 indicate entries in the reference listing's model directory at the back of the book.

a

b

c

t

u

v

w

x

y

z

Acknowledgements

INSTRUMENT OWNERS

The guitars we photographed came from the collections of the following individuals and organisations, and we're grateful for their help. They are listed here in the alphabetical order of the code used to identify their instruments in the Key below. **AR** Alan Rogan; **BB** Bruce Bowling; **CB** Clive Brown; **CC** Chinery Collection; **CM** Country Music Hall Of Fame; **DN** David Noble; **GA** Garry Malone; **GI** Gibson Guitar Corp; **GL** Gibson London; **GM** Gary Moore; **HK** Hiroshi Kato; **JB** Jeff Beck; **JP** Jimmy Page; **JS** John Smith; **LP** Les Paul; **MN** Marc Noel-Johnson; **MS** Mike Slubowski Collection; **PD** Paul Day; **PM** Paul McCartney; **PU** Paul Unkert; **RH** Rick Harrison; **SC** Simon Carlton; **SH** Shane's; **TA** Terry Anthony.

KEY TO INSTRUMENT PHOTOGRAPHS

The following key is designed to identify who owned which guitars at the time they were photographed. After the relevant bold-type page number(s) we list the model name followed by the owner's initials (see Instrument Owners above). **10–11** 'log', CM. **11** 'clunker', LP (photo Design Photography, Inc.; courtesy of the Rock and Roll Hall of Fame and Museum). **14** Goldtop, MS. **14–15** Goldtop, JS. **15** Goldtop lefty, TA. **18–19** 54 Custom, DN; 57 Custom, AR. **22–23** Junior, DN; TV, MS. **23** Special, CB. **26** 55 Goldtop, MS; 58 Goldtop, MS. **26–27** Goldtop lefty, PM. **30** TV, SC. **30–31** Junior, CB; Special red, PU. **31** Special 3/4, SH; Special yellow, MS. **34–35** Standard centre, AR; Standard bottom, MS. **38** Standard bottom, AR. **38–39** 'Number 1', JP. **39** Standard top, GM. **46–47** Standard, MS. **47** Standard lefty, PM; Standard centre, CC. **50–51** Standard, DN. **51** Custom, DN; Junior, SC. **58** Goldtop, MN; Personal, HK; Custom, JS. **58–59** Professional, MS. **59** Deluxe, BB. **66** Recording, PD; Jumbo, CC. **66–67** 'Oxblood', JB. **67** Recording, MS. **70** Pro Deluxe, SC. **70–71** 20th, MS. **71** Signature, GA. **74** KM, MS; The Les Paul, GA; Artist, GA. **75** The Les Paul, MS. **82–83** Heritage Standard, MW; Heritage Elite, MS; Heritage Award, MS. **86** Guitar Trader, MS. **86–87** Standard 82, MS. **87** Leo's, MS; Wallace, MS. **90** 84 Reissue, MS. **90–91** 83 Reissue, MS. **91** Custom, GI; Spotlight natural, MS; Spotlight sunburst, MS. **94** Studio Lite, GA. **94–95** Orville, MS. **95** 35th, DN. **102** Custom Plus, RH. **102–103** Classic Plus, MS. **103** Classic, GL. **106** Standard Centennial, MS; Classic Centennial, MS. **106–107** Standard Flametop, CC. **107** Custom Centennial, MS. **110** Page, MS. **110–111** Perry, GL; Ultima, MS. **114** Elegant, MS. **114–115** DC Pro, MS. **115** Flametop Aged, GL. **122–123** Betts, GI. **123** Frampton, GI; Marley, GI; Rossington, GI. **126** Allman, MS; Music Rising, GI. **126–127** Supreme, MS. **127** Page, GI. **130** BFG, GI. **130–131** Robot, MS. **131** Townshend, GI. **134** Bloomfield, GI. **134–135** 50th, MS; 2008 Standard, GI. **135** Traditional, GI.

Guitar photography is by Garth Blore, Matthew Chattle, Design Photography, Inc, Miki Slingsby, William Taylor, and Kelsey Vaughn.

ARTIST PICTURES are identified by bold-type page number, subject, and photographer/agency. **2** Page, Ian Dickson/Rex Features. **7** Slim, Michael Ochs Archives/Getty. **10** Paul & Ford, GAB Archive/Redferns. **27** Perkins, Michael Ochs Archives/Getty. **39** Flamingos, Michael Ochs Archives/Getty. **43** Clapton, Pictorial Press. **46** King, Michael Ochs Archives/Getty. **50** Bloomfield, Mick Gold/Redferns. **51** Richards, David Redfern/Redferns. **59** Beck, Robert Knight Archive/Redferns; Green, Pictorial Press. **63** Page, Ilpo Musto/Rex Features. **67** Allman, Michael Ochs Archives/Getty; Kossoff, Jan Persson/Redferns. **70** Frehley, Fin Costello/Redferns. **71** Bolan, Pictorial Press. **74** Marley, Estate Of Keith Morris/Redferns; Rossington, Ed Perlstein/Redferns. **75** Jones, Evening Standard/Getty. **79** Slash, Mick Hutson/Redferns. **83** Walsh, Pictorial Press. **90** Gibbons, Charlyn Zlotnik/Redferns. **94** Wylde, Mick Hutson/Redferns. **95** Clark, Ebet Roberts/Redferns. **99** Gossard, Marty Temme/Getty. **103** Moore, Mick Hutson/Redferns. **107** Young, Tim Mosenfelder/Getty. **111** Page, Tim Mosenfelder/Getty. **115** Bradfield, Ian Dickson/Redferns. **119** Wells, Steve Thorne/Redferns. **122** Perry, Paul J. Richards/Getty. **127** Morello, Jo Hale/Getty. **130** Armstrong, Gibson. **131** Mercer, Paul Bergen/Redferns. **135** Bonamassa, C. Brandon/Redferns.

MEMORABILIA illustrated in the book – advertisements, catalogues, patents, photographs – comes from the collections of Tony Bacon, Balafon Image Bank, Paul Day, *Guitar Trader's Vintage Guitar Bulletin*, *The Music Trades*, The National Jazz Archive (Loughton), and Alan Rogan.

ORIGINAL INTERVIEWS used in this book were conducted by Tony Bacon as follows: Jeff Beck, January 1984, February 1993, April 2005; Bruce Bolen, January 1993; Joe Bonamassa, June 2008; Jim Deurloo, October 1992; Pat Foley, March 2009; Robert Fripp, March 1991; Billy Gibbons, April 2008; Henry Juszkiewicz, March 1993; Matthew Klein, January 2002; Timm Kummer, April 2008; Marv Lamb, October 1992; Seth Lover, October 1992; Ted McCarty, October 1992; Tom Murphy, December 2001; Les Paul, March 1989, March 1993, April 2008; Stan Rendell, December 1992; J.T. Riboloff, March 1993; Tim Shaw, February 1993, March 1993, May 2008. Credits for other quotations where they occur in the text are given in sourced endnotes (see page 138).

THANKS to the following for help on this and the previous two Les Paul books (in addition to those named in Instrument Owners and in Original Interviews above): Julie Bowie; Michael K. Braunstein; Dave Burrluck (*Guitarist*); André Duchossoir; Pat Foley (Gibson); Roger Giffin; Dave Gregory; Dave Hunter; Mel Lambert; Brian Majeski (*The Music Trades*); Don Merlino; David Nathan (National Jazz Archive); Julian Ridgway (Redferns); Meredith E. Rutledge (Rock And Roll Hall Of Fame And Museum); Steve Soest (Soest Guitar Repair).

SPECIAL THANKS to Mike Slubowski, for allowing us access to his remarkable collection, which is strongly featured in this book; to Walter Carter, for updating the reference section and for all kinds of valuable assistance; and to Paul Day, for his contributions to the vintage *Gibson Les Paul Book* and its original reference section.

BOOKS

Andy Babiuk *The Story Of Paul Bigsby: Father Of The Modern Electric Solidbody Guitar* (FG 2008).
Tony Bacon *Million Dollar Les Paul: In Search Of The Most Valuable Guitar In The World* (Jawbone 2008); *The Fender Electric Guitar Book: A Complete History Of Fender Instruments* (Backbeat 2007); *50 Years Of The Gibson Les Paul* (Backbeat 2002); *The History Of The American Guitar* (Balafon/Friedman Fairfax 2001).
Tony Bacon (ed) *Echo & Twang* (Backbeat 2001); *Feedback & Fuzz* (Miller Freeman 2000); *Electric Guitars: The Illustrated Encyclopedia* (Thunder Bay 2000).
Tony Bacon & Paul Day *The Gibson Les Paul Book* (Balafon/Miller Freeman 1993); *The Ultimate Guitar Book* (DK/Knopf 1991).
Julius Bellson *The Gibson Story* (Gibson 1973).
Walter Carter *The Gibson Electric Guitar Book: Seventy Years Of Classic Guitars* (Backbeat 2007); *Gibson Guitars: 100 Years Of An American Icon* (GPG 1994).
A.R. Duchossoir *Gibson Electrics – The Classic Years: An Illustrated History Of The Electric Guitars Produced By Gibson Up To The Mid 1960s* (Hal Leonard 1994); *Guitar Identification* (Hal Leonard 1990).
George Gruhn & Walter Carter *Gruhn's Guide To Vintage Guitars: An Identification Guide For American Fretted Instruments* (Miller Freeman 1999).
Gibson Shipping Totals 1946–1979 (J.T.G. 1992).
Guitar Trader *Guitar Trader's Vintage Guitar Bulletin Vol. 1 (1982)* (Bold Strummer 1991).
Steve Howe & Tony Bacon *The Steve Howe Guitar Collection* (Balafon/Miller Freeman 1994).
Dave Hunter *The Guitar Pickups Handbook: The Start Of Your Sound* (Backbeat 2008).
Yasuhiko Iwanade *The Beauty Of The Burst: Gibson Sunburst Les Pauls From 58 To 60* (English-language edition; Hal Leonard 1998).
Joseph F Laredo *Les Paul: The Complete Trios Plus* – booklet with CD set (Decca 1997).
Robb Lawrence *The Early Years Of The Les Paul Legacy 1915–1963* (Hal Leonard 2008).
Stephen K. Peeples *Les Paul: The Legend And The Legacy* – booklet with CD boxed set (Capitol 1991).
Jay Scott & Vic Da Pra *Burst: 1958–60 Sunburst Les Paul* (Seventh String Press 1994).
Mary Alice Shaughnessy *Les Paul, An American Original* (Morrow 1993).
Tom Wheeler *American Guitars* (HarperPerennial 1990).

We consulted back issues of the following magazines: *The Amplifier*; *Beat Instrumental*; *Beat Monthly*; *Billboard*; *Disc International*; *Down Beat*; *Gibson Gazette*; *Guitar Player*; *Guitar World*; *Making Music*; *Melody Maker*; *The Music Trades*; *Music World*; *One Two Testing*; *Vintage Guitar*.

LISTENING to Les Paul can be a wonderful experience. We recommend *The Legend And The Legacy* 1948–58 (four CDs, Capitol 1991) and *The Trio's Complete Decca Recordings Plus* 1936–47 (two CDs, Decca 1997). We find the later Columbia material less interesting, and it's scattered over many CDs.

Updates? The author and publisher welcome any new information for future editions. You can email us at
lespaulguitar@jawbonepress.com
or you can write to
Les Paul Guitar Book, Jawbone, 2A Union Court, 20-22 Union Road, London SW4 6JP, England.

"Back then, the guitar person didn't know anything about electronics, and the electronic person didn't know anything about music. Now it's a marriage, and it's a very happy situation."
Les Paul, 2008